"I
dreamt
last
night ..."

A New Approach
to the Revelations of Dreaming—
and Its Uses in Psychotherapy

"I dreamt last night ..."

By Medard Boss

Translated from German by Stephen Conway

Introduction by Paul J. Stern

GARDNER PRESS, INC., NEW YORK
Distributed by HALSTED PRESS
A Division of JOHN WILEY & SONS, Inc.
New York · Toronto · London · Sydney

Gardner Press, Inc.
19 Union Square West
New York 10003

Distributed solely by the Halsted Press Division
of John Wiley & Sons, Inc., New York

Library of Congress Cataloging in Publication Data

Boss, Medard, 1903-
   "I dreamt last night . . ."
   Translation of Es traumte mir vergangene Nacht.
   "A Halsted Press Book."
   Includes bibliographical references and indexes.
   1. Dreams. I. Title.
BF1078.B57713   616.8'914'019   77-14988
ISBN 0-470-99330-8

Printed in the United States of America

Designed by Sidney Solomon

CONTENTS

Foreword

BY PAUL J. STERN, Ph.D.

In earlier works, Dr. Boss has demonstrated the power of the phenomenological method to illuminate large clinical areas, for instance, those of psychosomatic disease, of sexual deviance, and of schizophrenic disorders. To extend this approach to the realm of dreaming has, as the present book makes clear, far-reaching consequences. Dr. Boss' resolve to treat dream phenomena as largely autonomous and authentic, that is, as sovereign vis-a-vis the phenomena of waking life, leads him to reexamine, and redefine, the whole notion of *Reality*. And if Boss' phenomenological stance entails his taking dreams *for real* in a manner previously—if the pun may pass—undreamt of, it also enables him to discard, as irrelevant to the comprehension of dreaming, much that had been regarded up to now as the very core of the modern science of dreams.

Thus, to cite a particularly striking reversal, Dr. Boss has little if any use for the voluminous body of research on the neurophysiology and psychophysiology of sleeping and dreaming that has accumulated in recent years. The discovery of the multiphasic nature of sleep and the studies of REM- and NREM-states with multiple physiological correlates strike Boss, though he does not deny their anecdotal interest, as entirely beside the point where an

vii

understanding of the nature of dreaming is concerned. The same holds true for the more strictly psychological findings produced by these investigations.[1]

The findings of psychophysiology, Boss states, "tell us almost nothing about what they purport to investigate. They do not bring us one step nearer to an elucidation of dreaming as a unique mode of human existence." These findings merely establish temporal correlations; they entitle us to assert only the simultaneity of certain patterns of neural activity and of psychic states during which dreams frequently occur, or are subject to recall. To go beyond such bare "if-then" statements, to assert for instance, as many investigators are wont to do, that specific neural states "cause" or "explain" dreaming, is to indulge in unwarranted metaphysical speculation, the illegitimacy of which is not mitigated by the philosophical innocence of its perpetrators.

Boss' dismissal of experimental psychophysiology as unfit to promote insight into the nature of dreaming does not imply that he concedes much greater relevance to extant psychological theories of dreaming based on clinical observations. With a nice even-handedness Boss points out that the most potent of these psycho-clinical theories, namely the Freudian ones, are riddled with incongruities and dubious metapsychology to a degree that severely compromises their power of illumination. Anyone with doubts on this score has only to peruse the papers by Zane and other authors that Boss cites. To highlight the shortcomings of Freudian theory Boss quotes Ludwig Wittgenstein's comments about the "deceptive" psychoanalytic practice of disfiguring a patient's "beautiful dream," by means of far-fetched associations, into something unshapely. The point is not that Freud's psychogenetic method is morally or esthetically reprehensible but simply that it is logically (and epistomologically) deficient: ". . . genetic explanations never get a hold (not even a partial one) of the experiential content of a thing."[2]

In order to get at the experiential content of dream phenomena, Boss holds, we must first set about the radical "destruction of theories" that impede our vision. Theories look forever *behind* the phenomena instead of straight *at* them and thus estrange us from the directly observable. By downplaying what is given in immediate experience in favor of inferred "substrata" and quantifiable "processes," psychological theories based on the natural science paradigm overlook that "each thing is what it is, and nothing else."[3] Phenomology, on the other hand, seeks to apprehend as faithfully as possible what is actually there and to bare, with subtle accuracy, the internal and external articulations of the phenomenal world.

Boss introduces the reader to his phenomenological approach to dreaming by contrasting it with the widely known theory and practice of Freudian dream interpretation.[4] A major point of divergence concerns the psychoanalytic doctrine according to which most dream images are *symbolic*, a symbol being something that stands for something else but is in some way linked about what it stands for. The symbolic relationship, Freud held, is a vestige of a former archaic identity. He viewed the symbolic language of dreams as the primordial language of the psyche, which restores to words their full significance, their partly submerged original, and ultimately sexual, meaning. Freud derived this underlying sexual significance of language from a postulated common root of language and sexuality. For him, the word was sex, was vehicle of sexual desire, before it was anything else.

That the language of dreams is symbolic was for Freud such as self-evident assumption, supported by a widely held age-old tradition, that it hardly occurred to him to question its validity. Hence he marshaled his great powers of reasoning and persuasion mostly to prove that dream symbolism was basically *sexual* in nature and bolstered his case with clinical evidence he considered irrefutable.

Boss, however, questions not only Freud's narrowing of the realm of dreaming to preponderantly sexual themes (this criticism is hardly new) but also challenges the whole notion that symbolism is adequate or even relevant to the comprehension of dreaming. Dream phenomena, he holds, are not explained if we treat them as hieroglyphs and by means of ingenious cryptography strive to extract their *true* meaning. To understand dream phenomena we must, rather apprehend them in the nexus of their multifold spontaneous references, in their array of actual and latent properties that define their possibilities of interaction. Is it not symptomatic of existential impoverishment, Boss asks, of living in a denuded, dehydrated world, if most objects are seen as "naked factualities," torn from their natural contexts, needing synthetic enrichment, through symbolism, if they are to yield a modicum of meaning?

To bring this esoteric debate down to earth, Boss reviewed and repeated, in slightly modified form, some of the hypnotic dream experiments that had been adduced by Freud as proof for the correctness of his views on dream symbolism.[5] Schrotter, for instance, an investigator cited by Freud, had hypnotized a number of subjects, asking them to dream about designated sexual events while in trance and then to relate their dreams. In the dreams induced in this manner, the subjects seemed invariably to rely upon the mechanisms of symbolic translation that Freudian dream theory postulates. For example, a hypnotized woman was asked to dream about lesbian intercourse with a woman-friend. Sure enough, in the ensuing dream she met up with this friend, who was carrying a travel bag with a label that read "For Ladies Only." It was self-evident for both Schrotter and Freud that this travel bag with its restrictive labels was a *symbol* for the friend's genital organs.

Boss, however, challenging this ready assumption of self-evidence, raised some searching questions. Why was it, he asked, precisely a travel bag that the dreamer chose to "symbolize" her friend's sexual organs? Why not, instead, some other *symbolic* object more closely related to the sexual-erotic sphere? Why not, for instance, a silk purse of the kind worn with evening gowns at formal dances where sexuality, so to speak, impregnates the air? Does not a travel bag in itself, if we shed symbolic preconceptions, evoke themes of arrival and departure, of coming together and leave-taking, of extending and closing distances—themes of which sexual intercourse may in its turn be a "symbolic expression" (if we want to indulge in this sort of terminology)?

To shed more light on this problem, and on his divergent phenomenological approach, Dr. Boss devised some hypnotic dream experiments of his own, quite similar to those cited by Freud. He hypnotized five women—three healthy and two neurotic—and asked each to dream about a specific male friend who was in love with her and walking toward her, naked, aroused, with clear sexual intent. The three healthy women had dreams that corresponded in every detail to Boss' suggestion. Upon awakening, they related these sexual dream adventures without embarrassment, even with delight. The story was quite different for the two neurotic subjects; in them, Boss' suggestion induced anxiety dreams with markedly altered ("symbolically distorted," in Freudian lingo) content. Thus one of these women had dreamed that a uniformed soldier, a complete stranger to her, had come toward her, holding a handgun. While playing with his weapon, he had almost hit her; she had been so frightened that she woke up.

Now how does Boss, eschewing Freudian notions about symbolism, read these findings? The case of the healthy women is simple. Boss merely states that it was easy to *attune* them, by his hypnotic suggestion, to the theme of a loving sexual encounter; their dreams graphically presented these encounters, without disguises, symbolic or otherwise. As for the neurotic subjects, their hypnotic dreams also do not require interpretation as examples of symbolic cryptography. On the contrary, if we look at the dream reported above with open eyes, it reveals with stark clarity the infantile, narrow, fear-drenched world of the dreamer; such a world simply has no place for a sexually aroused, desirous lover; from within its confines, the approach of an adult man can be experienced only as intrusive, as a dangerous irruption. The extreme constriction of this world, the panic evoked by a man's approach, the perception of men as uniformed, intrusive, and faceless—these, according to Boss, are the relevant facts. What is gained, he asks, if we add that the gun actually symbolizes a penis? Very little. But by treating dreams as symbolic charades a great deal may be lost, namely the stark immediacy and the emotional charge of the phenomena that disclose themselves as we are dreaming.

An example that illustrates particularly well how Bossian dream interpretations differ from Freudian ones involves the dream of a psychology student reported by Boss.[6] This student had dreamed that the fiancee of a friend of his had just died of cancer. The dreamer had felt distant from this friend ever since the latter's engagement. The dreamer was shocked and saddened at the news of the young woman's death. After going to her funeral he found himself with other mourners in a self-service restaurant. He searched anxiously for some dessert or sweets but could not find anything of the sort. He felt discontent.

The dreamer had related this dream to a psychoanalyst whom he was seeing at the time. Predictably, the analyst had interpreted part one of the dream as an expression of unconscious death wishes toward the young woman brought on by his friend's engagement. Part two was interpreted, in equally orthodox vein, as a symptom of libidinal regression to the oral stage of psychosexual development. One is not surprised to learn that the therapeutic effect of these sterotyped interpretations was nil. In particular, the patient had little use for the analyst's insinuation that the dream betrayed his unconscious death wishes toward the fiancee; he could find no factual evidence for the presence of such wishes either in his dreams or in his waking life. Since he did not see eye to eye with his analyst on numerous other points, the patient left him to seek out a daseins-analyst.

When during the ensuing therapy the dream about the cancer death of the friend's fiancee came up again, Boss refrained carefully from imputing to the patient any unconscious death wishes; on the contrary, the dreamer's genuine sorrow upon learning of her death seemed to indicate, if anything, a wish that she stay alive. What seemed more important to Boss, though, than these speculations was the fact that the friend's engagement had attuned the patient to the theme of loving commitment. Even though the dreamer was not ready to realize for himself the intimacy of shared love, he was able to partake of it vicariously by admitting to his dream world a close friend involved in just such a relationship. Yet even in this distanced form an adult love could not endure in his impoverished existential sphere. With the young woman's death, it vanished from the scene to become merely a mournful memory. This disappearance of the promise of love made the patient's universe shrink to the extent that his dealings with the world were not restricted to the ingestion of food in a restaurant where each person must serve himself; and even within this narrow ("oral") sphere, there was a lack of plenitude— no dessert. At this stage, sweets were present, as it were, only in the mode of being yearned for. No wonder, then, that at the close of the dream the patient could no longer manage even a distant glimpse of the far richer sweetness of love or a woman.

This example and many others throughout the book illustrate how Boss, renouncing the use of theoretical constructs like libido, unconscious, orality, regression, censorship, etc., goes about *explicating* the phenomena of dreaming. His method is, simply, to let the dream phenomena unfold, to allow them to tell their own story. To be able to read this story the interpreter need not be steeped in esoteric knowledge about symbolic equivalences but does need a mind uncluttered by theoretical preconceptions. Above all, he needs the seemingly simple, yet extremely rare, ability to see, clearly and accurately, what is there, before his eyes. To those who possess or manage to acquire this phenomenological vision most dreams will reveal very directly the dreamer's existential condition. And the interpreter's close adherence to the dream phenomena will bring home to the dreamer, sometimes with shattering impact, the unacknowledged truth of his existential predicament.

That dreams *read* (rather than "interpreted") along phenomenological lines present poetically condensed images of a person's life situation at a given moment and also accurately reflect changes in this situation over time—hence serving as gauges of a patient's progress in therapy—is documented by Boss' expert use of his patients' dream series. A most instructive case, presented by Boss in his earlier book on dreams, involved a series of 823 dreams dreamt by a thirtyish engineer over a period of three years. The dreams of this depressed and impotent man sorted themselves into well-defined phases during which certain themes predominated, almost to the exclusion of others. There was an orderly, and progressive, sequence from stage to stage. Thus during the first six months of therapy, this man dreamt only of turbines, cyclotrons, automobiles, airplanes, and other machines. Then he began to dream about plants, trees, vegetables, and flowers. This botanical phase was followed, after a long, dreamless interval, by dreams teeming with animal life, at first only in the guise of harmful insects. (Over a six-month period he related more than a hundred insect dreams.) Next there was an extended phase dominated by toads, frogs, and snakes. The first warm-blooded animal that managed to enter his dream world was a mouse scurrying into a mousehole. The first human being to appear in his dreams, after two whole years of therapy, was an unconscious, gigantic woman in a long red gown, who floated in a large pond under a transparent layer of ice. Six months later he dreamt that he was dancing at a county fair with a woman who was also wearing a red gown but was, unlike the earlier dream figure, wide awake and full of life.

This man's waking life had first taken a visible turn for the better at the time he began to dream about plants. At that point his feeling that life was devoid of meaning had started to recede. His sexual impotence had completely vanished by the time he dared let lions and horses enter his dream world.

Most dream series are not as systematic and orderly as that of this mechanical engineer who had to graduate in his dreams through the whole phylogenetic scale before he was ready to realize his full human potential. But if there is forward movement at all in therapy, it is, as Boss' other dream series document, picked up most sensitively by dreams, especially in cases where the behavioral indications of waking life are still unclear and contradictory. Inversely, the recurrence of the same sterotyped dream over a long period of time is a reliable sign that therapy has come to a standstill.

Besides their practical value, dream series also possess great theoretical interest. They pose with particular acuity the problem to which Boss devotes the last major section of this book—the problem of the relationship between waking life and dream life.

In addressing this thorny question, Boss begins by telling us how *not* to approach dream phenomena. They are not to be approached as minor, truncated, spectral reproductions of waking life. Nor are they to be prejudged by the peremptory canons of daylight reality. Boss' discussion of the meaning of "realness," based on Heidegger's subtle ontology of Being, challenges the common assumption that our dream experiences lack, or are deficient in, the attribute of reality.

Boss repeats tirelessly that waking and dreaming are autonomous modes of being, neither one reducible to the other. In each of them, human existence articulates itself in characteristic ways. It is the enduring identify of the human being, now dreaming, now awake, the continuity of his life history, that ties together dreaming and waking, which forever exist only as the dreaming or waking of this particular person at this particular time.

As Boss, following in the footsteps of other philosophers, points out, it is extremely difficult to define criteria that clearly distinguish between wakefulness and sleep. The more than two-thousand-year-old riddle of the Chinese sage Chuang-Tse has not been resolved: Chuang-Tse, having dreamed vividly of being a butterfly and then having awakened into his human existence, had been life wondering: "Was I then a man who dreamed of being a butterfly, or am I now a butterfly dreaming that he is a man?" The perplexity of the Chinese sage was echoed by Rene Descartes who, in his *Meditations*, professed his inability to decide for certain whether he was awake or asleep. Descartes' uncertainty stemmed from the fact that "all the same thoughts and conceptions which we have while awake may also come to us in sleep." Boss, translating Descartes' insight into the language of modern psychology, has shown that all the modes of relating to the world that human beings display while awake are to be found also in their dreams, including the mode of dreaming[7], the ode of awakening[8], and the mode of interpreting dreams[9]. It is even possible "to dream that one is falling asleep and to have dreams during this dreamt dreaming state only to—while still dreaming—'wake up,' thereby becoming aware of the dream within a dream as a 'mere dream.' Only a second awakening, after a more or less prolonged dream state, will discharge the dreamer, now more awake, into his everyday world." In view of this curious *relativity* of the consciousness of awakeness, the cautious comparative "more awake" seems appropriate.

Though the seemingly clear common sense distinctions between waking and dreaming disintegrate under philosophical scrutiny, Boss' phenomology of dreaming proposes some less perishable touchstones for the two modes. For one, Boss suggests, the world of dreaming is, despite its apparent fluidity, narrower, more closed and hermetic, than the waking world. By this, Boss means that our dreams are pretty much limited to the temporal mode of the immediate present; the temporal dimensions of past and future, of self-conscious memory and anticipation, are usually absent while we dream. We distort Boss' meaning only a little if we propose the paradoxical formula that dreaming, at least as far as its temporal modes are concerned, is characterized by the absence of the imaginary.

But not only with regard to its temporal modes. The phenomena we encounter while dreaming usually present themselves in a very concrete, physically tangible form—not infrequently tangible to the point of being oppressive. (Here is the making of another paradox: the "immaterial" tissue of dreaming presents us mostly with "material" phenomena.) Abstract ideas, theoretical speculations, philosophical musings, psychological self-analysis are only rarely present in dreams. The concrete-minded realm of dreaming confronts us directly with sensations, perceptions, and emotions that grant us hardly any reflective distance. It is a universe of sights and sounds, with scant space for overarching insight or vision.

(Others have noted this predilection of dreams for the concrete. It was precisely this feature of dreams that seemed to compel the use of symbolism to assimilate their language to that of the everyday world. Boss does not deny that *some* translation of dream language is necessary but insists that it ought to be minimal. It ought to refrain from too vigorous manipulation of the dream texts, ought to adhere to them as closely as possible, transposing their imagery, ever so gingerly, into more inclusive existential statements.)

If Boss' analysis is correct, if the mode of awakeness surpasses the dreaming mode in existential richness and freedom, then it is clear why waking experience is the prime medium of self-realization, why the decisive advances and retreats, expansions and contractions of the individual's life history occur while he is awake. But this does not mean that the realm of dreaming is dispensable. If dreaming does not make history, it illuminates it. "A person who spent all his life dreaming would keep dreaming the same dreams. He might have a series of disjointed experiences, but not a true history. The person who led a dreamless life, who ignored the realm of his dream, would be, in an important sense, only partly awake. His life would be deficient in depth and scope; it would not be completely real."[10]

The main intent of the present book is to demonstrate, through a wide array of examples, how the phenomenological reading of dreams works in actual practice. In case after case Boss shows how to avoid the large inductive leaps that land other dream interpreters in the ditch of irrelevance. Boss' material amply supports the claim that his approach spotlights, with uncanny aptness, the existential condition of the dreamer, that it detects and explodes, in the most direct manner, the private myths and parasitic "life-lies" sapping the person's being.[11] The method seems mere child's play in the hands of a master like Boss. But the novice trying to emulate him soon discovers that its simplicity is more apparent than real. For most of us, it requires strenuous effort to discard, even fleetingly, the theoretical blinders we have come to take for granted.

Once we begin to master the *gentle* Bossian art of making the dream speak, we are rewarded by increased therapeutic effectiveness. What appears, from the perspective of waking, to be the pared-down, confined phenomenal world of dreaming is then turned to therapeutic advantage. The condensed, limpid poetry of the dream state, if allowed to prevail, confronts us, ineluctably, with existential tasks we have not sufficiently heeded in waking life. The dream matters, we are told, and it matters supremely because its agenda is the matter at hand. It not only presents our hidden agenda but *enacts* it, with vivid gestures. The meaning of such gestures becomes transparent to those who, in taking a phenomenological approach to them, have learned to read the signature of things.

Professor Boss is particularly adept at using the dream in therapy as a sort of *leading indicator* that foretells psychic developments not yet manifest in the patient's waking life. It quite often happens, we are told by Dr. Boss, that a person comes across up-to-then unacknowledged facets of his being *for the very first time* while dreaming. It is true that such potentialities not yet realized in waking life are usually met with, in these dreams, in the guide of "others" with whom the dreamer fails to identify, and in the enactment of events in which he fails to participate. Nevertheless, given the literal-mindedness of dreams, they are particularly suited, in the hands of a skilled therapist, to alerting the patient to as yet buried and, to him, alien modes of conduct that are about to emerge in his waking life. Especially for those numbed neurotics who seem more awake while dreaming than in their waking state, the encounter with the immediate reality of dream phenomena can have a truly cataclysmic impact.

The realm of dreaming, rescued by Freud from the contumelious disdain of the positivists, has been rendered opaque once more, of late, by the veils of a new (psychoanalytic) mythology. This mythology is no less tenebrous for its having been, initially, illuminating. Dr. Boss' new book on dreams constitutes a bold attempt to sunder this veil and to vindicate the full undimmed reality of the phenomena of dreaming.

Paul J. Stern

NOTES

1. Boss has equally little use for the presently fashionable statistical content analysis of dreams that aims at making dreams fit for computer analysis. These misguided efforts to computerize dreams stem directly, in his view, from the superstitious belief of scientists in the intrinsic virtues of quantification. What we stand to gain by quantifying dream phenomena is anything but obvious.

2. L. Wittgenstein, *Vorlesungen und Gesprache uber Asthetik, Psychologie and Religion*. Gottingen, 1968, p. 54.

3. L. Wittgenstein, *ibid*., p. 54.

4. M. Boss, see *Analysis of Dreams*. London, 1957.

5. M. Boss, *Der Traum und seine Auslegung*.

6. Chapter IV, comparison dream B.

7. The person dreams that he is dreaming.

8. The person dreams that he is waking up while he continues dreaming.

9. The person speculates while still dreaming about the meaning of his dream.

10. P. Stern, *In Praise of Madness*. New York, 1972, p. 60.

11. An impressive example is the case of Regula Zurcher in *Existential Foundations of Medicine and Psychology*. New York, 1977.

Preface

The present volume represents my second attempt to penetrate the nature of dreams; get a fresh, unbiased hold on their meaning; and arrive at practical applications for sociologists, educators, psychotherapists, and religious practitioners. The initial attempt, some twenty years ago, found expression in a book entitled *Dreams and their Interpretation (Der Traum und seine Auslegung)*. Long out of print, this work can only be located in its non-German editions. It is fitting that now, just as the present volume comes off the press, its predecessor should be given a second German edition in paperback.[1] For the content of this volume expands on ideas outlined in the older work.

In contrast with the more historical, classificatory, and theoretical intent of the 1953 study, the emphasis in *I Dreamt Last Night* is placed primarily on the practical. The present inquiry, being supplementary in nature, quickly proceeds to the heart of the matter. On the basis of diverse, concrete dream specimens, the reader is first reeducated to look at dreams without traditional theoretical bias, seeing in the dream experience only that which can be factually perceived to exist. Immediately afterwards follows a discussion of what this fresh understanding of dreams has to offer the reawakened dreamer in the way of practical-therapeutic, pedagogical, and spiritual benefits.

The present volume aims, then, at being a simple exercise book. But exercising involves constant repetition. Only by demonstrating the very same fact on a whole series of examples can the book serve its most important purpose. Only constant exercise can produce a novel understanding of dreams, one that is truly phenomenological and existential (*daseinsanalytisch*).

Of course, the final chapter does take up the "theoretical" subject matter first treated at the close of *Dreams and their Inter-*

pretation. The title given to the concluding chapter, back then, was "The Search for the Overall Nature of Dreams" (*Die Frage nach dem Wesen des Traumens in ganzen*). Lacking sufficient knowledge, I was forced to confine my efforts almost entirely to the formulation of the problem itself. I believe that, in the intervening years, examining several thousand new reports of dreams in light of this problem has taught me something more. The final chapter of the present work accordingly carries the title "The Nature of Dreaming, as Compared with That of Waking."

Among the dream reports are dozens given by non-Europeans, both healthy and ailing. Some of these people actually traveled to me for analysis; others entered the care of local therapists who permitted me to consult with them in the course of my overseas travels. The results are descriptions of the dream experiences of North Americans of every skin color: white, black, yellow, and red; of black and white South Americans; of Indians from the northern and southern extremes of that subcontinent; of male and female Indonesians, drawn from such large cities as Djakarta and Jogokata, but also from the innermost recesses of the island of Java; finally, there are dreams picked up in China and Japan. The "nature" of dreaming elaborated in the final chapter may with some justification be seen, then, as the nature of contemporary human dreams per se, not simply those of a geographically and socially limited group of people.

This final chapter, however, attempting to define the general nature of dreams, is written, specifically for the contemplative reader. Instead of having direct practical value, it forms a *background* for understanding and applying the above mentioned therapeutic practical directions. To be sure though, experience shows repeatedly that those, who believe that for the therapeutic application of a scientific understanding of dreaming a knowledge of superficially apparent technical rules suffices, regularly apply their techniques at the wrong time and in the wrong context.

As regards terminology, I should point out that I have endeavored throughout the book to use the substantive "dreaming" in place of the noun "dream," believing the former to be more descriptive of the activity itself. This choice was also made in order to avoid arriving at some hasty and ovelry narrow objectification of what dreaming really is.

The Swiss National Finance Foundation deserves special things for its financial support. I am also grateful to all of my students for their suggestions and corrections. Last but not least, I would like to thank my publisher for his customary careful attention to the putting together and printing of this book.

Medard Boss

NOTE

1. M. Boss. *The analysis of dreams.* (transl. by J. Pomerans.) New York: Philosophical Library, 1975.

CHAPTER I

The Present States of Knowledge about Dreams

DEPTH-PSYCHOLOGICAL "DREAM INTERPRETATIONS"

"I dreamt the other night . . ." is the beginning of a sentence that contemporary psychiatrists, psychotherapists, and psychologists hear many thousands of times. The reason they hear it so often is that usually they have a strong interest in their patients' dreaming. Yet the interest in dreaming is not restricted to modern psychotherapists. It is as old as man himself.[1]

Nevertheless systematic research, of the sort that can claim to fit in with modern science, has existed only since Freud's pioneering work. *The Interpretation of Dreams* was published at the turn of the century. Here Freud enjoys comparing his method of construing dreams to the deciphering of ancient scripts by archeologists. Even these cuneiform decoders, he goes on to say, were until the middle of the last century considered visionaries or swindlers. In time, however, critics were silenced by the remarkable agreement shown in interpretations by various archeologists of the same text. By precise analogy, interpretations of one and the same dream by numerous "correctly schooled analysts" were to justify the highest expectations of those employed in Freud's branch of science.[2]

Yet it was precisely in this, his greatest scientific hope, that Freud and all of his merely imitative students would find themselves sorely disappointed. Notwithstanding the immense expenditure of theoretical labor in past decades, today—three-quarters of a century later—critical opinion is increasingly eroding depth-psychological theories of dream interpretation. The most skeptical of these critics come from the ranks of the analysts themselves. Their remarks carry incomparably more weight than the whole lot of rash, emotional reproaches leveled at psychoanalysis in its infancy by colleagues of Freud who had no inkling of analytic methodology.

The following four examples, drawn from a large body of critical evidence, sufficiently expose the catastrophic situation in which the "art of depth-psychological dream interpretation" finds itself today. All four come from thoroughly unimpeachable, expert witnesses. The first, Ludwig Wittgenstein, labels himself a "disciple" and student of Freud. He is also one of the fathers of modern scientific logic and therefore singularly qualified to evaluate the scientific validity of Freudian dream theory. This he does, painstakingly. The three critics cited subsequently are "correctly schooled," practicing psychoanalysts. Therefore, they too know very well what psychoanalysis is. Within the German linguistic sphere, Ott[3] has preceded me in calling attention to Wittgenstein's testimony.[4] The second critic cited here is Richard M. Jones.[5] The two final judgments were made by psychoanalysts M.D. Zane and M.H. Eckhardt and can be found in a book edited by J.H. Masserman.[6]

In the third of his "Lectures on Aesthetics," in which this term is employed in its broadest sense to mean "the perception of content," Wittgenstein illustrates his notion of the limits of scientific language through a criticism of Freudian dream theory. He mentions an example that Freud has called a "beautiful dream." In this dreaming a patient descends from an elevation, catches sight of flowers and shrubs, breaks off a branch from a tree, and more. Freud, writes Wittgenstein, would interpret this dream on the basis of purely sexual associations, "the coarsest sexual material, the foulest indecencies—indecent from A-to-Z, so to speak."[7] "But," Wittgenstein immediately counters, "*wasn't* the dream itself beautiful?

I would tell the patient: 'Do such associations make the dream ugly? It was beautiful, and why shouldn't it have been?' I am inclined to think that Freud deceived his patient." Naturally, Wittgenstein does not mean to say that Freud intentionally led his patient astray. He means only that Freud has offered her an explanation that simply does not conform with the content of her dreaming experience, an interpretation that pretends to be an explanation but is not. *"For genetic explanations never capture (not even partially) the experiential content of a thing."*[8]

In a later section of the same lecture, Wittgenstein returns to the problem of the "beautiful dream" and says: "It is those sentences, above all, that tell us 'This is *in reality* something else' which assume the form of persuasion, meaning that we are persuaded to neglect certain distinctions that actually exist." Wittgenstein concludes his critique of the scientificness of Freudian dream theory by remarking, "I am reminded of the wonderful saying that 'Every thing is what it is, not something else.' "[9] But here Wittgenstein the logical is already referring to an entirely different methodology, one no less capable than natural scientific research of unearthing truth, the elaboration of which forms the single aim of the present volume. For presumedly Wittgenstein had in mind, with his "wonderful saying," Goethe's aphorism: "Do not look for anything *behind* phenomena; they themselves are the lesson!"[10] and also Husserl's cry to "Return to the things themselves!" Both are initial invitations to a new manner of thinking, one that we can call phenomenological. This new thinking means to turn away, radically and permanently, from all previous scientific procedures. These natural scientific investigators tend to abandon as fast as possible, their objects with their different qualities as they are immediately perceived in favor of quantifiable "substrata" and energetic processes merely presumed to exist somewhere behind the observable qualities. The phenomenological approach, by contrast, strives to avoid exclusively "logical" conclusions and to adhere instead entirely to factually observable things, aiming to penetrate their significances and contexts with ever greater refinement and precision, until the very essence of them is fully recognized.

On the other hand, R.M. Jones undertakes the gargantuan task of giving a comparative overview of all modern dream theories, from Freud's to Erikson's. His research culminates in the resigned admission that dream literature to date has been nothing more than a multiplicity of speculations, none of them deserving preference over the others. Jones, echoing Snyder, compares dream investigators to the proverbial blind men who try to discover the nature of an elephant. Each of the blind men probes a different part of the elephant's body. One, taking hold of a leg, mistakes the elephant for a column; another seizes the tail and concludes that the elephant is a furniture tassel; and so on.

Still more depressing are the criticisms of Freudian dream theory appearing in the articles of psychoanalysts M.D. Zane and M.H. Eckhardt. Both of these articles are included in the final chapters of the book edited by Masserman, *Dream Dynamics*.[11] The authors proceeded along lines similar to those once taken by the Royal Asiatic Society, when its investigations into ancient cuneiform scripts inspired Freud with such great hopes for his own dream theory. The difference is that the results produced by Zane and Eckhardt were the very sort that might have confirmed the critics of the cuneiform interpreters. Zane and Eckhardt reported on the results of a dream symposium that was carried on, over a five-year period, by members of the American Academy of Psychoanalysis. Zane's evaluation of the symposium begins with the eyebrow-raising remarks: "Nothing seems more important for our field than to confront the recurrent finding in our workshop over its 5-year existence that regarding the same dream psychoanalysts derived very different meanings, took very different approaches, and had striking difficulties in communicating with each other, and that our divergences actually increased when, in addition to the manifest dream, we provided clinical material about the dreamer and his therapy." Zane draws the only conceivable conclusion when he closes this paragraph with the words: "Should we, then, not take a closer look at how we work with dreams as individual psychoanalysts, if what we leave our patients with meets so little support from our colleagues? . . . In my view the persistence of such differences for so long may well signify something fundamentally wrong with how we psychoanalysts work with dreams,"[12]

Zane buttresses his harsh assessment of the contemporary art of dream interpretation with a concrete, extremely impressive illustration. Considering the serious situation in which the science of dreams finds itself today, we would be remiss not to reproduce this illustration in its entirety.[13] Zane begins by introducing word-for-word the tapescript he assembled for the seminar participants from a physician—patient dialog of 1967. It reads:

*Patient:*A couple of Saturdays ago, I decided to stop in at the barber-shop and get a haircut. The barber was talking, talking, talking, talking, talking, which I hate with barbers—but since then I've been having dreams. I've had this dream about three times now, where there is a great big patch back there; it's about the size of a soup plate now and getting larger all the time. Uh, this is crap. I suddenly start worrying about something I've never worried about in my life.

Dr. Zane: Can you go over the dream precisely as you had it?

Patient: I'm just seeing my own head from the back and there is something back there about 4 inches in diameter and it's bald except for a few straggling strings of hair across it. I've seen it on [laugh] the back of a lot of guy's heads.

Dr. Zane: How did you feel when you saw it in the dream?

Patient: Terribly frightened. I wake up. I'm terribly frightened of throwing myself out the window and grab the sheet.

To this dream account Zane appends the interpretations of five different seminar participants, all based on Freudian dream theory:

1. *Dr. A:* Why did Manny not pursue the issue of the barber and the barber pole?

2. *Dr. B:* I think the barbershop incident is related to some incident that happened in childhood in relationship to the patient's father. And also to the therapist.

3. *Dr. C:* I think that this guy's major worry is to ward off any attack that will be a blow to his omnipotence or narcissism.

4. *Dr. D:* Wouldn't it be a good idea to devote some time to exploring the metaphor or the dream—the loss of hair?

5. *Dr. A:* I don't think it's a loss of hair. In the dream the patient is describing a bald area with a few straggling hairs. Now from the dream and in the little that we had in the dream report and the rest, he mentions the word "crap" and the words "back of" kept recurring with this image of a bare area with a few hairs. My association to it, if you will, was "behind," so that the image of the dream was "I cannot cope with my homosexual impulses."

6. *Dr. C:* I think that the patient was saying: "I cannot cope with my

loss of control, my rage; so I'll have to submit into a feminine homosexual position in order not to precipitate a fight that will destroy me."

7. *Dr. A:* It may be that one could view homosexuality as just something feminine. But on the other hand, one might say it's the aggressive homosexual role that's threatening to erupt from the patient.

8. *Dr. E:* If you are going to use your interpretation of the backside and all that, how do you deal with these extra facts that are there—that it's all getting larger and larger?

9. *Dr. B:* I would take the increasing size of baldness as increasing anxiety and increasing rage.

10. *Dr. A:* One could also say that the patient is increasing, that he is enlarging on the problem. He is writing it first in small letters and then in large letters.

11. *Dr. D:* I am concerned about the fact that this dream ended up in a moment of profound panic. And I am saying that we ought to know the dynamics of that panic.

12. *Dr. A:* This is the kind of fragmentation or dissolution of the self or ego or whatever terms you would want to use that accounts for this overwhelming panic. So one could see it as a homosexual panic.

13. *Dr. C:* That is exactly the area of dissolution that is so pregenital. That is why I object to your use of the term homosexual as such. It's—it's an identity crisis.

To these "dream interpretations" of his five colleagues, quite self-contradictory in many respects, Zane added only that the patient himself had shown no homosexual tendencies during the entire course of therapy. Zane concludes his remarks by telling us:

> Unless we can resolve the unsettling phenomenon of irreconcilable difference in response to the same dream disclosed in our workshops, I feel that qualified psychoanalysts will continue to give highly individual responses to the same dream and the field of psychoanalysis will continue to presume knowledge of human behavior while its practitioners, when they convene to study an important clinical area, will barely be able to understand and communicate with each other.

Eckhardt is of the same opinion, remarking further that:

> Many of us have discarded essential ingredients of Freud's theories, as, for instance, the concept of dream as wish fulfillment, or the concept of the dream as the guardian of sleep, or the concepts pertaining to the distinctions between manifest and latent content of dreams. Yet we have retained the term "interpretation" for our manifold therapeutic activities with

dreams and we thus continue to act in obeisance to concepts which intellectually we have to come to doubt.[14]

Perhaps we psychotherapists behave so irrationally because our pure theory has blinded us to the bedrock of experience upon which we human beings stand even in our dreams. Not only do we avoid the data that would allow us to question the theory, but we are ruled also by a host of other vague notions about the human mind, each of them doing its part in obstructing our view of the nature of dreaming.

My first study of dreams contained a detailed description of Freud's psychological assumptions, along with an account of why he felt obliged to invent them.[15] I also have indicated ways in which the pillars of Freudian dream theory cannot stand up to *scientific*, that is, empirically rigid, criticism. I maintained that in the observable phenomena of dreaming, there is not the slightest factual evidence for the existence of either the "dream-work" postulated by Freud, or any "infantile instinctual desires" of the sort supposed to produce dreams from within an individual unconscious. Even the central notion of "dream symbolism" collapses as soon as undemonstrable suppositions are no longer confused with empirical facts. Proof is provided, in the same book,[16] that the ideas upon which Carl Jung built his dream theory—a somewhat modified notion of symbol, speculations concerning "archetypes" in a "collective unconscious," and "interpretation on the subjective level"—are fundamentally far less different from Freudian precepts than has generally been supposed. Like these, the Jungian ideas had to be characterized as empty speculations. Comparisons of "interpretations" by Jungian psychologists of a single reported dream tend to reveal the same variances that Zand and Eckhardt have found among Freudian "interpretations."

But "depth psychologists" were prone to lose confidence in their methods of dream interpretations long before Zane and Eckhardt came along, with the result that original and innovative impulses in the area of scientific dream research began to wane. Furthermore, a real loss of interest could also be seen in relation to the more traditional ways of treating dream phenomena.[17] Interest ebbed more and more, until it was given a powerful new impetus by an entirely different, neurological method of sleep and dream research carried on by three Americans.

NEUROLOGICAL SLEEP AND DREAM RESEARCH

Between 1953 and 1955, E. Aserinsky, N. Kleitman, and W. Dement all made the discovery that human sleep is not a condition that remains homogeneous throughout the entire night.[18] They found out that in all mammals, including man, several highly distinct cerebral states could be seen to follow each other in an orderly succession. They found this by monitoring the electrical potentials of the patient's brain, during the entire sleep period, on an electroencephalograph. This method of dream research immediately caught on with countless other scientists around the globe. Among them were some students of Jung, who proceeded to construct a laboratory for experimental sleep and dream research in a private psychiatric clinic in Zurich. C.A. Meier has given us a synopsis of the scientific fruits of the Jungians' work with dreams[19] and, before him, R.M. Jones has produced an excellent overview of the American efforts in this field, with the promising title *The New Psychology of Dreaming.*[20] It also contains a bibliography that is nearly exhaustive for English-language publications. Numerous similar works are also available in French. Five of the best have been collected in an issue of the *Annales de Psychotherapie*, under the title "Psychophysiologie du Reve.[21]

In all of these publications, a clear distinction needs to be made between results obtained from actual neurological processes and observable dream phenomena, on the one hand, and, on the other, what the authors have interpolated on the basis of their own, preexistent dream theories. Some of these theories hold with Freud's notions of the dream, others with the corresponding Jungian hypotheses. In their secondary theorizing, consequently, the writers of these publications diverge significantly from each other. The same criticism applies to their interpretations as was leveled at those of their intellectual lodestars.

These writers agree, however, in their empirical findings. We may now say with some certainty that, for all adult human beings, each night's sleep can be divided into four to six cycles, each containing intermittent phases of different sleeping states. Detection of this pattern is based solely on the distinction between sleeping states characterized by concomitant rapid eye movements and those lacking such movements. The former sleeping state seems more important for dreaming, because research subjects awakened during, or immediately after, this phase report dreams far more frequently than those awakened from the second sleeping state. But this does not permit us to conclude that periods of sleep without rapid eye movement occur with fewer dreams. We can say only that if a research subject is awakened out of the sleep phase not accompanied by rapid eye movement, he is generally less capable of *remembering* any immediately preceding dream experiences.

Many different names have been given to the sleep phase exhibiting rapid eye movement and frequent dream recollection. The Americans call it "D (Dreaming)-State" or "REM (Rapid Eye Movement) Sleep." The French abbreviate it as "etat R" or "P.M.O." (*phase de mouvement oculaire*). Everyone seems to have labeled it the "paradoxical" state, because it shows a strange admixture of voluntary and autonomic processes and stands somewhere inbetween dreamless deep sleep and waking.

For the moment we can let the matter rest by saying that the EEG-observation method allows us to establish the simultaniety of one special cerebral state of sleep, on the one hand, and dreaming, along with a large number of autonomic bodily processes, on the other. Another valuable discovery is that human beings do much more dreaming than can be assumed on the basis of memories upon awakening in the morning. Using this, EEG dream investigators from both camps, the Freudian and the Jungian, have reached a conclusion that has some astounding implications for Freudian and Jungian theory. That is, when the sum of a night's dreams is examined, both dreams remembered casually in the morning and those obtained from experimental awakening from REM sleep phases, the vast majority of dreams have an unpleasant atmosphere, producing little evidence for Freudian wish-fulfillment.[22] Then again, most dreams are concerned with everyday things to which the dreamer has an everyday, banal relationship. There are no traces of Jungian "compensation" for waking consciousness. As for Freud's idea of dreams as the guardians of sleep, R.M. Jones, himself a Freudian, shows convincingly that only by ignoring essential distinctions can dreams collected through EEG observation be seen as supporting the Freudian theory.[23]

The findings from sleep research are certainly highly interesting in their way, and even necessary. But they tell us almost nothing about what they are supposed to represent. Not one of them brings us a single step nearer to an explanation of dreaming as a unique mode of human existence. They merely establish a "when—then" relationship. While the cerebral aspect of human existence is in a state that allows certain electrical patterns to be recorded on an electroencephalograph, *then* dreaming occurs more frequently, or at least it is remembered more often by the dreamer. It exceeds the proper limits of the EEG research methods to claim something more, or something other than a mere correlation of simultaneity between neurological evidence and the dreaming perception of entities and behavior in dreams with respect to those entities. Such a claim is no longer based on scientific findings, but on a kind of mystical thinking.

Even the definitions Jones delivers with such self-assurance, of dreaming as a *process*, as the "mentation" of a specific cerebral state, are philosophical speculations of highly questionable kind.[24] They are philosophical inasmuch as they attempt to characterize the nature of dreaming. But they are poor philosophy, because they rest on an objectification of human beings that inherently obstructs our vision of the specifically human dimension of dreaming. "Processes" can only occur in things preconceived as being present at hand materially, or immaterially, and as having some definite location within space. Dreaming can never be reduced to this. It must be recognized as a mode of human existence on a par with waking life. A final criticism of Jones concerns his coinage "mentation," whose meaning remains totally obscure.

Nevertheless, Jones' work is highly valuable, both as a summary of results available to date of EEG-observation experiments, and because of the strict division Jones makes between dreaming as such and individual dream contents. Yet, if what we have said is true, the book has a misleading title. For there can be no talk of a "new psychology" of dreaming. When Jones states that dreaming is an "augmentive response" of the human psyche to the D-cerebral (dreaming) state peculiar to all mammals, he still owes us an explanation of how this supposed psyche is capable of responding to the dreaming state of the brain. Response can only be made to something the significance of which has been perceived. Yet no one can perceive the D-state of his own brain as such. Equally inadequate are Jones' other formulations, which make dreaming out to be a phenomenon that is neurologically "causated" or "neurologically regulated in basis."[25] They clearly transgress the statement of a mere synchronism which is—as already mentioned—the only scientifically permitted relationship to be seen between neurological findings and the simultaneously occurring perceptions of significant things.

On the other hand, C.A. Meier may be right when he says that we cannot understand dreams without first getting a better grasp of their natural antecedent: sleep.[26] But there are two assumptions I would question in his claim that EEG sleep research can make a positive contribution to our objective understanding of dreams. Just as the dreaming person's perception of himself and of the meanings of all the other entities in his dream-world cannot be learned from scientifically recorded EEG-patterns, so we cannot expect these patterns to provide us with an understanding of the sleeping state as a meaningful mode of human existence comparable to waking existence. And as far as the relationship between electrical currents and sleep as a human behavioral mode is concerned, we again can do no more than establish a simple "when—then" relationship. In any case, it is difficult to imagine what is meant by the phrase "objective understanding of dreams."[27]

Growing insight into the limitations of neurological findings concerning dreams has in the past decade found wider expression in "dream psychology."

As might be expected, contemporary statistics about dream contents are still based in great part on the statistical results of neurophysiological dream research.

STATISTICAL DREAM RESEARCH

Even Freud's *Interpretation of Dreams* contains some statistical information on "dream contents." Freud was familiar with a number of statistical analyses of "dream contents" dating from the second half of the last century. This research showed that dreams of painful content outnumbered pleasant dreams (by) at least 2 to 1.[28] So Freud himself noted the very fact that has been rediscovered by contemporary EEG dream experimenters, and that has been occasionally brought to bear against the Freudian theory of wish fulfillment. Still, he confidently viewed the statistical findings as faulty criticism of this theory, believing that they failed to take into account his own postulated distinction between manifest and latent dream content.[29]

Among the latest works in the field of (psychological) dream statistics, that of C.S. Hall and L. Van de Castle stands out for its scope and thoroughness.[30] It may be seen as highly representative of the statistical approach. The so-called manifest content of no fewer than a thousand dreams of university students has been sorted for the statistical frequency of diverse aspects of their contents, such as a particular physical setting, the emergence of a specific character trait, or interpersonal relationship, or mood.

The book was written in the express hope "that it would take dreams away from the analyst's couch and put them into the computer."[31]Why such a move is desirable remains unexplained. The motive behind an enterprise of this kind must arise exclusively out of the superstition of the modern technological mind, according to which quantifiable things are inherently "truer" than those which can only be grasped qualitatively, since only the former submit to calculation. Whatever the case, however, the practical benefits of computer dream storage are not immediately apparent.

"PHENOMENOLOGICAL" DREAM STUDIES BY OTHER RESEARCHERS

Since 1953, the publication date of my own initial phenomenological study, only a small number of scientific writings has appeared that address the true qualities of the dream experience. Most authors do not even bother to question the older dream theories of Freud and Jung, preferring instead simply to adopt the traditional hypotheses as axiomatic bases for their own dream theories. To my knowledge, the only recent dream studies that have attempted to strike out on new paths have been Von Uslar's *Der Traum als Welt*[32] and *Dreams and Symbols* by Calinger and May.[33]

The authors of both works tend to rely, implicitly or explicitly, on my 1953 study,[34] likewise calling themselves "phenomenological" dream investigators. Yet their efforts are so half-hearted that they are quickly drawn into the current of the old "metapsychological" dream transformation, in the Freudian–Jungian sense of the term.

Rollo May chose as a point of departure for his "phenomenological" dream research the dream accounts of a woman who was in analysis with his friend Leopold Calinger. May himself knew only that the dreamer was a woman in her thirties who had undergone psychotherapy once before; that she had had a love affair with a friend of her husband, Morris by name; and that at another time she had fallen in love with a psychiatrist named David. May's colleague Calinger had made detailed recordings of every dream he had heard in the course of the analysis. Calinger had even taken down, word for word, everything that he and his patient had said about the dreams. Yet May opted to dispense with these last materials, adhering, for "phenomenological" purposes, strictly to the pure descriptions of the dream events themselves. He felt, as soon as he had studied the patient's first dream, as though he knew her personality; the insight afforded by subsequent dream accounts seemed to produce a nearly complete picture of a real person and her transformation in the course of psychoanalytic treatment. So truly, May commented, do people reveal themselves in dreams.[35]

May realizes that he is contradicting the views of Freud and Jung, who both believed that dreams could be understood only through a previous knowledge of the life of the person in question, and with the aid of that person's spontaneous, waking associations to the dream material. With true phenomenological intent, May expressly condemns the customary psychoanalytic "interpreting" of dreams. This, he says, inevitably translated the dream material into *our* (psychoanalytic) symbols, instead of paying attention to the language of the dream experiences themselves. The net effect of this is to force the dream material into the jargon and rationalizations of a particular school of psychiatry—the analyst's. Dreams thus translated express, at worst, the therapist's opinion rather than their own inherent significance, and at best, the opinion of the patient, put into terms and categories given him, ready made, by the therapist.[36]

For these reasons, May agrees wholeheartedly with me, writing that future analysts should take a purely "phenomenological" approach to their patients' dreams, adhering strictly to the dream material as it presents itself. The progress of his dream investigations taught him, in fact, that he needed to take an even more rigorous phenomenological tack than he had originally set out on. for he had discovered that almost everything contained in traditional dream studies—the entire physician—patient discussion of the dream contents and of the patient's childhood associations to them—lay far afield of the dream material itself. It was therefore necessary to expose the countless stages by which traditional psychoanalytic dream interpretation distanced itself from the dream material. In May's investigation of a concrete case, for instance, the following could be ascertained: first, that the dreamer, Susan, had a dream; second, that she remembered the dream, and that her memory might already have partially distorted the dream material. Next she related the dream to her analyst. In doing so, she involuntarily stresses certain elements, while omitting some and even partly falsifying others. Fourth, the patient and analyst discussed the dream material. This discussion almost always introduces theoretical terms that lead further away from the dream itself. After he had set down in writing his "phenomenological" study of Susan's dreams, May finally read what she had told her analyst *about* the dreams: her impressions immediately upon awakening, along with her own interpretations of the dreams. As a rule she introduced her associations and "interpretations" with the sentence, "I think the dream means this, or that," and in nearly every instance these associations and interpretations consisted entirely of psychoanalytic cliches and banalities, very logical sounding, but in fact no more than an intellectualization that severely diluted what the dream itself had to say, particularly with regard to the dreamer's behavior. To his great surprise, May discovered from the detailed protocols of the analytic sessions that such "dream interpretations" were regularly followed by new dreams in which the patient was given the phenomenological warning, by herself or another party, "Let's call a spade a spade," or "This is a soap opera we've gotten ourselves into."

And so Rollo May resolved to predicate his study solely on the dream material itself, allowing it insofar as this was possible, to speak to him directly. No phenomenological enterprise has ever had a better prescription for its essential character and basis. The problem is that, in the practical execution of his phenomenological intent, Rollo May falls short of his prescribed goal.

The extent to which he treats dream material in an unphenomenological manner, yielding to that "despised" psychoanalytic brand of dream translation, is evident from any one of the concrete illustrations May employs. Whenever the patient Susan dreams of a man, for instance, whether this man is a supervisor or a stranger named Scotch, May reinterprets the dream figure as the analyst (whom he has given the pseudonym Caligor).[37] If in the dream Susan falls down a flight of stairs and lands on her feet, May translates this into a "clear wish-fulfillment dream.[38] If Susan dreams she walks into a house and spots some sections of pipe on the floor, May takes the pipes to be "ever-present sexual, excretory symbols." No justification is ever given for such a conclusion.

No less than May, Detlev von Uslar shrinks back from a thoroughgoing execution of his phenomenological intentions. In Chapter IV of this work I examine in detail a concrete specimen of Uslar's dream interpretation, which follows Freud's old scheme to the letter. (I also present comparisons between Freudian dream interpretations and strictly phenomenological dream evaluation.)[39] For the moment we must be satisfied with Uslar's own admission that his dream ontology does nothing to further either our general understanding of dreams, or their therapeutic application. He makes this confession while advocating that, even today, the implications of Freudian and Jungian dream theory should determine the course of our dealings with dreams.[40]

Looking back over the present state of the science of dreams, we cannot get around the fact that no dream theory—depth—psychological, statistical, or neurological—begins near enough to the beginning. All of them start out with the unquestioned assumption that there must be, in preexistent space, some encapsulated "psyche" in which the dream process occurs. Even researchers who intend to proceed "phenomenologically" fall in with this conception, a "dream psychology" being, after all, a science based on the notion of a "psyche." Yet not one of them can supply any information about the nature, operation, or location of the much-discussed human thing, called "psyche."

NOTES

1. An historical retrospective on the highly fluctuating valuation of derams through the ages may be found in my first book of dream studies: M. Boss. *The analysis of dreams.* (transl. by J. Pomerans). New York: Philosophical Library, 1975. Pp. 11ff.
2. S. Freud. *Gesammelte Werke.* Vol. XI. London: Imago Publishing Co., Ltd., 1940. P. 239.
3. H. Ott. Daseinsanalyse und Theologie. In G. Condrau, ed., *Medard Boss zum 70. Geburtstag.* Bern, Stuttgart: Hans Huber Verlag, 1973. Pp. 104ff.
4. Ludwig Wittgenstein. *Vorlesungen und Gesprache uber Asthetik, Psychologie und Religion.* Goettingen: Vandenhoeck, 1968. Pp. 73ff.
5. R.M. Jones. *The new psychology of dreaming.* New York and London: 1970. Pp. 187–188.
6. J.H. Massermen. (Ed.) Dream dynamics, scientific proceedings of the American Academy of Psychoanalysis. *Science and Analysis,* 1971, Vol. *xix*, Grune & Stratton, New York & London. 174, 186ff.
7. Wittgenstein, *op. cit.,* p. 49.
8. My italics.
9. Wittgenstein, *op. cit.,* p. 54.
10. Wolfgang von Goethe, *Maximan und Reflexionen,* Vol. 13. Ges. W. Inselverlag. Leipzig. 1922, p. 595.
11. Masserman, *op. cit.,* pp. 174 and 186.
12. Masserman, *op. cit.,* p. 174.
13. M.D. Zane, Significance of Differing Responses among Psychoanalysts to the Same Dream. In J.H. Masserman, ed., *op. cit.,* pp. 174ff.
14. Masserman, *op. cit.,* p. 187.
15. M. Boss, *The analysis of dreams.* (transl. by J. Pomerans.) New York: Philosophical Library, 1975. Pp. 35ff.
16. Ibid., pp. 52–76.
17. Compare the discussions of post-Freudian, post-Jungian innovations in depth-psychological methods of dream interpretation in: M. Boss. *Der traum und seine Auslegung.* (2nd. ed.) (paperback). Kindler-Verlag, Munchen 1974. Pp. 68ff.
18. (a) E. Aserinsky and N. Kleitman. Regularly occuring periods of eye motility and concomitant phenomena during sleep. *Science,* 1953, *118*, 273–274. (b) W. Dement. Dream recall and eye movements during sleep in schizophrenics and normals. *Journal of Nervous and Mental Disorders,* 1955, *cxx*, 263–269. (c) W. Dement and N. Kleitman. The relation of eye movements during sleep to dream activity. An objective method for the study of dreaming. *Journal of Experimental Psychology,* 1957, *liii*, 339–346.
19. C.A. Meier. *Die Bedeutung des Traumes.* Olten and Freiburg: Walter-Verlag, 1972.

20. Richard M. Jones. *The new psychology of dreaming.* New York and London: Grune and Stratton, 1970.
21. *Annales de Psychotherapie,* 1972, *III*(4). Les editions ESF, Paris.
22. Compare Section 3 of this chapter.
23. R.M. Jones, *op. cit..,* p. 33.
24. Ibid., p. 119.
25. Ibid., pp. 118 and 142.
26. C.A. Meier, *op. cit.,* p. 62.
27. C.A. Meier: *op. cit.,* p. 64.
28. Compare p. 15.
29. S. Freud. *Gesammelte Werke.* Vol. II/III. London: Imago Publishing Co., Ltd., London: 1942. P. 139.
30. Calvin S. Hall and Robert L. Van de Castle. *The content analysis of dreams.* New York: Appleton-Century-Crofts, 1966. P. x (introduction).
31. Idem.
32. Detlev von Uslar. *Der Traum als Welt: Untersuchungen zur Ontologie und Phanomenologie des Traums.* Pfullingen: Gunther Neske Verlag, 1964.
33. Leopold Calinger and Rollo May. *Man's unconscious language.* New York and London: Basic Books, Inc., 1968.
34. M. Boss: Der Traum und seine Auslegung. 2. Paperback Autlage. 1974, Kindler, Publ. Munchen. pp. English Translation: The Analysis of Dreams. Pomerans 1958, New York, Philosophical Library.
35. Callinger and Rollo May, *op. cit.,* p. 12.
36. Ibid., p. 8.
37. Ibid., p. 91.
38. Ibid., p. 89.
39. See Chapter III.
40. Uslar, *op. cit.,* p. 307.

CHAPTER II

The Phenomenological or *Daseins-* analytic Understanding of Dreams

INTRODUCTION

Since the role of symbolism has been so significant in dream theories up to now, we shall return for a moment to an earlier critique of traditional dream symbolism with the intent of making a completely new beginning in our analysis of dreaming and elements of dreams.[1] Let us begin by orienting ourselves around a very simple example, a flesh and blood dog meeting a waking human being. Now, why don't we let the dogs that inhabit our dreaming world likewise be the flesh and blood dogs *they* show themselves to be? Why can't the dogs we encounter in dreams remain merely dogs? "*Merely*" dogs? you may ask. But why question "merely?" Any dog, whether the person perceiving it is awake or asleep, assembles a rich nexus of meanings and contexts of reference. They all point to the animal kingdom as a whole rather than to the vegetable kingdom, or the mineral.

But what is this living creature we call an animal? How does animal life differ in essence from, say, human "nature," or from the being of a lifeless stone? Perhaps the only genuine characteristic of animals we human beings can come up with is some "indefinable otherness." Or should we say that animals stand midway between human beings and inanimate objects? Certain philosophers, professional and amateur, would place animal nature very near that of inanimate material objects—not a rock, perhaps, but a rather complex (equally unliving) machine. These philosophers hold that animals must be radically separated from human beings because they cannot speak. If animals existed like people in a world like the world of people, then, these philosophers reason, animals would also be capable of using words.

There are other philosophers who would accuse these of being unsympathetic, and myopic, regarding animals. They emphasize that human beings and animals both are living creatures and, as such, closely connected. True, this group concedes, animals cannot form words that human beings understand, but aren't some people born mute? And is it not true that the most highly developed animals (dogs, for instance) have an extremely differentiated language of sound and gesture, whose capacity to communicate meaning is hardly less differentiated than the verbal language of humans, and probably more expressive?

Yet what does this second group of philosophers know about the "innermost" essence of the "lifeless" matter from which the first tries to derive the nature of animals? Lifeless matter communicates with us much less by language than do animals.

The debate between these philosophical persuasions, both of which no doubt exaggerate, will never be resolved to our satisfaction. At any rate, the very nature of animals will remain fundamentally beyond the grasp of human understanding, because animals *are* speechless; they cannot express themselves in words we understand. They will never be able to tell us just how they experience what they encounter in the world. In fact, it is dubious even to speak of the "experience" of animals.

Even if we were to replace the word "animal" with "creature" and defined this creature as the "mere" animal in contrast to the "animal rationale" that is man, these old Latin distinctions would not make us any wiser regarding the "mere" animal's nature. At most, "creature" is a word that proclaims an article of faith supporting a belief that animals were created, in particular by some god. And we gain nothing by denying animals rationality as long as the nature of reason, and thus of unreason, too, remain as obscure as they have so far.

The nature of inanimate objects, in contrast, is set apart by distinguishing features that are universally apparent. A stone, for instance, is present at a specific location is a space conceived of as preexisting, hollow, and three dimensional. It occupies the space described by its own volume. Its surface separates it, within and without, from whatever else is there. Finally, it is separated from these things in measurable distances.

A living animal, by contrast, does not end at its skin. For instance, the perception of dogs extends far beyond their physical boundaries to everything their senses of sight, hearing, taste, touch, and smell can apprehend. How could dogs ever notice anything if this were not so, though in the absence of spoken words the mode of their sense relationship to what is somehow affecting them is totally obscure. Yet if animals were not, like human beings, receptive enough at least to distinguish one thing they perceive from another, we would never see dogs leaping up at their masters and barking or hear them yelping, in completely different, at treed cats. Whether dogs can understand their masters as human beings, and cats as cats, as we would is another mystery.

In any case, dogs, like people, are drawn to things around them, and *one* characteristic of the way a dog relates to what it perceives does stand out clearly. In contrast to the diverse relations freely available to human beings, animals seem to be limited, wholly or almost wholly, to a single potential way of relating, which shows as a fixed, unfree, "instinctive" bond that compels the animal to offer always the same "response" to the same phenomenon under the same circumstances. This one potential way of relating for animals would seem to correspond most nearly with that one among many possible and freer human relations which is characterized as "enslaved," "compulsive" submission or addiction to something.

Something—and it is something from dreaming—argues that this is in fact so. For if there were not some kindred affinity between people and animals at least regarding this one mode of relationship, how could it happen so often that a human dreamer sees himself unexpectedly changed into a dog and running around on all fours, only to revert just as suddenly to human form and behavior? How else could the actions of animals encountered in dreaming generate, in the more seeing mind of the awakened dreamer, immediate insights into enslaved relationships that plague his own existence?

We shall return to this in a moment, but let us make one remark in passing. If all this is true, then animal nature is to be understood as a primitive form of human existence. In that case, all attempts to grasp human behavior on the basis of its animal counterpart would be doomed from the start, being predicated on an inappropriate anthropomorphism of animals. It would be scientifically sounder, then, to go in the other direction, trying to understand animals on the basis of human behavior, regarding them as primative forms of human existence.

Now, of all animals, dogs in dreaming or waking existence communicate with us most expressively, being as highly domesticated as, but more dependent on us, than cats and birds. They confront us with such diversity, each breed distinct in shape and behavior from all the others and each individual having a particular immutable character. Any dog, though, whether we meet him in our waking state or while dreaming, is still much more expressive. His four legs refer to the earth on which he stands and runs in daylight and night's darkness, the sky's winds and rains touching him. His obedience to his master connects him with mankind. His being born out of another dog speaks of the divine principle or the ancient "physis" that generates living beings from "nature's womb. In this sense, then, one dog (like any other thing in waking and dreaming) refers from its own nature in a fourfold way to human beings, to the creative divine transcending everything that is, to the sky's limitless expanse and to the earth. If a dog is to communicate so much, a person must have a corresponding sharpness of sight and hearing— the person who dreams and the "dream interpreter" alike. But it is precisely this ability to watch and listen that has become so difficult for people now. Our "vision" has become largely restricted to perceiving only that of the encountered phenomena which is quantifiably measurable when they are taken as isolated objects. Above all, we have lost to a great extent the capacity of seeing what is qualitatively essential in them, including all their inherent qualitatively meaningful references to the rest of the world. Only with long and patient exercise can we recover this prerequisite for a genuine appreciation of dreaming.

Crude as our sketch of the nature of dogs has been, it conveys the nature of dreamed dogs, too, which are like any other dogs we might encounter, nothing more nor less. How, then, can "dream interpreters" justify asserting that dreamed dogs, along with their observable nature, represent the "personification" of the dreamer's own animalistic traits? Where, we wonder, would the dreamed dog ever get such "symbolic" significance—unless, of course, we are assuming from the start that the dreamer himself has made the dreamed dog inside himself and has outfitted his creation with more significance than any God himself would be in a position to do.

However, there is no evidence for the existence of such a hidden, endopsychic dog manufacturer. All the ways in which we experience what we encounter in our dreaming states coincides—as long as the dreaming state is lasting—exactly with the ways we see the entities of our waking life. Also in dreaming, dogs encounter us from their places in the open realm which is our world, just as they do in our waking lives. In the absence of factual evidence, any additional alleged "subjective" meaning attached to dreamed dogs, along with the necessarily posited "intrapsychic" agent producing this meaning, must be labeled the mental construction of the "dream interpreter." Such constructions have nothing to do with the reality of dream experience itself.

It is only when we let a dreamed dog simply be a dog that it begins to stimulate our thought: The very fact that the human dreamer perceives a dog rather than, say, a wild lion or a fish, a domesticated, warm-blooded creature rather than a plant or a stone, tells us awakened dreamers something essential. It lets us recognize that, at least during the dreaming, something about the nature of a dog is affecting the dreamer deeply. The dog's mere presence shows that the dreamer's existence is open enough to admit the phenomenon "dog" into the world-realm of his dreaming perception. But we can also discover something else important. The dreamer can let us know how he, a perceptive being, responds to what he has perceived, how he relates himself to the dog.The dreamer can approach the dog happily, react with indifference, or flee from it in terror.

We can learn a great deal about any human dreamer by attending to these two circumstances. We must first consider exactly for what phenomena the dreamer's existence is so open that they may have entered and shone forth into its understanding light. This in turn tells us what phenomena are not accessible to the perception of his dreaming state, or, in other words, for the entrance of which phenomena the dreamer's existence is still closed. As a second step, we need to determine *how* the dreamer conducts himself toward whatever is revealed to him in the clearance of his dreaming world, particularly the mood that predicates this way of behaving. If both of these can be accurately described, we reached a full understanding of the dreamer's existence during the dream period. Any comment over and above those potentialities amounts to arbitrary padding, because human existence is by nature a series of particular attunements and responses to the meaningful presence of phenomena that reveal themselves in one's world. A human existence obviously involves many more potential ways of perceiving and acting than any given moment of waking or dreaming shows, and these possibilities are all very important to the person in question. But when they are not involved with the dreamer's Being-in-the-world as it is existing in his dreaming, they contribute little to our understanding of the dream phenomena as such.

The phenomenological approach to a dreaming existence is not only scientifically viable but can also be a source of great value in therapy. However, *the therapeutic application should not be confused with the phenomenological understanding of the dreaming elements in their entire meaningfulness.* It is one thing to understand the particular mode of human Being-in-the-world occurring while, and reported after, dreaming; it is another thing entirely to apply this understanding therapeutically to the awakened dreamer, though of course the understanding has to come before the application.

We can avoid distorting dreaming elements with our personal speculations only when we stop assuming hidden and different meaning behind the significances that disclose themselves to us directly from the given dream contents. We must, instead, let the elements of the dreaming world remain exactly as they were when they revealed themselves to the dreamer. If, for example, the dreamer encounters a dog in his dreaming world, we simply are able to state that the meaningfulness of a dog's manner of living is showing itself to the dreamer, is approaching him, is telling him about itself from somewhere, near or far *"outside"* the dreamer. The most we can allow ourselves without falsifying the dreaming experiences is to ask the patient afterwards, if his perception, now that he is awake, is not a good deal clearer than it was in his dreaming state? We may ask the reawakened dreamer in particular: "Since you dreaming experience belongs as much to your existence as your waking life, can't you now see, that you have awakened, that a dog-like subjection to things you encounter not only exists in your world as a relationship of an external animal but also as a feature of your own existence?" A follow-up question would be: "Now that you are awake, don't you sense an attitude of panic toward your own tendencies to fall prey, like an animal, to what is encountered by you, like the panic you experienced toward the 'external' dog in your dreaming?"

In this way we avoid asserting that the canine manifestation of the dreaming world has an "inherent significance" beyond that of just a strange dog; or that it incorporates, represents, and "symbolizes" some canine aspect of the dreamer's own nature. Any such talk of "dream symbolism," and any dream interpretation on either the subjective or the objective level, presupposes the existence within the dreamer of some "unconscious," already existing double, equipped with powers far beyond his own. There would have to be some such double to recognize, as the dreamer himself could not while dreaming, that doglike modes of behavior lay within him. The double would also have had to want to keep this knowledge from the dreamer, and would have to be able to enforce his will through the techniques of camouflage and "psychic projection outward."

Where practical therapy is concerned, it is no matter of indifference whether a dream element is reinterpreted on the subjective level, as a depth-psychological "symbol," or used phenomenologically to guide the reawakened patient toward a sense of his own doglike potentialities. For all symbolic reinterpretations fail to take into account the limitations of the dreaming state as to a more accurate self-appraisal. The dreaming patient's distance from himself is seen in the fact that dream phenomena which do not belong to his own existence nevertheless have the power to cue him to potential ways of his own being.

At best, the patient grasps symbolic reinterpretations of dreamed phenomena on a superficial, intellectual basis. But if an awakened dreamer is simply asked whether he can sense existential possibilities of his own that correspond to the meaningfulness of the features of dreamed phenomena, the proper insight will reveal itself out of the patient's heart and be embraced.

Once again, the proper question is whether the awakened dreamer perceives "doglike" existential possibilities of his own more clearly now than he did in the dreaming state. Such phenomenological adherence to actual experience renders all hypothese of a "psychic unconscious" superflous. Later we will point out in detail why depth psychology's supposition of a "psychic unconscious" is not only unnecessary for an adequate dream theory, but very harmful in any theoretical or practical application of knowledge gained from dreams.

For the moment, however, we need keep in mind only that the supposedly complex problem of "dream interpretation" can be reduced to two simple questions. To what phenonema is a person's existence at the time of dreaming sufficiently open, that they may shine forth into it and so come into being? The second question concerns whether, now that he is awake, he is able to recognize features of his own existence which are identical in essence with the traits of the phenomena which he could perceive in his dreaming state only outside himself, from "external" objects, animals, or fellow human beings?

If we do this, we will no longer need to take one particular mode of existence, dreaming existence, and objectify it as some concrete "dream" that people can "have." Even less will we be tempted to personify dreaming existence as a homunculus in the dreamer's mind that can mobilize a will of its own and engage in strategic maneuvers against the dreamer.

Freed of the misleading and superfluous additions of modern psychologistic dream theory, we will be ready to begin training for an undistorted view of the Being-in-the-world of dreaming human beings. An approach so simple is often criticized as "banal," but as our sketch of canine nature has shown clearly, this reproach falls back on the critics themselves, people who have become blind to the wealth of meaning in every phenomenon we encounter, whether waking or dreaming. It is precisely an attachment to the banal that restricts their vision to seeing only impoverishment in things.

Our new dream theory can be called a phenomenological approach, as opposed to the traditional causal and deterministic attitudes, since it keeps strictly to the actual phenomena of dreaming. It aims to set forth an increasingly clear picture of these phenomena—phenomena that could always be seen, however indistinctly, from the first.

We will begin our practical exercises in the phenomenological understanding of dream elements by examining very simple dream sequences and going on to progressively complicated ones. Of course, as we have stressed already, any exercise must be based on repetition.

Dreams of Persons Considered Totally Healthy by Themselves and Others

EXERCISES IN THE PHENOMENOLOGICAL APPROACH TO DREAMING, WITH ILLUSTRATIONS FOR THE PRACTICAL APPLICATION OF THIS NEW UNDERSTANDING OF DREAMS

Example One: Simple Dream of a Healthy European

I'm eating lunch with my old friend, M.H., in the Hohe Restaurant in Zollikon. The room is moderately occupied by people of both sexes. The voices of some women and of a few children can be heard somewhere, too. Sunlight is filling the dining room, warm and bright. We're very happy to be able to meet again in a place that's so peaceful and relaxed. We both order the same thing, an *entrecote cafe de Paris*. We eat heartily and talk about our children. I notice with satisfaction how much my guest is enjoying his meal, how he is really going at it with his teeth. Then I wake up, a little sad that my friend's visit has only been a dreamed event. The day before I had wished very strongly that he'd visit me again.

At first glance this dream sequence seems to be one of the kind Freud called "undisguised symbolic wish-fulfillment dreams" and used to "prove" two key points of his very complex dream theory. "Such undisguised dreams," he stated flatly, "*naturally have inestimable value as proof* that the true nature of dreams in general signifies wish-fulfillment."[2] But as we stated in an earlier book on dreams, this one "proof" Freud mustered is as suspect as the inference that because some roses are white then all colored roses are essentially white roses, their color being merely disguised whiteness.

Freud also believed that such dreams as this one could be used to illustrate one of the four processes which he attributed to unconscious dream-work, this one being the transformation of wishes and desires into completed actions. As the dreamer himself admitted, the day before he dreamt he often had the wish for his friend M.H. to visit him again as soon as possible. Now, might even this way of stating it be a subjectivistic-psychologistic violation of actual experience? Can wishing be called a thing—a "wish," a psychic configuration existing of itself somewhere in a person? Is there, "in" a person, even one desire that is attached to some endopsychic representation of an external object? We have pointed our before that there is no evidence in the actual phenomena of human existence for the existence of such endopsychic entities as representations, or affects attached to them. Yet not even the most important precondition for these assumptions has yet been explained: No one knows where or what that "psychic" container is to which "in" might refer. If the reply is "in" a psyche, it must first be demonstrated that we human beings possess psyches, entities that exist somewhere at hand in some hollow space. Second, we would need to know the nature of this "psyche" into which "affects" and representations of the external world might enter as though it were a capsule.

If we follow the phenomenological, or Daseins-analytic, approach and keep to the facts of the experience itself, we find only that several times the day before his dream, the dreamer consciously entered into a very specific relationship to his friend: he wanted his friend nearby. No "wishing," however, constitutes an independently existing isolated endopsychic configuration that can transform one thing into another.

All wishing is inherently a wishing *for something*. This means that our dreamer's wishing is a specific way of relating the whole person to some phenomenon on a basis equivalent to other ways of relating, such as touching something and smelling it. The relationship to the wished-for thing differs from other potential modes of relating mainly in that the wishing person is content to sustain a passive longing for a thing, whether it is present to the sense or perceived remotely. In either case, he dispenses with bringing it into his immediate presence because there are insurmountable obstacles or because his desire is not strong enough to overcome lesser obstacles. Endopsychic representations play no more a part in wishing than they do in, say, physical contact. A person who wishes for something is, like one who is touching it, already dwelling "out there" with that thing—human Being-in-the-world open to the phenomena it encounters where they reveal themselves in the clear realm of perception.

This is how matters stood with our dreamer *before* he went to sleep. Speaking scientifically, it can only be said that at that point his perception recognized a relationship to the friend, but only in the form of wishing for his presence. And that presence was the limited one of visualizing the friend far away at his home in Hamburg. But *once sleep and dreaming had begun*, his wishing for his friend to be near vanished; the dreamer's existential realm opened out, allowing him to perceive his friend as an immediate, sensed presence.

In the state of dreaming, then, there was no need for the first step of *wishing* for the friend to be near. And no hypothetical endo-psychic desire had to transform itself into some other endopsychic entity, the representation of a physically perceptible external object, for example. This whole process is unnecessary as well as ground-less: How can some wish arise "in a sleeping mind," only to be trans-formed through some assumed dream-work into an actual presence? How could an endopsychic desire, a thing for whose ex-istence there is absolutely no proof, ever be transformed into some-thing else? What had happened, in the passage from waking to dreaming, was a change of the dreamer's whole mode of existence, which includes the character of the realm of perception that made up his existence and the way in which his friend was present.

Is it really this simple? Is this all we can learn from our pseudo-wish-fulfillment dream? Whatever the case, the dreaming did show that the subject's untroubled daytime relationship to his friend did not change in the dreaming mode of his existence. A close examina-tion of the dreamer also revealed that before going to sleep he had very much wanted something else, too, something to eat, because an upset stomach had made him fast all day. The connection between the waking wish for food and the actual eating during the dream that followed is the same as that between the wish for the friend and the friend's physical presence in the dream. Before the subject fell asleep, food was available to him only as something desirable, but as being there for him only in that mode of presence which we call a visualized or represented one. By contrast, while dreaming he en-joyed the immediate, sensed presence of two *entrecotes cafe de Paris*. This simple approach to things keeps one from empty, and therapeutically harmful, speculation and leads to an abundance of fruitful theoretical and therapeutic insights into the makeup of the dreamer—more insights, in fact, than we could ever fully exhaust.

Even the simplest dream therefore reveals the two fundamental principles that allow us to penetrate the existential mode of a person during sleeping. First, we must notice what phenomena the dreamer's *Da-sein* is open to during the dream and how they affect him. Second, we must scrutinize the dreamer's response to what reveals itself to him, how he conducts himself toward what he sees.

Our simple illustration also lets us see how much of the manipulation involved in the generally recommended method of dream interpretation is superfluous and misleading. In our effort to enter into the dreamer's existential state, we managed without his supposedly indispensable "free associations." In fact, those "free associations" might have led us far off the mark, missing the meaning inherent in the dream elements themselves. That danger is all too often present with "free association" from individual dream elements. First, such "associating" must usually wait a few days to happen, until the patient's next session, and in the meantime, other experiences may have put the patient in a completely different mood. Furthermore, the course "free association" follows may be strongly influenced by any number of waking situations at a given time, not the least of which is the presence of the analyst. The analyst's theoretical expectations, which cannot stay hidden from the patient for long, are particularly active in codeterming the direction "free association" takes. This helps explain why the "free associations" of patients in Freudian analysis regularly head toward instinctual desires, while in Jungian patients they lead to archetypal structures and mandalas. And if patients in Daseins-analysis were encouraged to practice "free association" (in the Freudian sense), no doubt they would keep coming up with typically existential ideas.

Even the "amplification" of "dream contents" Jung preached generally harms the understanding of dreams and, more important, the therapeutic process itself. For instance, the dreamer in our illustration might have introduced various myths and legends to "amplify" his dream of eating *entrecotes*, and these myths and legends might have led us to abstract an archetype, such as "*cornucopia*," which would be supposed to exist in a psychic unconscious. But such "amplifications" only divert the dreamer from his own world and the personal existence to which he is responsible and presuade him to savor "interesting" accounts of distant worlds and ages instead. While such activity is not harmful in itself, the time the dreamer spends thinking about mythical heroes will not be spent working on his own way of being.

However, if "amplification" is taken to mean explicating, opening, and revealing the meanings and frames of reference that belong directly to concrete elements of the dreaming world, or to the way the dreamer conducts himself toward these elements, it is indispensable. Such "explication" requires that the awakened dreamer give an increasingly refined account of the dream sequence, but this should be elicited only by letting the subject supplement his first sketchy remarks with more detailed statements. The goal is to be put together as clear as possible a waking vision of what actually has been perceived in dreaming. "Faulty memory" is naturally a factor here, but no more than it is in the recall of events in waking life. Note that this has nothing to do with the Freudian concept of secondary revision, or interpolation, or with the Jungian concept of "amplification" as retrieval from ancient myths and legends. It is simply getting a full account of just what kinds of things can reveal themselves to the dreaming person, as well as an equally complete description of the ways he has responded to them. In other words, the aim is to make visible the dreaming subject's whole Being-in-the-world: the particular way of being open (or limited) that characterized—and was—his *Da-sein* for the duration of the dreaming.

Thus, if we wish to see our dreamer's existential makeup, we had best dispense with "free association." Nor do we need any prior knowledge of his life history. This is true for all dreams and assumes only that the wakened dreamer describes his dreaming with enough detail about significance and context. The latter includes biographical materials to which the dream elements themselves point—but only materials drawn from actual experience. If, as once happened to one of Jung's patients, the dreamer sees a table that he recognizes, even in the dream, as the same table whose cold surface glared at him twenty years earlier when his father was berating him for poor academic performance, then the reference to the angry father comes out of the dream table itself. This contextual significance belongs to the table itself as it assumes thematic presence in the open realm of the patient's dreaming world.

Once a neurotic becomes aware of the peculiarities of his *latest* conduct in dreaming, he tends to recall earlier situations in which he has conducted himself in the same way. He also begins spontaneously seeing the pathogenic behavioral patterns of the mentors who since his infancy have brought him up in a neurotic way and who continue to deny him freer choices in the way he is.

But now we are already discussing the *therapeutic application* of dream theory, and our first dream example can offer little insight here. The dreaming subject shows no neurotic symptoms when he is awake, nor does any neurotic compulsion show in his dreaming of eating *entrecotes* with his friend. He did not feel pressed for time in the dreaming, and he was not given to boredom. In space, he was neither hemmed in nor spanning the cosmos in near-psychotic anxiety. Instead, he was serene, at ease, and engaged in a mutually warm relationship with a friend. The children of both the dreamer and his friend were present, too, in the conversation. At most, it could be indicated that women were conspicuously absent from the dream phenomena. This absence might move us to question the awakened subject cautiously—and only cautiously—regarding the openness of his waking existence to women. Such considerations have merit only if the subject's distance from women was manifested in *both* dreaming and waking. But though there were no women in the thematic foreground or visible to the eye, even this dream world was not entirely devoid of feminine influence, for the dreamer heard women's voices from somewhere in the dining room.

It would certainly be possible to attribute the friend's visit to a homosexual drive and then derive the shared lunch from a libidinal regression to the "oral stage of development." It is possible to assume anything one wants to assume. But such a mental construct has no basis in the actual phenomena of the subject's existence and could therefore never be verified. Moreover, such speculations generate new pseudo-problems that are as impossible to solve as they are easy to avoid. There is the concept of libidinal energy: How can the whole world of a human being, waking and sleeping, ever be constructed from this notion? For the essential quality of the human world is its unbroken connectedness to the meaning in whatever it encounters. Physicalistic concepts, which include energies of any sort—even libidinal energy—do not conform to this fundamental aspect of the human world, because they all are "blind." If we try sidestepping the dilemma by claiming that drives and libido refer to "psychic" energies, we simply raise the new question of what the term "psychic" really means in this context.

Examples 2−7: Dreams from Healthy Swiss Army Recruits

Young men around the age of twenty who are fit for active duty are presumably in robust health and may be expected to exhibit "normal," uncomplicated dreaming behavior. We owe the following dream specimens to the industry of a captain in the Swiss infantry, who has recorded them randomly from accounts given by his recruits during a four-month training period. A psychologist in civilian life, the captain needed material for his statistical work.

Example 2

Today I had a dream about my first great love, a girl I haven't thought about while waking for at least two years. In the dream, I accidentally meet up with her. We sit down on a bench. The thing I remember best is that I am allowed to hold her hand. But by then, I'm sorry to say, the brief dream is already over.

In this dream, this young man engages body and soul in the tender relationship to his first love. His entire being is involved in that single dreaming relationship. He is happy that he may hold the girl's hand. A human existence is attuned in itself as a whole to happiness, whenever it is able at the given moment to carry out one of its essential inner possibilities. To make sense of this we should have no need of any additional explanatory device, such as, for instance,

an endopsychic "affect," the presence of which can never be demonstrated. The sector of the world that the dreamer's existence is
able to hold open is broad enough to grant to his first love a very intimate, highly sensible presence. But she could never have suddenly
appeared to him in this fashion—not even while dreaming—had she
not remained a part of his world all during the two years when he
had, as he put it, "never thought about her." The answer is, of
course, that her presence during those years was not perceptible to
his senses. Nor was she "there" any longer thematically in his
"thoughts" or "imagination." Instead she persisted in his world
only at the edge of his vision, as a peripheral presence, not an entity
with central thematic importance.

The sudden transformation of that peripheral presence into a
sensory one, such as occurred in the dream, is usually "explained"
through a peculiar imaginative model. It is said that a "cerebral
engram coding" has been activated. Of course, that kind of talk
clearly belongs in the realm of the contemporary mythology of the
brain. Not that molecular biology won't soon unearth some empirical results concerning how once perceived entities are
"remembered," or better "retained," in the open realm that comprises our human world. But the connection can never be more than
one of mere simultaneity. For, if the recruit's first love had not persisted, as the person she is, in her proper place within his open realm
of perception, if she had really been no more than a material-
energetic "cerebral engram" for two years, how could that mere
engram ever have accomplished the miracle of reconstituting the
perception of the young girl as the first love during his dreaming?

All that our dreamer needed for his happiness was to hold the
girl's hand. Had he been a somewhat older man, and had he not
spent his youth in central Switzerland—a region where abhorrence
of sensual love is practically made official—his dream might have
pointed to a neurotic fixation requiring therapy. In that case, the
analyst would probably have communicated his astonishment that
the love relationship in the dream had gone no further, never expanding into a more erotic one. The analyst's surprise might have

made the subject realize for the first time that the limited behavior he accepted in his dreaming was not just a matter of course. This would probably have come as a shock to the patient, because he had probably never known that freer behavior toward women was permissible, or even possible. The mere utterance of surprise on the part of the therapist is generally enough to indicate to neurotically inhibited patients the possibility of a freer existence. They are encouraged to experiment when the therapist is "stunned" by their "decency." The therapist's reaction is therefore an aid in therapy.

But our recruit considered himself completely normal and healthy. That is exactly what he was within the protective circle of his local peers. There is good reason to expect that in just a few years he will have learned a much freer way of behaving toward women, without the necessity for therapeutic intervention, and will carry this new behavior right into waking life.

Example 3

I bought a new motorcycle, this fantastic Honda CB 450. When I got it home, my mother told me and the bike to go to hell. She was burned up because I spent so much money on it. So I rode out into the world, and somewhere I met a girl. I fell in love with her right away. She was crazy about my racy machine. After a while I took her back home with me on the bike. My mother ran over and put her arms around me. When I turned around, suddenly my old BMW R 51/3 was there instead of the Honda, and the girl had disappeared. It was a funny dream.

Now, a Honda CB 450 is not a "symbol" in the "depth-psychological" sense of the term. Instead, we all recognize a Honda CB 450 as the very thing that it is in itself: a device having considerable power and allowing for extremely rapid locomotion. What the rider actually mounts, and becomes physically joined to, is the force of a multihorsepower motor. No wonder that a Brigette Bardot loves to pose on motorcycles while crooning verses about the sensuous thrill of their rattling and vibration. Such impressions are by no means merely secondary and subjective; they are not "symbolic" meanings out of a subject's unconscious psychic layer tacked onto some underlying "pure actuality" of the Honda. Instead, they are fundamental to the Honda, the significance that comprises its essence. That is just how the Honda addressed the recruit in his dream, by revealing its essential features. But his mother would have nothing to do with any machine that could be used to race away on. She became angry when her son showed up on the bike, consigning him to hell. For all too often, at least in the eyes of their sons, mothers seem bent on preventing their children from making independent decisions. At the start of his dream, our recruit doesn't pay much attention to his mother's scolding. It does not occur to him to abandon his bike, return home to his mother, and appease her anger with protestations of remorse. As a matter of fact, he roars out into the world without a care. Once out there, he is struck by the possibility of erotic behavior toward the opposite sex. Freed of his mother, he finds someone his own age to love. Her excitement over the powerful new machine echoes his own lust for adventure. However, his newly won freedom is not yet strong enough to stand on its own. The young man's mother quickly draws him away from the girl and into her own arms. She still is so powerful that she is capable of banishing this young girl as well as the Honda out of her son's vision at which he is existing at that moment.

In the case of this recruit, a painstaking therapeutic application of phenomenological dream theory would be in order. It would need to confine itself, however, simply to eliciting actual entities as they appeared to the dreamer and to clarifying his behavior toward them. Strong emphasis would need to be placed on the transformation that occurs in the dreamer's relationships to the dreamed girl friend and his own mother. A simple retelling of the dream by the analyst would probably suffice to enlighten the patient to the inconsistencies in his dream behavior. His immediate reaction upon awakening, a studied indifference toward the "funny dream," would indicate the need for a thorough consideration of his waking relationship to his mother.

This would in turn have represented for the waking subject, impelled as he was by his highly expressive dream, a first step toward a more permanent curring of his ties to his mother. It would have done so, I say, except that here the patient himself did not seek out therapy. He had never felt the slightest pang of suffering. For a man of his age and background, the dream was not really pathological. A man such as he will no doubt mature until he is capable of keeping his Honda and actually racing out into the world on it, whether in dreams or waking life.

Perhaps it might also have been wise for the analyst to point out that the dreamer had made use of a technological device, the motorcycle, rather than leaving his mother on foot, or on the back of some living animal such as a horse. The subject might have been asked to compare his waking relationship with machines to that with his fellow human beings, himself included, and other animate creatures. But here again, in the present age of technology even a waking preoccupation with machines cannot be labeled abnormal. There are quite a few young men who think of motorcycles, both in their dreams and while awake, as far more animate and desirable than, say, horses or young girls. Creatures of highrises and asphalt that they are, young cityfolk are hardly able to countenance an intimate relationship to the life of nature anymore. Or if they can, it is likely to consist in an attitude of flight, or defensive aggression, as witnesses the following example.

Example 4

All of a sudden I find myself in a primitive jungle. Everywhere I look, I can see only trees and dense undergrowth. I am cutting a way through the brush with a machete. Suddenly I hear a rustling nearby. Thinking little of it, I push on into the jungle. But that's where I go wrong. A snake bumps into me and bites me in the calf. Instinctively, I pull out my gun and begin shooting at it. The snake cringes a few times, but then it's dead. I open up the bite with my machete, then start sucking out the wound. I begin to feel terrible, but I know I have to keep on sucking or else in a few moments I'll be dead. But then I go unconscious. When I awaken, I'm in a jungle hospital. Sitting next to my bed is a nurse, dressed all in white and looking at me with a mother's loving gaze.

Like the motorcycle in the preceding dream, the jungle here is no mere "image." It is as little a "symbol" in the Freudian sense of being a camouflaging cover for something quite different, as it is in the Jungian sense of some metaphorical expression of a significance which the waking subject has not yet fully grasped. There is, for example, no evidence, indicating that the jungle in the dreaming is merely a symbolization of a "collective unconscious" presumed to exist in the depths of a concrete psyche. Once more we must stress that all dream theories subscribing to this view lack any proof for the existence of an "internal symbol generator." Yet every symbolic theory of dreaming inevitably posits just such an internal, symbol-making counterpart of the dreamer, someone who knows more than the waking or dreaming subject, who recognizes his aims and capabilities, and who can disguise that knowledge by wrapping it in symbols, then project these outward.

But if we stay away from this brand of speculation, all we can say is that the existential state of the dreamer has allowed him an immediate sensory/sensual perception of a primitive jungle, a machete, a revolver, a snake, and nothing else. To an unbiased observer, the jungle that presented itself to the dreamer's senses is nothing more than a jungle, but nevertheless as "real" as any jungle can be perceived in his waking state. Likewise, the dreamed snake is "only" a snake; it does not "really signify" anything other than itself. The machete, similarly, is "just" a machete, and the revolver a "mere" revolver, not some "penis symbol." They are no "images" of something else. The killing of the snake is experienced by the dreamer as just that. The hospital he awakens in is a hospital, and the nurse is a kind, maternal woman in sharp contrast to the destructive presence of the snake.

Any jungle, whether it appears to a waking or a dreaming person, evokes a superabundance of significances/meanings and frames of reference. It is inherently a dark, untouched region of nature, teeming with plant and animal life, aand barely permitting access. Our recruit bravely forged ahead through the jungle in his dream, clearing a path for himself by destroying plants with his sharp machete. Soon enough, however, he was stopped by a poisonous snake that slithered toward him out of the jungle's darkness.

Now, a dreamed snake is not simply an emblem for the male member, nor is it a "symbol" of the dreamer's own autonomic life processes. It exists, as it is immediately experienced in the dreaming, on its own, without the help of a psychic unconscious. If one thinks about snakes one peculiarity that sets them apart from mankind is their cold-bloodedness. Then again, snakes are bound to the ground, having no legs to raise them above it. Few humans are at all familiar with snakes' habits. One thing, though; snakes can be extremely dangerous to unprotected humans. They spring out of a hole in the earth without warning to capture their prey, and their winding movement is unpredictable, therefore frightening. In his dream, our recruit experiences all of these traits of the snake and the jungle as comprising their innermost natures. He perceives that there is, in the sector of the world open to his dreaming existence, a dark, unfamiliar realm of living phenomena. His curiosity, his thirst for knowledge, induce him to bully his way into that realm. Being unsuspecting, however, he exposes himself to lethal danger: the snake suddenly shooting out at him to regard the undomesticated life of the jungle as a hostile force. So powerful is this force, in fact, that it renders him unconscious and might easily have stamped out his human life, had it not been for his quick thinking after the attack and the chance to kill the snake with his revolver. The subject then "awakens" in his dream, no longer in a threatening jungle, but instead in the protective environment of a dreamed hospital room. No snake has access to this asylum, only a tenderly maternal nurse clad in immaculate white.

Such is the story of our recruit's experiences while dreaming. It hides no additional "symbolic" meaning behind its immediately perceptible elements. Furthermore, these elements impress the dreamer solely with the significance they have always carried for him. Neither he himself, nor any miraculous creature supposed to exist within him—i.e., "the unconscious,"—knows anything more. For only entities that reveal themselves directly, with the same meanings they hold in the subject's waking environment, can gain admittance to his dreaming mode of existence.

It may also be true, though, that this same person is sharper, more insightful after waking than he has been during the dream experience. We cannot dismiss the possibility that his waking existence may be open and responsive to much more diverse and richer world phenomena. This is especially likely if the analyst encourages the patient to begin to think about a possible relationship between the dreaming and waking life; for instance, now that he is awake, might he not well sense other dark and unfamiliar forces in addition to the overwhelming jungle life which was present in the dreaming state. He might be asked whether he now—during his waking state—realizes that it is not only nature, but his own existence which contains a primeval realm full of untamed possibilities for living, one that only appears to him now, in his present state of existential development, as consisting of dangerous and threatening forces. It might then be wise to follow these questions by reminding the patient that destruction of those forces would also rob him of their vitalizing influence. The matter would be very different, of course, if he, the patient, were able to recognize that "dark," animal-like behavior also belongs to his own existential possibilities. Then he may learn to stand to it and to manage it responsibly. The reawakened dreamer might also be directed to that moment in his dreaming when he could see himself only as a helpless, infantile being under the hospital care of a motherly protector. Could the patient tell the analyst more about this now that he was awake? Did he recognize now, waking, any persistent infantile attachment to his mother, something resembling his dreaming relationship to the hospital nurse?

The analyst is entitled to ask such questions, as we have said before, because a person's dreaming and waking existences, though they seem to have different "worlds" and "realities," nevertheless inhere in the one and the same *Dasein* of that person.

By the same token, the questions just recommended to the analyst do not constitute "dream interpretation" in the usual sense. They are not "dream interpretation," on either the "subjective" or the "objective" level. First of all, our approach never posits anything like subjectivity; there is no internal subject, in the Cartesian sense of a "thinking substance," nor is ther a "psyche" or "subjective consciousness capsule" to hold any endopsychic images. No "theory of cognition" could ever explain the way in which such an encapsulated "inner subject" would ever be able to transcend itself and reach the objects of the "outside world." We will examine this more closely in the final chapter of this book.

Example 5

Suddenly I see a horrible-looking giant about a hundred yards behind me. He's running after me, and I'm running away from him as fast as I can, but the distance between us keeps getting smaller. Soon he's so close that he'll get me with his next step. He actually steps on me with one of his giant feet, so that I end up wedged between his toes. It's just a matter of seconds until he squashes me altogether. He bellows out a scornful laugh. That's when I wake up.

We can quickly get to the heart of this dreaming by applying what we learned from our third example, the dreaming of the motorcycles: here again we shall proceed in a strictly scientific manner; this means adhering only to what can actually be observed about the dreamer's existential behavior toward the entities that appear to him in his dream world. In any such phenomenological, or *Daseins*-analytical examination of human activity—whether that activity belongs to a person's waking or dreaming existence—it is best to begin by clarifying precisely and succinctly the person's moods that prevail at various given moments. It is always important to consider the mood to which his existence as a whole is momentarily attuned, for it is this mood that determines the characteristics, the breadth or narrowness, of the perceptive realm which the existence is able to hold open and *as* which it "exists" at that given moment. Our latest recruit is attuned, while dreaming, to a panicked anxiety of death. Such an attunement reduces the dream world so drastically that, out of all conceivable human counterparts, the dreamer is able to countenance only a terrible giant who pursues him with intent to kill. The only thing in the dream world besides the giant is the dreamer's own *Dasein*, which now appears helpless and ridiculously tiny, hardly as big as one of the giant's toes, and which must engage itself in a vain attempt to escape being crushed beneath the giant's feet. But in the dream world of this subject, there is no savior and no successful rescue. Just as his fear of dying reaches its peak intensity, the dreamer is awakened by the scornful laughter directed at his plight by the giant.

The giant's laughter is so intensely real and is perceived at such an enormous volume, that it throws the dreamer's entire existence out of its dreaming mode and into the waking one. The same effect could have been had by an "external" stimulus of equal intensity, one that could be heard by any other waking person who happened to be in the same room as the subject. There would have been little point in calling the dreamed laugh "unreal" while labeling the other "real." The distinction is pointless unless we are able to specify what we mean by "reality."

That is all that the phenomena of the recruit's dreaming tell us on their own, nothing more. With a precise description of what was perceived during dreaming, the "dream interpretation" is ended. Anything added to his falls outside of the actual dreaming and adds nothing to our understanding of the dreamer's existence at the given moment. Above all, there is no justifiable way to claim that the strange giant is not "really" the giant he appears to be, but something quite different, although veiled by him. No evidence exists in support of the common interpretive transformation whereby a giant becomes not "really" a giant but a veiled, symbolic projection of the dreamer's internal images of his evil father, or his military officer, or—when the dreamer is a patient in therapy—of the analyst, or some amalgamation of all three authority figures. Equally without foundation is the statement that the dreamed figure was the pictorial expression of the so-called "animus" or of some "archetypal" giant. The mere fact that such giants have appeared in the dreaming of the most diverse peoples, all across the globe and throughout time, constitutes neither theoretical nor empirical proof for the actual existence of endopsychic archetypes belonging to a collective unconscious. That such giant figures have shown themselves so universally is an incontrovertible "empirical" fact, but this does not warrant the interpretation that in the depths of every human "psyche" there would rest a pan-human "archetype." Rather, the notion of "archetype" represents only one of the many possible abstract logical conclusions that might be made on the basis of actually experienced facts. As such, it has only the most minute chance of corresponding to something that actually exists. Why couldn't it be that giants have appeared in similar form as directly sensually perceptible presences to all sorts of people since prehistory, simply because there are such things as giants, although they never have existed in those modes of presence which are accessible to natural scientific investigations? At any rate, giants do not exist as images or patterns of force within an alleged "psyche"; we must revise our view and see them appearing independently out of the open realm of human existence, that is, engaged in dreaming, imagining, or hallucinating relationships to that which is encountered. But where do giants originate, then, if not in the interior of a human "psyche" and if not being produced by this allegedly existing thing "psyche"? Answer: out of Be-ingness as such, i.e., out of that great darkness (*Verborgenheit*) that rules all that is, heaven and earth, God and man, and out of which these things "come to light." Compared with the grandeur of that darkness, all notions of an endopsychic "unconscious," whether individual or collective, seem the gross distortions of a subjective reductionism, one that cannot even clarify its own subjective basis.[3]

Still another arbitrary addition to the actual dream phenomena would be to call the frightened coward in the dreaming a figurative personification of the dreamer's "ego." Now, the "ego" is a term that is constantly being bandied about today by psychologists; yet it does not have its basis in any demonstrable phenomenon of human existence. Such things as "egos" exist only as objectified abstractions of certain human behavioral possibilities. As a man untutored in psychology, our recruit would never have said, "My ego ran away from the giant." What he said, instead, was simply, "*I* ran as fast as *I* could." When a person says "I" very naturally like tha, whether waking or in dreaming, he does not have in mind any objective entity, material or immaterial. He means the sum of all the behaviroal possibilities that presently belong to him, and of all the modes of perception and behaving that make up selfhood.

If such psychological ego-constructs are empty and unfounded in fact then, they cannot contribute, within the framework of "dream interpretation," to a better understanding of actual dream phenomena. The traditional psychology of dreams has never been interested in that kind of understanding, anyway, since the theories, structured as they are around the natural scientific approach, have always aimed at something entirely different. They have set out, first and foremost, to establish some underlying, hypothetical causal explanation. In doing so, they followed the early lead of Freud, no matter whether they agreed with the remainder of his dream theory or not. "In our opinion," thus Freud describes the basic intent of his whole psychology, dream theory included, "perceived phenomena *must* give way to the assumed interplay of drives and impulses."[4] Freud, however, never gave reasons for his rather surprising "opinion" that the phenomena as they are immediately perceived *must* and have to recede behind the merely assumed tendencies. He was not capable of answering this crucial question, because he remained completely unaware of the underlying philosophy of his way of scientific thinking.[5]

Causal relationships, no matter how complete the chain of cause and effect, never deliver an understanding of anything. The leading natural scientists have already recognized that all that is registered in a causal relationship is a regular temporal succession of events, the succession in itself having no intrinsic meaning. Meaningfulness and understanding only exist in the realm of motivated relationships that constitutes a human life. Consequently, any inquiry into the nature and meaning of a dream sequence should aim at locating the place it occupies in the development of a human life history. Here, of course, we can return to the early Freud, for did he not open his pioneering *Interpretation of Dreams* by stating that all dream contents were meaningful psychic entities whose relation to waking existence he would establish? But Freud could not keep his promise, for he had at his disposal, in his attempt to understand specifically human phenomena, only the necessarily inadequate principle of causality. An adequate understanding of the character of human existence was not available to him.

Today, thanks largely to Martin Heidegger's insights into human nature, we can channel Freud's early attempts to penetrate the meaning of dreaming into a more directed search for the relation between the waking state of existence and its dreaming counterpart. The simple fact that waking and dreaming are experienced as two distinct existential modes, that we distinguish between them, suggests an intuited basis for doing just that. Two things can be distinguished only on the basis of a third thing that encompasses them both. We can tell red from green only because both partake of something we call color. Until we have grasped the nature of color, neither red nor green can exist for us. The question facing us now is, what particular thing unites the waking and dreaming states? Where our recruit's dreaming about the evil giant is concerned, to take an example, we can legitimately ask—though our question is not directed toward any "dream interpretation"—what common element found in the waking states before and after the dreaming might have given birth to the world of the dream itself. We noted at the heart of the "giant"-dreaming a mood of anxious panic. What might have brought about such an onrush of fear? Our first hint is the uncommon frequency with which dreams of annihilation visit army recruits as a group. For many recruits, being inducted means being suddenly lifted out of the pampered kind of family life that typically exists in the modern social welfare state. That is why so many see their induction as a forced conversion to a life of subordination; it is an involuntary submission to the absolute discipline of a male military hierarchy, which, thanks to the enormous power it wields, can demand superhuman achievement from new recruits. All things considered, then, the mere start of basic training was sufficient to create in our subject the sort of depressive, anxious mood that would precede a dreaming about a menacing giant. One recruit tried, of course, to conceal his mood while he was awake, but the existential mode of his dreaming state belied that effort. Not only did the mood of anxiety persist, it actually erupted in the dreaming state, flooding over and permeating the dreamer's whole existence. In any attunement to anxiety, e.g., in panic, the perceptive open world realm as which this human being basically exists is narrowed down to such an extent that only the threatening traits of all that is encountered can now enter into the existence's "field of vision." Thus our dreamer's existence was rendered unreceptive to anything except some mammoth threatening force.

In that mood or attunement determine the state of world-openness of the *Da-sein*, an understanding of mood is important not only where the present dreaming example is concerned, but for the therapeutic worth of any sound theory of dreaming. For again and again, it happens that a dreamer experiences with unprecedented intensity, and becomes engulfed in, some mood that has prevailed during the preceding dreaming state but which has lost any compelling impact in the everyday existence, with its division into a multitude of diverse world relationships. It repeatedly happens that a dreamer commits himself to a mood or world-attunement with an intensity and wholeheartedness unparalleled in his waking existence. A mood that is not adequately wakingly admitted can then predominate and call forth dream beings and events that correspond to it, whose significances are appropriate to it—in our example a dream Goliath—and which achieve an impressive, ineluctable, and sometimes uncomfortable closeness to the dreamer. When a patient in therapy is made aware of such dream happenings, he can no longer overlook his own corresponding waking world-attunement and moods.

If the dreamer in this instance had been a patient in analysis rather than a healthy recruit, he should have been asked the following questions: "While dreaming, you saw adult manhood only in the form of a strange giant who threatened your life. Now that you are awake, do you begin to sense that the same sort of adult manhood also exists as a possibility in your own life? Do you view your own coming to maturity with an attitude resembling panic? If you do, can you attribute your fear to the fact that you gauge your entire existential promise according to the self you already know, that of an immature young man? Such an unrealized existence must naturally be destroyed when it is forced prematurely to confront the powerful adult that will be your future self."

One thing we should keep in mind is that the anxiety experienced by our recruit in the face of the giant is not an isolated accidental phenomenon. In any momentary attitude of fear, such as this one, all the fears that the individual has ever felt in his past life emerge into the present behavior. For in the realm of human existence, past experiences persist, speaking into the present and codetermining a person's future behavior. By its very nature, human existence is never other than unfolded in its three temporal dimensions, which are not merely a bygone rigid petrified past, an isolated present, and a future of "not-yet." Since the *Daseins*-analytic theorist and practitioner is always working within this perspective, there is no substance in the oft-heard complaint that he does not concern himself with the life histories of his patients.

Example 6

Last night I dreamed about something I've dreamed about many times before. No one else existed, and I had the whole world to myself. I could take and use any car, any ship, anything there was. By taking over all the banks, I got hold of a pile of gold. Now, when I had appropriated everything in these dreams, I could decide who should be resurrected, usually my father, mother, brothers and sisters, and of course a beautiful girlfriend for me. In this narrow circle of people, I could really enjoy life. But the dreams usually ended with the thought that the new life was lonesome.

In the dream sequence reported above, the young man grants himself a godlike omnipotence over the things and creatures of his world. Anything that doesn't suit him, he simply does away with. Here there is no hint of the self-annihilation that figured in our previous example, the dreaming of the giant. After this dreamer has seized power, in fact, he allows his immediate family to be brought to life. But in the end this group is so small that the dreamer continues to feel lonely.

Is is easy to see why such a dream sequence would occur in an adolescent who has yet to attain independent selfhood and is still overwhelmed, each waking day, by the massiveness and complexity of those worldly beings, which are other than he himself. At this age, a person should not be considered unhealthy or abnormal simply because his chief aim, waking and dreaming, is "narcissistic" self-discovery and self-assertion. After all, any true, productive philanthropy invariably issues from an abundance of self-assurance, not a lack of it.

Our dreamer feels at ease only with his immediate family. He feels equal to these people, and it delights him to resurrect them again and again while dreaming. But whether awake or dreaming, the young man can experience as bringing happiness and comfort only those situations to which his own existence is able to confront and respond. Yet a sense of loneliness arises at the end of each of his related dream events. This loneliness is an indication of the dreamer's inherent inclination toward a fuller interpersonal existence. For only someone who needs others can know what it is to be lonely.

On the other hand, any repetitive dream sequence points toward a halting of the growth process in a person's waking existence. When this process begins again and the person is able to take a new step forward, the repetitive dream sequence promptly disappears.

If the young man ever decided to enter therapy because of his loneliness, he might be made aware of the limited realm of his existence shown in his dreaming. His interests are restricted to completely egotistical aims and his interpersonal relationships end with his immediate family. Perhaps this is in itself would be enough to provoke an expansion of his waking existence. But the therapist should take care not to intervene too soon, for doing so could harm a patient who is exceptionally un-selfreliant. If such were the case, it would be better to let the dreaming rest and to point instead to the potential for broader self-assertion in the patient's waking existence.[6]

Example 7

> I crawled through the streets and killed a woman by strangling her with a cord. It wasn't the only murder that night. In all I committed three murders, just for the fun of it. The other two women I stabbed instead of choking. After a long time I got caught and, in spite of my stubborn denials, was sentenced to death by hanging. I woke up terrified just as they were slipping the noose around my neck.

This is the most suspect of all the dreams reported by young men who are considered completely healthy, both by themselves and by others who know them. The twenty-year-old in question exhibited no neurotic or psychosomatic symptoms in his waking life, nor was his character particularly striking. He had female acquaintances, furthermore, whom he never thought of murdering while he was awake. But at night in his dreaming, he did away with any woman he encountered, not out of revenge or even rage but "just for the fun of it."

Since this is a dream which in the Freudian view would be labeled one of wish-fulfillment, it provides an excellent opportunity to dismantle the concept of wish-fulfillment as well as illustrate the phenomenological approach. No evidence of wishing exists in his dreaming behavior; wishing is superfluous, seeing that the dreamer discovers himself already in the process of murdering women. And even if he had felt an urge to kill women in his waking life, which was not the case, still it would be misleading to call his dream a wish-fulfillment dream. It is not even fair, solely on the basis of this dreaming, to attribute "unconscious death wishes" to the dreamer in his waking existence. Considering how easily modern psychology uses the phrase "unconscious desire," we cannot stress often enough that it refers to something that cannot exist. To speak of *unconscious* wishes has the logic of speaking of *wooden* iron. There is no such thing as isolated wishing. Wishing must exist in relation to some desirable thing, to some presence whose significance has been recognized at least as something desirable. Every act of wishing presupposes knowledge of a significant entity. How can it be that a person knows a thing and, at the same time, does not know it, is "unconscious" of it? Imagine what contortions are required to give this paradox an appearance of feasibility. But more about that later.[7]

What remains incontestable is that the recruit murdered all of the women he met while dreaming. Of all the possible ways in which a young man can behave toward women, only that of killing was available to our young man while he dreamed. This single mode of behavior is diametrically opposed to the conduct of a normal love relationship. Mature love entails recognizing all of the potential for life present in the love partner, and a willingness to fight with one's whole being for the full realization of that partner's existence.

But our recruit not only *kills* women, he takes pleasure in it. Now, a human *Dasein* is attuned to pleasure whenever it is allowed to engage in a fundamental relationship to what it encounters, and thereby approach self-fulfillment. Even the process of preparing to eliminate obstacles to fulfillment brings joy; it is a state of anticipatory pleasure. The dream sequence in itself speaks only of the pleasurable killing of three women, and of a resultant death sentence, apart from the single additional circumstance that the misdeeds occur at night. In taking in the entire dreaming existence of the recruit, at the moment of his misdeed the above account encompasses the sum content and significance of the dream. There is nothing else besides, either hidden or manifest. Whether in the subsequent waking state he is able to see much more significance in his dreamed murders, and in the sense of guilt he comes to feel while dreaming, is another matter entirely.

A therapeutic procedure based on *Daseins*-analytic dream theory would begin by having the reawakened dreamer tell whether he had anything against women in his waking state. Experience shows that the patient would then start to visualize more and more specific incidents from his past waking life which continued to cast a dark shadow over the patient's present, and reduce the full range of his existential behavior toward women, until it included in dreams only the possibility of killing. The motivational context of the patient's waking life history would make it clear that adult females had always stood in the way of his developing to an independent and self-reliant selfhood and, consequently, could only appear worthy of annihilation, never deserving of love.

Finally, the patient would become aware that one of two sets of circumstances is decisive for his latest dreaming. Either his mother and her successors had done him violence in impeding his human growth, or he would be struck with the knowledge that his own infantile attachment to his mother had allowed him to see her only as a prison denying him access to his maturity. Perhaps he would simultaneously recognize both circumstances as motives for his recent dreaming of killing women. Of course, his mother never comes up in the dream, which centers on three females who are total strangers. There is nothing about these women to back the contention that they all really "meant" his mother: the dreamed women are strangers, and nothing more. If a person, as a result of his mother's pathogenic behavior or some personal weakness, remains a subordinate child long after he has attained his official majority, he is commonly left with a perception that is not only childlike but pathologically reduced as well. From infancy onward, his existence has become rigidly set as a restricted "field of vision"; which explains why as an adult he continues to see all women in the role of mothers and, if his own mother's behavior was poisonous and imprisoning for him, as evil creatures deserving of death. What happens here is not, however, a change "within" the dreamer, meaning specifically a "carrying over," a "transference" of affects actually belonging to an "internal" representation of the mother. On the contrary, the existing of the person *as* a realm of perception, of seeing, persists as it was in infancy, so that he has to see all women just as he saw them and experienced them in his childhood.

The dreamer commits his murders exclusively at night. In the dark of night, he himself sees less, and he is less well seen by others. Presumably, our dreamer makes the most of the second circumstance. In his subsequent waking state, however, the recruit becomes aware that he would much rather hide his destructive desire to triumph over women from himself.

As for the second, decisive portion of his dreaming, in which the dreamer was sentenced to death, the recruit could possibly see much more while awake than he could during the dreaming itself. To be sure, he would need a therapeutic hint before he would be able to understand how strange it was to feel no guilt while he killed people during the dreaming, and that he had to be pronounced guilty by somebody else, by a judge, someone he did not even know. Waking, the recruit would sooner or later recognize that the reduction of his existing to a single mode of behavior leaves him existentially indebted to the totality of his own given possibilities of living, which are constituent for his existence. For he would learn to recognize that any arresting of the rightful development of any being shining forth into the open realm of perception as which he is existing is equivalent to suicidal behavior. Human existence can mature only by allowing itself to be engaged by whatever impinges on it, so that the encountered entity can come to its full being in the open realm of the human world. If a person does away with anything that claims his existence to serve as the open perceptive realm into which it may shine forth and thus come to be, he also deprives himself of carrying out any of his possible relationships toward it. This means to kill also part of himself as human existence. For human existence is basically made up of its possibilities to relate to what is encountered. It is this spirit of mutuality of any human existence and all other beings which counters any possibility that the notion of a phenomenologically understood *Dasein* represents an egotistical philosophy.

The *Daseins*-analytic approach also provides an insight into all of the other varieties of "guilt dreams" that occur in healthy or neurotic human beings, even though many of these people remain totally unaware of what it is they feel guilty about, or are charged with having done, in their dreaming. Such people often know less about themselves while dreaming than does our murderous recruit, never recognizing the source of their guilt. With expert therapeutic interrogation the significance of all sorts of "guilt dreams" can be understood. In the light of their waking existential mode, patients can realize that the guilt they have experienced while dreaming— whether that guilt is revealed in their dreaming through a specific person, a concrete task, or something even more vague—is grounded in the more fundamental, existential guilt of mankind.

The ontological guilt of human beings in general is one of omission. It arises because people never manage to develop all of their innate existential possibilities and therefore build up a debt to themselves. At any given moment, a human being is capable of engaging in only one of the myriad of possible relationships that constitute his existence. All other possibilities remain unexercised at that moment. In addition, new demands are constantly reaching him from the direction of his future, demands to which he is not yet able to respond and whose fulfillment must be deferred. Guilt is therefore an inherent part of human existence; it can never be expunged either by Freudian psychoanalysis, Jung's analytic psychology, or Daseins-analysis. Freud's old dream of using psychoanalysis to restore man to the presumed innocence of the savage of primitive times, or a young child, is worn out. Yet not all people have to suffer through guilt dreams, despite man's universal, existential guilt. Experience tells us that guilt dreams torment only those whose debt to their existential development is considerable greater than is absolutely necessary. It may be that they stubbornly refuse to yield fully to the call of beings with which an engagement in a relationship toward them would be very important to their existential development. It may also be that some pseudo-moralistic, neurotic reduction in their existential receptivity was acquired at an early age, preventing them from relating freely to the same entities. Neurotic guilt dreams regularly disappear when such people have succeeded in reliberating their existences through therapy. For then they are permitted to respond with all of their being to whatever addresses them; that is, they learn to live in a truly human fashion.

Yet no matter how many spectacular insights may occur to a dreamer after he has awakened, they fall outside the experience of the dreaming itself. Or, to put it another way, none of the significations recognized after the dreaming was originally "there" in the world of the dreamer, and certainly none was secreted away in some corner, or level, of a psychic container. This applies to the "ideas" that occur to patients undergoing *Daseins*-analytical treatment, as well as to the hypotheses and conclusions of more traditional dream interpretations. On the other hand, significances brought to light during a *Daseins*-analytic investigation of dream elements may induce the reawakened patient to visualize thematically every *analogous* significance that has a place in his past, present, or future life. In this way, of course, dream content may contribute in an important way to the existential enlightenment of an individual even *after* he has reawakened; and, as Freud himself realized, in the realm of the so-called neurotic and psychosomatic ailments, self-enlightenment is equivalent to healing.

Example 8: Dreaming of a Healthy, Twenty-four-Year-Old Black American Female, in Advanced Pregnancy

I found myself in the middle of a magnificent, dense African jungle. Sunlight poured down through the foliage of the tall trees. Birds were singing and chirping all around. I felt a great peace within me, a mood of happy tranquility. Gradually I became aware that I was an elephant, a big heavy elephant. I only took this fact in; it didn't surprise me at all. I moved through the jungle just the way elephants are supposed to, powerfully, deliberately, but gracefully. I was filled with an intense feeling of total peace and calm contentment.

Next I started to build a kind of wall out of tree trunks, piling one on top of the other. Each of them was carpeted in a heavy of layer of wild vines. To do this work, I used my elephant's trunk, which was very long and strong. I kept picking up trees from the ground with it, and placing them carefully on top of each other. That went on for a while. The work gave me a lot of pleasure, only I didn't understand why I was doing it. Yet I was filled with the deepest peace. I got a kind of esthetic satisfaction out of the work. My trunk was taking the place of my hands in the dream, but I didn't think anything of it. It seemed natural, as if it had always been that way. While I was building my wooden wall, I was fully aware of the spectacular beauty of the jungle. A wonderful feeling of bright relaxation pervaded my whole being. I was also becoming increasingly aware of my female nature. Just when that feeling reached its peak, I started to give birth to a little elephant. Even this didn't surprise me, though now I realized that I had been constructing the wooden wall as a kind of nest, or fortress, for the newborn baby. I experienced the actual birth in great detail, but without any pain at all. I immediately had a second elephant baby. During the births, I had been lying on my side. Now I got up and started to look after my newborn twins, still immersed in a marvelous feeling of fulfilled femininity.

A bit later I continued the work on my wall, keeping both elephant babies near me at all times. Realizing that I had attained the highest moment of satisfaction in my life, I took my time with the work, so much time, in fact, that I began to be overcome by a feeling of endless eternity. I knew that my life would always go on this way. For all eternity I would go on bearing more children and building new nests, all with an unchanging attitude of love.

The chief characteristic of the dream was that I never needed to think things over logically. I sensed everything in a direct, intuitive, or emotional way, feeling that I had a boundless knowledge of all things.

We shall never know what goes on in an elephant's world, or for that matter, whether elephants have a world, as we conceive of it. Like every other animal, they cannot speak our language and tell us how they experience their being. Therefore one thing is certain; they are not placed in the world in the same way as we humans. Of course, elephants are related in their own fashion to whatever impinges on them. Yet owing to their lack of speech we must always remain in the dark as to the manner of that relationship. Whenever we believe that we understand such animals, we have merely applied human standards to them and thereby inadvertently anthropomorphized them. Our dreamer, however much she felt and behaved like a *bona fide* elephant, was much more than that; she existed as a *human* elephant. Her existence, despite its elephant's outward form, was truly human. Her perception was held open to the presence and significance of entities that impinged on it in a uniquely human way; that is, she perceived things "linguistically," in the most profound sense of the word "language": the jungle, the sunlight, each shadow and tree trunk as a universal "jungle," "light," "shadow," "tree trunk," etc. Otherwise she could never have perceived herself and her infants as "elephants," creatures having their own specific significance. Very different things spoke to her of their meaningfulness as well: great joy, bright relaxation, contentment as a female, and time beyond the finite. That is how the dreaming woman experienced the affiliation between her creative-feminine self and timeless animal nature. The experience was so intense that the smallness of the human form could no longer do justice to it; the colossal feelings evoked the colossal form of the elephant and the limitless expanse of a primitive, teeming jungle as thematic elements of the dream worlk. Even the time frame of the dreamer's existence stretched accordingly, extending from the finiteness belonging to human isolation, to the borderless infinity of immutable nature.

Although as a rule perception in dreaming does not nearly equal that of the waking state, here the dreamer was in advance of her waking self in the realization of her feminine existential possibilities. That notwithstanding, however, a large part of the subject's being remained hidden from her while she dreamed. For she perceived herself then predominantly—though not totally—as living ahistorically. Her temporal frame of reference did expand, true enough, but only in the sense that finite time was overcome by an endless repetition of the same thing, the endless child bearing and nest building. We should keep in mind, though, that human nature is essentially finite and historical. It is finite by virtue of the fact that it is at the service of something other than itself, that something then constituting its borders. It is historical in the sense that what has happened in the past never simply disappears and is gone, but is retained and continues to speak in a person's present and future lives.

No human being remains the same during two successive moments, since in the second moment he is already filled with the first. This fact leads to the important consideration that humans are not fit objects for natural scientific experimentation. All that natural scientific experiments can ascertain, strictly speaking, is whether a given set of circumstances will always produce a given result. The first prerequisite of natural scientific experimentation is therefore the possibility of repetition, which entails beginning each time with the very same situation. But since human beings are inherently historical creatures, and constantly in flux, they preclude that possibility. Even batteries of psychological tests designed to quantify, and experiment with, human phenomena can never do more than touch the bare periphery of human existence.

Dreams of Persons Considered Mentally Disturbed by Themselves, Others, or Both

The phrase "mentally disturbed" is used here to refer to persons whose free exercise of one or more vital existential possibilities has been pathologically impaired. By "pathological," I mean that the impairment is accompanied by behavioral disorders sufficient to cause suffering in the affected persons or fellow humans, particularly love partners. Such suffering can assume very diverse forms, ranging over the following nosological groupings:

1. Classic hysteria or obsession showing specific symptoms.
2. Hysterical or obsessive personality with no obvious specific symptoms, only disturbed behavior toward the self and others.
3. Those ailments commonly (but incorrectly) termed "psycho-somatic.
4. The neurosis of persons suffering from a general, otherwise symptomless discontent with civilization.
5. Slight and severe depression.
6. Attitudes of general indifference, ennui, desperation over the meaninglessness of life.
7. Psychoses.

The therapeutic suggestions and formulations reproduced below in the form of direct speech are literal transcriptions of advice given to, and easily understood by, patients. It should be kept in mind, though, that the patients whose dream experiences appear here are, for the most part, of above-average intelligence and therefore equipped with good insight into their own natures. For patients of considerably lesser acumen, the form of questions should be tailored to fit average understanding and colloquial speech, but their content must remain unaltered. If such concessions are not made, therapeutic measures are likely to fall on deaf ears.

Last, the reader is expressly warned against *blindly* adopting the measures outlined below as new weapons in his or her own therapeutic arsenal.

Dreaming of Neurotically Disturbed Persons (Examples 1—22)

Example 1: A thirty-year-old married woman with two children, who began *Daseins*-analytic treatment because of frigidity.

I dreamed I was supposed to decline a Latin noun, one of the ones whose masculine ending disguises its feminine gender. I was supposed to decline it with an adjective, so that the feminine endings of the adjective would betray the true gender of the noun, despite its masculine forms. But I had a hard time performing this task; in fact, I never managed to finish it. Even while I was dreaming, I wasn't sure just which word was involved.

The *Daseins*-analyst first simply reiterated as follows:

So, while dreaming you were supposed to take a Latin noun that is feminine, but hides behind masculine-looking endings, and decline it together with an adjective, so that, in spite of its masculine endings, the noun can be recognized as feminine by the feminine endings of the adjective. But you weren't up to the task.

Here the therapist takes an initial step by just repeating the substance of her dream to the reawakened dreamer. Even this little proved sufficient, however, to make clear to the patient that she had been concerned in her dreaming state with demonstrating the innate, but hidden, feminity of a Latin noun that was masquerading as masculine. All that the dreamer had on hand for that purpose was a feminine adjunct, something extraneous, a mere "ad-jective." She finally had to face up to the fact that she had failed in her task of unspecified origin.

In order to allow the patient to gain an insight into her present overall condition on the basis of her dreaming behavior, it was imperative not to distort her dreaming Being-in-the-world with symbolic interpretations. For otherwise the actual matter at hand would escape both the dreamer and the therapist. Both would then overlook the extent to which the dreamer failed to perceive that *it was she herself* who was hiding her feminity behind a masculine appearance. The hiddenness of a femininity behind a masculine facade was known to her only through an alien component of a "dead" language: a Latin noun whose presence was incontrovertible but whose meaning was left vague. Consequently, she was not yet able to grasp, either waking or dreaming, that she needed to change, to "decline," *her own* masculine demeanor, so that her femininity could begin to shine through, at least first through something peripherally affixed to her, something adjectival. But the details of her dream convinced the therapist how very far she was from realizing that her true feminine being could not manifest itself but was covered by a masculine facade. It was still less apparent to her where the demand for change came from, even the mere changing of the masculine-looking Latin word. She did not even wonder, while dreaming, who had asked her to demonstrate feminine gender in the distant realm of Latin grammer. Like a schoolgirl, she gave unquestioning obedience to a strict, invisible teacher. But she could not complete the task assigned her. Waking or dreaming, she hadn't the slightest inkling as to the origins of the commandment.

Whenever a therapist uses symbolic interpretation on the socalled subjective or objective level in such a case, he fails to see and to evaluate correctly how far the patient still is from becoming aware of that existential trait of his own existence whose significance corresponds with the meaningfulness of a dreamed object or a dreamed fellow human being. By such a therapeutic intervention he is therefore committing a common, yet unpardonable, therapeutic error. Why should the vaguely perceived Latin word in the woman's dream be anything other than just that? What reason is there for claiming that the Latin word, because it is a noun-subject, "actually refers to" the dreamer's own "human ego?" Where is the proof for such a statement? Who, or what, could have hidden a "symbolic meaning" behind the Latin word, knowing in advance precisely to what the "actual meaning" would refer? For only something that exists and is known can be hidden. Furthermore, there would need to be some agent existing within the patient's existence who would have to decide on the importance of concealing it. Yet we have repeatedly indicated how meaningless and unsatisfactory it is to invent endopsychic sages, such as the "unconscious," or the "unconscious censor," and then assign them the role of concealer.

All that our patient knew while dreaming was what she actually experienced. If she wanted vision deeper than her dreaming perception allowed, she would probably have to consult an analyst, schooled in the perception of the basic nature of whatever he encounters, an analyst who is existentially free to recognize what significances pervade a thing, making it to what it is. Such an analyst may not seize on events from outside the dreaming itself, pointing to these as indicators of the dreaming's "actual," "unconscious," or "symbolic" content. Then he would be guilty not only of falsifying given phenomena, but of an unthinking prejudgement of their basic nature. Yet there is something worse than the theoretical inadequacy of any "scientific" procedure that does violence to the dream contents by "interpreting" them as symbols: namely, disruption of therapy. To see what great harm may result from this, we have only to consider the extent to which our subject is cut off, while dreaming, from any essential insight into her existential state, and how she can respond only to a peripheral command having to do with grammar beyond her ken. This fragile self-knowledge should suffice to suggest what injury might be brought on by symbolic interpretation violating the actual dream phenomena. If the woman has been fortunate enough to avoid an "education" in psychology, the symbolic content which the analyst suggests for the Latin word will simply to in one ear and out the other. If the therapist pushes his interpretation, she may find it at best "very interesting." This will make her begin to think about it. Yet it is this very "intellectualization" which prevents her from actually experiencing feelingly important insights into the foundations of her being. Only on the basis of such insight does a person come to have no choice but to transform his behavior towards the encountered beings of his world to correspond to the "expansion of consciousness" gained in therapy.

In sum, then, only the following inquiries and suggestions have enough scientific and therapeutic value to be addressed to the reawakened dreamer:

a. As a person who doesn't know what to live for in your waking life, might not the appearance of a task in your dreaming state signify a first step toward a freer, more meaningful existence? In the world of your dreaming, that task even consisted in a most precise claim on you, i.e., in declining a Latin noun that looks masculine, but is really feminine, as the adjective accompanying it shows.

Any intervention on the part of the therapist should take the form of questions, not specific declarative statements, since the former allow the patient much more for agreement or disagreement. Positive declarations of what something "means" tend to force the therapist into the role of authority figure, at the same time thrusting the patient into subordinate, infantile behavior.

b. After the analyst made reference to the positive content of the dream, making no effort to restrain his own appreciation of that content, he should ask:

On the other hand, does it not strike you as strange that in your dreaming you are given a task so separate from yourself, involving only a word from a dead foreign language, and that the task entails highly abstract, intellectual labor, namely, a grammatical declension?

Once the patient became aware of her dreaming distance from the Latin word, she spontaneously remembered dozens of things, dating as far back as early childhood, toward which her behavior had been similarly distant. It was not long before she began to see the reasons behind her behavior: her parents had encouraged her to maintain an unnatural distance from things so many times that it had become second nature to her.

If, by contrast, the therapist begins searching for early childhood memories before the patient has had a chance to grow fully aware of the behavioral modes that govern her present waking and dreaming existence, the therapy is liable to wind up a Sisyphean labor. But if the patient is led to question her distance from the things she encounters, instead of taking it for granted, she may sense the possibility of establishing much closer relations with the entities of her present world. In the light of this freedom, patients (not just the present one) find that they can effortlessly remember when their neurotic impairments originated. This insight into the historicity of them is in itself highly liberating. It makes the patients become aware of the fact that their present pathological structure of existence is not immutable and once and for all given, but has become as it is now in the course of their life experiences. This means at the same time that it can be changed.

Now the time had come when the *Daseins*-analyst had to repeat and to complete his therapeutic interventions by the following statements and additional questions:

All that happened in your dreaming state had nothing at all to do with your own existence. During the whole time of your dreaming state you were only able to hear of a task referring to a Latin word. But now that you are awake could you not already be more clear sighted than you were while dreaming? Could it not be that now you are able at least to have a presentment of quite a different task which is awaiting you; a task, though, of a quite different, practical, concrete nature, but one having nevertheless the same essential content of meaningfulness? Could there be a task, for instance, faintly appealing to you and demanding of you as a waking person to bring to light the femininity not only of an external distant Latin word, but the feminine character traits of your own existence? In your waking states you have showed up to now only a decidedly masculine bearing. Has not the moment come when your own possibilities of feminine ways of relating toward that which you encounter have to be carried out? Your dreamt task was of unknown origin, but can you not feel that this task of your waking clearly originates from the essential claim of your own existence, i.e., its demand to carry out all the relational possibilities of which your existence is made up?

c. At last the therapist may add the encouragement:

Do you not think yourself that this task will be one which you shall be able to accomplish, in sharp contradiction to the purely intellectual task of your dreaming state, where you finally failed in spite of all your efforts?

Again, much stress would have to be laid on the fact that although the two tasks were essentially of the same meaningfulness, namely, a demanding of the patient that she change something, each of them belonged to two completely different worlds. In the world of her dreaming existence there was nothing else but the task to decline a Latin word. The task of changing her own existential bearing from a masculine way of relating to a feminine one simply did not exist as long as she dreamt. Nobody in the whole universe knew anything of such a task, before she had told these dreamed events to her analyst. How, then, could the contention be justified that this second task nevertheless existed already or was present "in" her while she was still dreaming? Naturally, since Freud, psychologists are used to deriving a welter of mental conclusions from the given phenomena. But none of them is capable of actually proving that their logical conclusions and derivations correspond to something really existing. To the contrary, in spite of their mental constructs of ever so many psychological unconsciousnesses, nobody is able to say exactly what the verbs "to exist" or "to be" can signify without somebody's awareness of the particular existing being.

Example 2: Dreaming of a twenty-nine-year-old single woman with numerous hysterical symptoms

While dreaming the patient sees her analyst, who in her waking life has always been clean-shaven and immaculately clad in a white labcoat, suddenly enter the treatment room wearing street clothes and with an unkempt, wild growth of beard. The beard seems eery to her. She is afraid of the analyst and runs away. On the contrary, while awake she had always stressed that she saw her analyst exclusively as a rational, intelligent, trustworthy, unbiased medical advisor.

Obviously, this woman sees something more in her analyst while dreaming than while awake. But how does that something extra, that wild growth of beard, get into the dreaming? Subjectivistic psychology would calmly reply that the dreamer must have produced the beard from within her "unconscious," then affixed it to a homemade dream image of the analyst. Yet there is, in this person's existence, no evidence to indicate that the beard is a product of endopsychic imagination, assuming "hallucinatory" reality when projected outward onto the dreamed image of the analyst. That is pure psychological speculation, without the slightest basis in fact.

As far as the dreamer's perception is concerned, all that really happens is that a decidedly bearded analyst manifest himself in the light of her dreaming existence. The beard is attached to the analyst from the very start, somewhere "out" there in her dream-world, not anywhere "in" her. Furthermore the dreamt beard is not at all experienced by the dreamer as being only an "image" of a beard but as being a real beard made of the stuff actual beards are made of. Also, the beard is not an isolated object, of specified volume and existing in a vacuum. Rather, it is a growth emanating from an existing male. Without the help of interpretation, one can agree that the wild exhuberant growth stamps the analyst as a naturally manly man. It belongs on the sort of "uncultivated" male whose behavior toward women would contrast sharply with that expected from a clean shaven analyst in his labcoat.

As a dreamer, the patient receives more information about her analyst than her waking self ever perceived. No longer is he locked into the frame of the intellectually superior, distant medical guardian. Now he appears in her dreaming as a sloppy, uncouth bearded man. Her dreaming response to that man, ending in terrified flight, is worthy of notice.

The therapeutic application of the phenomenological approach to dreaming outlined above might give rise to the following questions:

a. "Isn't it comforting, at least, that in your dreaming you no longer restrict your analyst to the role of the clean-shaven, distant physician, a mere brain in a white frock, who treats you dispassionately like an object? In your dreaming, fortunately, your eyes open to something vital, unpolished, inherently masculine about him."

b. "On the other hand, isn't it surprising that you are forced to

see such a man as a dangerous, threatening creature who leaves you
no alternative except flight?"

c. "What is it you think you have to run away from?"

There would be no scientific justification, or therapeutic value,
in saying more about these dream events. In particular, there is absolutely no basis for saying that the bearded analyst in the dreaming
really "signified" something other than himself, and making the entire dreaming a "transference dream," wherein the analyst appeared
as a symbol for the woman's own father, who had worn a beard
when she knew him. It may well be true, however, that the errant
behavior of the father had pathogenically altered his daughter's
perception from an early age, so that even now her existence is open
only to perceiving dangerous, cruel male behavioral possibilities.
That notwithstanding, however, the patient's latest dreaming involved only the analyst himself, not her father or some "endopsychic father image." Its content in no way warrants the designa-
tion "transference dream." First of all, we can't prove the existence
of any endopsychic affects that may be transferred from one endopsychic representation onto another. Second, we ought to repeat
here what has been said about the notion of "transference" in our
discussion of the recruit who killed women in his dreams. It is
characteristic of neurotics that they do not practice transference in
the sense of transporting something from one place to another within a psyche. Indeed, they characteristically change nothing. For the
neurotic, everything remains as it has always been for him. It remains for him just as he had to experience his world as a child. The
neurotic, then, remains fixated in his infantile ways of perceiving, so
mistaking and distorting the beings of his adult world. Figuratively
speaking, it is as if the cornea of his mind's eye was deformed so that
he ever afterwards sees only a distorted world. As a result, even after
they have attained their official adulthood, neurotics still see everyone they meet with the limited vision given them through the errors
of their patents. As a consequence of this restriction and distortion
of their ability to perceive, their perception of the analyst is also

necessarily distorted, and indeed the more humanly close he is, the more intense the distortion. No matter what their general intellectual development in other areas, they can only see him as either a cruel, rigid father—though not their own—or a violent, unloving mother. But in thus misjudging other adults, neurotic people do not "actually" have in mind their true fathers or mothers. Though their vision may be clouded, it never strays from the people who are standing before them. What makes it so imperative to be rid of the theory of transference for good, in fact, is that the beginning relationship to the analyst is often the most genuine one available to the severe neurotic, the only pillar holding up his or her world. If the therapist debases this emotional relationship for the sake of the tranference theory, labeling it a "false connection" or a "deception," he only further confuses the patient. All too often, in fact, such analytic mistakes have led the patient to suicide.[8]

Example 3: Dreaming of a twenty-eight-year-old single male, suffering from a sense of loneliness and of the meaninglessness of life.

Last night I dreamed that I was sleeping. I woke up in my dream, and looked out the window of my parent's house. Two hostile armies were in the fields. They began to fight. They were getting closer to the house, and I was afraid they might get in, so I ran around closing all the doors, than ran into my mother's bedroom. She was lying in bed. I climbed in. Suddenly everything was peaceful and quiet. The shooting outside stopped. I could sleep again.

One advantage of the phenomenological approach to dreaming is that it gives an immediate consideration to that worldly dwelling place in which the dreamer finds himself. In this case, the dreamer "awakens" in his parents' house. He declares, after being asked to provide a more detailed description of his dreaming experience, that he felt while dreaming like a boy of about twelve years. Now, it is most important to remember that the time at which the patient experienced the dream is *now*, last night to be more precise, when by the standards of the waking world he would have been twenty-eight years old. That means that right then, at the moment of his dream, he was existing as a child in his parents' house, dependent on the mother into whose bed he had climbed. As a matter of fact, he was a *sleeping child* who had awakened for only a brief period. The therapist misses the decisive import of these dream events if he sees in them primarily a summons to search for some pathogenic experience that must have occurred during waking some sixteen years before, and which functioned as the cause producing the dreaming of the previous night.

The only really helpful line of therapeutic inquiry would begin with the question: "To what extent are you, the awakened dreamer, aware that even today you still exist fundamentally as a child sleeping in immediate closeness to a mother?"

Then the following questions would be appropriate:

a. "Doesn't it surprise you that, when you opened your eyes in the dream, the whole world outside your parents' house appeared to you as a dangerous battlefield?"

b. "Even given a world ruled by warfare, isn't it still surprising that, instead of mixing in the fray, you exist only as a frightened infantile observer?"

Experience teaches, by the way, that patients who assume an observer's stance while dreaming, distancing themselves from active participation with others, require especially stubborn, persistent therapists. That aside, however, Question b would naturally lead to the following one:

c. "Does it not seem odd to you, finally, that even the observer's stance remains frightening, causing you to flee further, namely to your mother's bed and into renewed, dreamless sleep?"

It would be a mistake, by contrast, to attribute the dreaming retreat toward the mother to an unconscious Oedipal wish, a "psychic cause." That would be wrong, first and foremost, because the patient himself never experienced anything of the kind; but also, of course, because the notion of a "psychic cause" leaves unspecified the meaning of its two constituent parts, the terms "psychic" and "cause."

Merely by asking Questions a, b and c, the therapist would have done all that he could usefully do. Any theoretical speculation without a factual basis in the dream experience itself could only be harmful. The three simple questions, however, led the patient to pay attention, and to begin to sense that, even in his waking life, he went around as a daydreamer, filled at all times with a pervasive feeling of anxiety toward the outside world of strange adults, whom he could see only as destructive combatants. The patient may come to realize that he is forever on the point of taking asylum in his mother's arms, as a sleeping infant.

Example 4: Dreaming of a thirty-year-old male, suffering from a severe anxiety neurosis, married, with two children.

In my dream last night, I was in the house my family lived in from the time I was thirteen until I was eighteen. My mother was standing over the stove in the kitchen. I had just come back after leaving her years before to marry the woman whom I actually did marry in my waking life, and with whom I had my two children. While dreaming, I was wondering whether I should apologize to my mother for leaving her. I was also considering whether I should tell her that I had done so only out of duty to my wife, who seemed so helpless. I knew that coming right out and apologizing would erase the bad feelings that still existed between my mother and myself from the time when I left. The temptation to apologize was great, because my mother was exerting a powerful attraction on me. I could feel that she wanted to draw me into a state that was very warm and beautiful, where all problems and difficulties disappeared. But at the same time I knew that giving in to that maternal attraction would mean the annihilation of myself as a distinct personality.

Here again, there is no justification for going beyond what the dreaming experience has revealed to the dreamer, in order to dredge up things supposedly hidden behind the dream manifestations. The meanings of occurrences and entities in the dreaming are in plain view. The dreamer experiences in a direct fashion how little his heart has been with his wife during the time of their marriage. Just as directly, he realizes while dreaming that his decision to marry and leave his mother arose exclusively out of a sense of duty, a feeling that "that's what people do," rather than a mature love. Now in his dreaming, however, the patient resumes close relations with his mother. He does not fail to recognize the terrible danger of his all too strong attachment to his mother to his developing to an independent self-reliant existence. This existential circumstance had never become clear to him in his waking life. It was only after he had wakened from the dreaming that he was struck by what he had learned about his state of mind. The message of the dream so overpowered the patient that the therapist needed only to sit back and listen. Had he wanted to do something more, it would have been advisable only to reiterate the sequence of the dreaming experiences, or at most, lay some stress on the positive import of the fact that the dreamer was able to resist the pull of his mother.

Example 5: Dreaming of a forty-year-old male, married, childless.

This patient suffered from an inability to ejaculate and have orgasms, despite full and easy erection; he was employed and successful as a technician

Last night I dreamed I was woken up by church bells at five in the morning. It was the pastor who was ringing them so early. I walked right over to the church and cursed him for waking me with all that noise. I also told him not to do it again.

Here again, as in our third example, we are dealing with someone who "wakes up" within his dreaming, then exhibits a specific kind of behavior. Initially, he is enraged at being wakened prematurely. That experience in the dreaming prompts the therapist to begin the next session by asking the patient whether there may not be some other awakening that is disturbing him in his waking life. The patient immediately replies, "Yes, *you're disturbing me* with all those questions that make me see things about myself that I don't want to see." This confession betrays far more awareness than has been available to him in his dreaming rage at the pastor. The confession arises not out of the dreaming, but out of the patient's waking existence. In the dreaming state, the significance of being awakened, and of resistance to it, addresses the dreamer solely in a peripheral way: It takes the form of a "physical" awakening occasioned by the pastor's church bells. It is then, all the more important for the therapist to make repeated mention of the reawakened dreamer's annoyed response to his tremendous resistance to increasing his self-awareness in his waking state. To accomplish this, the therapist need only reiterate, whenever possible, the patient's own reported anger at the pastor; he must stubbornly hold this fact under the patient's nose.

But in the dreaming it is not the analyst who awakens the patient but a pastor in no way resembling the analyst. Is it then not so that the analyst is hidden or veiled in the form of the pastor, perhaps because the dreamer dares not express openly his aggression toward the analyst? Is it then not necessary to "interpret" the figure of the dream pastor, which in the language of modern dream theory is tantamount to "reinterpretating" him? Has not one to assert that the dream pastor does not really mean the dream pastor, but actually means someone quite different, namely, the analyst? But what right does anyone have to make such pronouncements? We must ask here, as we have so often before, what personal and conscious agent exists within the dreamer's personality capable of disguising the analyst, hiding him behind the figure of the pastor, so that therapy is required to reverse the process of transformation? In the dream itself, the pastor is experienced only as the actual clergyman known to the patient's waking self. If, in accordance with the precepts of phenomenological dream interpretation, the pastor is allowed to remain just what he appears to be, and additional insight is gained which escapes the more usual forms of dream interpretation. The great scientific—therapeutic significance of this insight was mentioned in the foreword to Chapter I of the present work.[9]Granted, the patient probably would never have dreamed of being awakened abruptly had he not already experienced therapy in his waking state as a rude awakening to unpleasant insights concerning his own existential makeup. The pastor's appearance in the dreaming state and the existence of the analyst in the patient's waking world are therefore not totally unrelated. What remains doubtful, is the precise nature of the relationship between the two figures drawn from the patient's life. The mere fact that a relationship does obtain is not sufficient reason for declaring one figure to be more real than the other or deriving one from the other, thus introducing an implied cause and effect relationship between them. If the dreaming and waking experiences are not arbitrarily intermigled, if the pastor and analyst are permitted to remain distinct, independent phenomena, aside from their common connection to the theme of premature awakening, the analyst is brought before a decisive question. The fact that the dreamer sees himself awakened not by the analyst himself, but by a pastor, prompts the analyst to ask:

If you really think about your dreaming of the pastor, can you not feel that you also experience analysis as basically a kind of religious intervention, a conventionally ethical summons to specific behavioral modes given by a representative of public, social morality?

It was precisely that question which had an astoundingly therapeutic effect on the patient, greater than anything else done or said by the analyst during the entire course of therapy. Yet the question would not even have occurred to the analyst, had he been blinded by "depth-psychological" dream theories. For then he would simply have confused the dreamed pastor with the analyst.

Example 6: Dreaming of a twenty-six-year-old female, married five years, but still childless.

This patient exhibited infantile conduct, was frigid, and had overwhelming anxieties

The night before last I dreamed I had finally gotten pregnant and could become a mother. I was brimming over with joy. Then I had to go home to my parents. Full of excitement, I told them about my pregnancy. But they immediately doubted that I could ever become pregnant. Suddenly, then, my pregnancy went away.

While dreaming, this patient for a brief time achieved an existential openness and maturity that accommodate the possibility of her becoming pregnant. According to the expansion of her *Dasein* (existence), her whole existence was attuned to happiness and joy. Yet the dreamer could maintain such open freedom only a little while. A "summons" from her parents, to whom she is enslaved, carried her back into their immediate physical presence. At the same time, her own existence shrinks, retreating to the prepubescent state of childish dependence. While dreaming, in fact, the patient shows such a lack of freedom that she cannot return to her parents' home of her own free will. She does not know why she could think of nothing more grown-up and intelligent to do than return to her overbearing parents. "Then I had to go home to my parents," gives the picture of a person who has no choice but to obey unquestioningly an alien force that is other than herself.

It is this, and only this, that the therapist should tell the reawakened patient. His job is to make her see, more clearly than she has ever been able to before, just how things stand with her. This clearer insight to her existential state would suffice to make her previous infantile subservience to her parents questionable for her and, in itself, would be an encouragement for her to adopt freer modes of behavior. Of course, even in *Daseins*-analytic therapy, a single battle does not win a war. Farther along in analysis, dozens of similar dreams may come to light. The analyst must never tire of taking each of these opportunities to point to the patient's special type of enslavement. He must be many times more obstinate than the most entrenched existential restriction of his patients.

Example 7: Dreaming of a thirty-two-year-old female, single, under *Daseins*-analytic treatment for an anxiety neurosis for a year.

My dream last night began with me in my mother's house. I saw my pet turtle, Jacob. Some force started to tear the turtle apart, pulling the top shell away from the bottom one. It was torture for me to watch, so I screamed and said to my mother: "There is only one way to free the animal from its pain, by killing it."

The dreamer finds herself in her mother's house. Mothers only exist where there are children: the very word "mother" implies "children," and vice versa. Consequently, the dreamer's presence near her mother lays stress on her filial situation in and of itself. She is engaged in a close mother–child relationship. She is existing as such a relationship. That is the first hint that the therapist can offer the patient. Meanwhile, the open realm of her dreaming world also has room for the presence of a beloved animal, the pet turtle Jacob. Animal nature, as we have said, is distinguished from human nature chiefly in that it is "instinctive"; that is, animal life is firmly embedded and unfree in its relations to what shows itself from its environment. It has always and already fallen prey to the somehow preceived beings. So the dreamer perceives that kind of enslaved "living" only going on outside of herself, in her beloved pet. "Nevertheless," the therapist might say to her,

Animal nature does somehow come close to you in your dreaming, if only in the form of a creature that is cold-blooded, harmless, and very well armored. You can only enter into a close relationship with a creature that is distant from a human mode of existing. It is no mere accident that, both in your waking life and your dreaming, you selected a turtle as a pet. Yet a relationship to even such an animal is very much more than none at all. But then an uncanny, unknown power suddenly appears and begins to tear your armored pet apart, so that you and it suffer terribly.

A phenomenological approach to this patient's dreaming would consist in asking her: "Now that you are awake, do you still sense the presence of some force that is out to tear open other armored creatures?" If the answer is no, she might then be asked: "Doesn't what you have to go through in therapy seem like a kind of tearing apart of yourself, one that is equally painful for you?" Here again, the therapist must strictly guard against the self-contradictory contention that, in the dreaming state, the turtle's armor "really" was the dreamer's own existential barriers, or that the tearing apart of the turtle "symbolized" the analytic exposure of the patient's waking life. If this were so, the patient herself, or some superperson within her, would have had to realize the "subjective meanings of dream entities," though such awareness would have had to be an "unconscious one." Also she did not experience the turtle simply as an image; instead, she recognized it with all of her sense as her flesh and blood pet, Jacob. Once again, it is of paramount importance that we note the great distance from which her dreaming existence viewed a process of being opened up. For it was not she herself, but a turtle with a life all its own, that was being torn open. An insight into this existential distance from herself would not occur to anyone who used a prescribed "symbol" theory of dreaming to reinterpret the dreamed result. The dangerous impact of such blindness on therapy has already been pointed out.[10]

Another essential feature of the explicit significance of the dreaming is the unspecified source of the power that tears open the turtle. Whatever it is, it has a magical character. Then again, we should pause to consider that the dreamer dares not undertake to put the suffering pet out of its misery herself but merely cries out helplessly to her mother that someone ought to do it. Magical power is only experienced by people whose existences are impotent in relation to the entities that impinge upon them. We have already mentioned that the dreamer was residing in her mother's house; she was an immature being engaged in a mother–child relationship. There is a further feature of the dreaming which would lead a therapist to review the analytic situation: namely, the fact that the magical force tearing open the turtle is so unendurably cruel that the dreamer sees killing the turtle as the only possible solution. When someone dreams in this way, the therapist is well advised to observe whether his analytic attempts to free the patient in her waking life do not also constitute unbearable torture. And even where suicide does not appear likely, there remains a grave risk that an oppressed patient will abruptly break off her treatment. When such dreaming appears, an ill-considered, too rapid progression motivated by the therapist's therapeutic ambitions could have irrevocable consequences. In general, the therapist must confine his efforts, and especially in the case of the present patient, to indicate with unending patience whatever impairments of existential freedom are revealed in the patient's dreaming Being-in-the-world. To this end, the reawakened dreamer should be cautiously asked the following questions:

a. "Doesn't it surprise you that in your dream you are not in your own house with your husband, but with your mother in your parents' house?"

b. "Isn't is striking that the only animal that gained admittance into your dream world was one with a shell of armor?"

c. "Now that you are awake, does the potential for animal-like bearing, and for living in the small space of animal, speak to you only from the presence of a cold-blooded armored creature, remote from human modes of existing?"

d. "Are you, waking, now perhaps more aware than you were in your dreaming that the meaningfulness of being torn apart has something to do with your own existence and not only with a turtle in your external environment?"

e. "Is not the most astonishing thing of all the fact that a totally alien magical force intervened while you were dreaming and began to tear off the turtle's armor pitilessly, oblivious to all your screams?"

f. "In your dreaming existence only an alien omnipotence disclosed itself to you. Might it not be that your waking Being-in-the-world is already so much more clear sighted that a tearing open of your own shielded *Dasein* could reveal itself to you, a tearing open brought about by the process of the analytic treatment?"

g. "Does it seem to you as if that procedure is so overwhelming and so painful in your eyes that suicide is the only way out?"

A therapeutic procedure using dreaming in such a way is nothing more than resistance analysis (*Widerstands analyse*), which in turn is the highest form of therapy to which Freud was able to develop psychoanalysis. Wilhelm Reich gave resistance analysis a special importance with his formulation that only "ego-proximate defense mechanisms" should be called into question, not the "id contents" hidden behind them. The latter would surface in an ordered and natural fashion, once the "ego defenses" had been worked through. But if the reverse process were followed, and the analyst dealt immediately and directly with the repressed "id contents," the analysis would inevitably end in terrible chaos.

The insights that are afforded by *Daseins*-analytic examination of human existence significantly further the kind of "resistance analysis" espoused by Freud and Reich. They do so principally by eliminating the ballast of inadequate and unsuitable theories and presuppositions that serve only to conceal and distort the phenomena, and which have a disastrously deleterious effect on the therapy.

Example 8: Dreaming of a twenty-three-year-old female student, suffering from a disturbed relationship with males.

In last night's dream I was walking, along with my mother and my brother, toward the lake, since we were supposed to take a boat trip, or some similar outing. Just as we were about to cross a heavily traveled street, we stopped short in horror, seeing that an accident had occurred. One (or two) motorcycle riders lay on the ground. One body was an amorphous mass, dark and round; its head lay to one side, separated from it. Then I saw a second man's head (or was it the same one?) that had been severed right down the middle. All of the anatomical structures along the wound were displayed in exact textbook fashion. I woke up very disturbed after that.

The dreamer's initial situation, or worldly dwelling place (*Weltautenthaltsort*), was one in which her existence was attuned to a pleasurable, almost festive mood and was engaged in walking along the circle of her immediate family. The plan was to take a boat ride and enjoy the lake together. The dreamer's initial carefree mood indicates to us that she was mature enough to meet the demands posed by a communal outing in the company of her family.

She was able to engage freely in that particular relationship to the world. But then a heavily traveled cross-street, open to the world, puts a heavy dent in her plans. No sooner do men from outside of her family cross her path, than catastrophe strikes. The only male who gains access to her dreaming world, aside from her sexually un-obstrusive brother, is the horrible twisted corpse of a man who had presumably just been seated astride a powerful machine. His body has been crushed into a dark, round, amorphous mass; only his head keeps its external, though dead, form in the dreamer's field of vision. He is not even sufficiently "alive" in the dreamer's eyes to appear as a blood-smeared corpse. Even the head, the center of rational thought and reflection, has been denatured to become a textbook-like diagram, a model described by sharp boundaries.

It would be wise, from a therapeutic standpoint, to provide the description of the dream catastrophe with a few focal points by asking the following questions:

a. "Do you realize, even now that you are awake, that you are only happy as long as you remain within the circle of your immediate family?"

b. "What do you feel now about the way in which vital young men are warded off from your world immediately after they enter it?"

c. "Does it not seem odd to you that only the head of the motorcycle rider manages to retain its shape, and that even this head appears only as a representative, textbook-like anatomical cross-section? Does that dreaming experience perhaps lead you more clear-sighted waking existence to a deeper awareness in regard to you waking relations with the opposite sex?"

d. "Does it become clear to you now in your waking existence, for instance, that your relations with the men you encounter are confined to a distant, rational, dead, intellectual formalism, wherein the entire realm of powerful masculine physicality is perceived as merely a dead, amorphous mass?"

It is not so important that the patient be able to offer an im-

mediate answer to such questions, nor that she ponder them seriously at once, or even that she may push them aside as so much non-
sense. From a therapeutic standpoint, what matters is that the questions have been raised, and that the analyst keep them open, utilizing every analogous opportunity to do so.

Example 9: Dreaming of a thirty-year-old single male, suffering
   from depression and lack of relationships to fellow human
   beings.

Last night I dreamed I was standing at a hot dog stand. I had just
finished ordering a hot dog and was having a pleasant conversation with the
vendor, when a young woman appeared beside me and began to snuggle up
to me. I became violently afraid of her and ran away as fast as I could, even
forgetting to take along my hot dog in the rush.

The recommended line of therapeutic questioning might read as
follows:

   a. "I think it is wonderful that, at least while dreaming, you allow yourself the deep, though unshared, sensual pleasure of eating a
juicy hot dog, and that you are bold enough to enjoy it right out in
public, at a stand on a busy square.
   b. "On the other hand, don't you find it at all strange that when
a woman approaches you in a highly erotic way, you see her only as
a frightening, anxiety-producing creature?"
   c. "Are you aware of the extent to which anxiety overwhelms
you in the presence of the young woman, forcing you to run away
and preventing you from enjoying the sensual pleasure of consuming
the hot dog in peace?"
   d. "What is it that you concretely fear, in your waking life,
about the sensual, erotic presence of women?"

There is nothing easier, of course, than to make the dreamed hot
dog out to be a Freudian "symbol" for the male member. But where
is the justification for such a trick? Besides, translating the object
"hot dog" into a penis, or pseudopenis, would preclude a paramount

insight: Neither the analyst nor the patient would be able to recognize that therapy had so far permitted the patient to open up sufficiently to eat something alone, but not far enough to accomodate the sort of interpersonal erotic pleasure into which relationship the male member really belongs as a part of its bodily sphere. Here we have yet another example, then, of the advantage gained by allowing a dreamed object, such as a hot dog, to remain just what it appears to be. Of course, even a hot dog has manifold meanings and frames of reference, and those should be brought to the attention of the patient. Among other things, our dreamer's hot dog points directly to the food stand at which it is bought, the butcher who has made it, and the jolly vendor. Then again, a street-corner hot dog stand is the very opposite of a fine dining room in a first-class hotel. No matter how modest the stand or its fare, however, the process of eating a hot dog constitutes an assimilation of something fleshy and animal-like, rather than something bloodless from the vegetable kingdom.

In the psychoanalytic libido theory, the eating of the hot dog in this dream would be taken as a sign that the dreamer was fixated at the "oral-drive stage." But no theory of drives can ever be broad enough to explain even an existential activity as simple as hot dog eating. Like any other human endeavor, eating a hot dog presupposes that the presence and significance of the object at hand has been perceived. No libido, no instinct or partial instinct, possesses the ability to perceive the significance of an object at that which it is: it cannot recognize a hot dog as a hot dog. As mere "blind" energy quanta, such things as libido and drives can never generate the kind of perceptive openness that is the basis of our human existence. Whether the particular activity is hot dog eating or something else, human phenomena cannot be accounted for by an energy that mysteriously seeks out an external-world object, then libidinally "cathects" it. No, the activity arises out of an inseparable union of human perception and the perceived entity, such that the entity can only shine forth and assume presence in the light of human perception. A genuine understanding of any human behavior must see the relation between man and object not as a bipolar one, that is, existing between two separate inanimate objects, but as an integral unity in which the entities of the world claim human existence, engaging it as a site in which they present themselves. For they come into being only by entering the open realm of human perceptivity.

Example 10: Dreaming of a frigid, twenty-six-year-old female

I dreamed I was trying with all my might to cover a young man with wisps of straw. He was lying in front of me on the ground but wouldn't keep still. He kept moving around, each time exposing another part of his body. Besides that, all I had to cover him with were short, thin pieces of straw. But it was very important to cover him completely, I remember; in fact, it seemed as if it were a matter of life and death to keep him covered up under the straw. He didn't see it that way, though, and asked me all of a sudden for a slice of bread and butter. It really burned me up that he picked that very minute to ask for a slice of bread and butter.

After the dreamer had insisted that her dreaming told her nothing at all, the analyst ventured the following opinion:

The thematic foreground of your dream world is made up of a complex pattern of human relations. During your dreaming, a young man lies naked at your feet. Your behavior consists in trying to hide his nakedness at any price. What you want to do, and in fact must do, is to protect him from the public, or "other people." All you have on hand, apparently, is a very unsatisfactory material for camouflage, just a few meager wisps of straw. The young man's behavior is strikingly different. He, too, has a relationship to "other people," but one which says, in effect, that he doesn't care what they think. It means nothing to him that he might be discovered naked in your presence. As far as his relationship to you yourself is concerned, it is characterized by the fact that he keeps crossing up your plans. Then on top of that, he has the nerve to ask you for a slice of bread and butter. Apparently, he is hungry and wants to satisfy his appetite right away. There is no doubt that you and your dream partner do not see eye to eye. Your actions couldn't be more diametrically opposed. You become enraged at the naked young man's failure to understand your pressing concern to conceal his nakedness from the gaze of "other people."

The commentary above represents a good example of the way in

which the analyst might begin to apply his phenomenological understanding of the dream experience. He might continue by asking the
patient whether in her waking life she had a similar relationship
toward naked young men and public opinion. If her answer were
yes, she might then be asked:

> Well, then, why are you so prudish? Why do you allow "other people"
> to influence you in such a decisive, enslaving manner, that you don't dare
> face up to the presence of a naked young man?
>
> Doesn't it occur to you that the naked young man in your dream world
> was lying at your feet, so that you were standing above him, at least
> physically? Is it also true of your waking life that you have to get men under
> your control? Is your waking behavior toward young men limited to the
> single dimension of superiority and inferiority?

The following remarks on the part of the analyst would un-
doubtedly also be beneficial in therapy:

> Your dream partner's unabashed behavior shows that you too, at
> least in your dreaming, see the possibility of a very different, freer mode of
> behavior. In fact, that new mode of behavior drew uncomfortably close to
> you through the person of the young man. You, however, are apparently
> still far from adopting that behavior yourself. It will probably be quite
> some time before you are ready to utilize that kind of behavior in a respon-
> sible manner of your own. You still fight it off desperately, even when you
> only see it in others. Even when it occurs outside of yourself, you want to
> suppress it forcefully. But the fact that in your dreaming you are given only
> thin wisps of straw to hide it may signal that the end also of your waking
> prudishness is fast approaching, its power running out. Whatever the case,
> it is noteworthy that you are not yet open to conceive of any erotic
> relationship of the naked young man with you in the dreaming. His appetite
> shows itself to you being aimed solely at the consumption of bread and but-
> ter, and therefore as a purely self-centered sensual desire.

Naturally, analyzing a single dream experience would not be
enough to free the neurotic woman once and for all from her
prudishness and dependence on "other people." It would also be absolutely necessary to make the patient aware of all the factors in her
life that have contributed to her restricted behavior toward the opposite sex, and that still cast their shadows over her from out of the
past.

As we already have mentioned above, gaining an insight into the neurotic restrictions one has acquired through upbringing and life events represents in itself an important liberation, for it permits the patient to realize that a limited existence in the present does not necessarily indicate an immutable, God-given constitution that must be accepted fatalistically. That same insight hints at the possibility of radically new and freer ways of behaving, whereas previously patients have been led to believe that their neurotic behavior is the only behavior possible for them, something to be taken for granted.

Example 11: Dreaming of a thirty-five-year-old male, a self-willed intellectual, with an unconsummated marriage of five years' standing.

This patient can only realize an intimate relationship to a woman in fantasy, and even there never goes beyond an exchange of tender caresses. He reported one of his dreams as follows:

> I'm hitchhiking on a country road. A very powerfully built man, about my age, has me get in his car, and drives on. While he's at the wheel, I shoot him. I really don't know why, and I don't feel any remorse. But then I start worrying about the police. If I don't get rid of the body, they'll convict me of murder. Luckily, the body beside me turns into a burning match on its own. I'm thinking, I just have to let it burn down, then I can toss the ashes out of the window and no one will be the wiser.

This dreamer's dwelling place is an unfamiliar country road. To be on a country road is to be enroute somewhere. But our dreamer knows neither where he is coming from, nor where he wants to go. Above all, he does not intend to travel under his own power, using his own two feet. Nor does he have the use of a personal car that *he himself* could drive. He wants to be driven around by someone else, at the other person's expense: He is hitchhiking. As if in answer to his wish, another person instantly happens along—an especailly powerful, vital man—to offer the dreamer a ride in his car. But no sooner has the trip gotten underway than the dreamer murders the driver, without recognizing any real motive for his action. The murder just seems to happen, and the remainder of the trip is shrouded in darkness. The dreamer's only interest now is to hide all traces of the deed, so that no judge can sentence him to prison. Miraculously, the corpse is transformed into the easily disposable ashes of a burnt-out match.

Thus the therapist recounted the dreaming for his patient. He then began to offer some helpful questions and hints:

a. "Now that you are awake, do you see yourself in any situation similar to that of the dreaming? Do you perhaps suspect that it was not only for a given moment that you were on a country road, but that you find yourself traveling without direction in a much more comprehensive sense, an entire human existence without origins or goals?"

b. "Do you not also realize more profoundly now than in your dreaming, that you are in an encompassing existential sense not standing on your own two feet and moving under your own power, but prefering instead to be carried around at other peoples' effort and expense?"

c. "While dreaming you perceive yourself murdering your driver, a vital young man, for no discernible reason. Can you now in your waking state see more clearly that the way you have been living up to now has effectively killed not some stranger, but the potential in your own existence for vital, masculine behavior?"

Responding to Questions a and b, the patient timidly confessed that his waking behavior did in fact correspond to that of his dream, only in a far more pervasive manner. Yet it was only after the dreaming and subsequent questioning that he had been able to see this fact clearly. Most importantly, he could now see that the passive, parasitic bearing he had shown as a hitchhiker while dreaming characterized all of his waking relationships. The patient at first tried to sidestep the third question, having to do with the murder of the car driver, by insisting that he had no enemies in his waking life and harbored no death wishes against anyone. Only when the therapist pressed the patient, by asking how things stood with his waking masculine behavior, did he make the dumbfounded admission that at some point in the past his existence as a robust male had vanished into thin air. His parents had told him that he had been an unusually active, vivacious child. These thoughts led the patient to ask himself whether the killing off of his existential possibilities was responsible for the persistent feeling that he had done something wrong, and for his fear of being found out. The therapist ended the discussion by remarking, "Could be."

It would have been wrong, factually and therapeutically speaking, for the therapist to have made statements along the lines of traditional "dream interpretation." The murdered driver was not "actually" the dreamer himself, nor any part of the dreamer. The driver was perceived, and existed, only as an unknown stranger as long as this dreaming state lasted. The driver in the dreaming was not simply a "symbolic" stand-in for something about the dreamer himself. The driver disclosed himself to the dreamer and, therefore, existed only as an unknown stranger. Once again, the fiction of "dream-work" that would be needed to accomplish such a transformation of the dreamer himself into this driver whom the former killed would, inevitably presuppose once more that there exists within the dreaming patient an "unconscious knowledge" of his loss of masculinity. For, if such knowledge were not lodged in some supra-person within or behind the dreamer, then who (or what) would have been in a position to realize that something needed to be concealed? Besides which, if there were no homunculus present to perform the act of concealment, the "dream image" which was projected outward could never come into being. But the facts of the matter are very different. In reality, the patient exists in his dreaming state in an integral fashion, his vision terribly obscured, but his existence nowhere divided into distinct "psychic identities." His dream perception is reduced to such an extent, actually, that the human life he takes has deteriorated to become merely the remains of a burnt-out match, and the destructive act of taking life is not recognized as something affecting himself, but only a total stranger. In any case, though, it is the dreaming that first makes him realize that he is a murderer, enabling him afterward to gain a clearer insight into his destructive behavior. Thanks only to prompting by the analyst, the reawakened dreamer becomes profoundly aware that he has committed a kind of partial suicide in the course of his lifetime.

If a strict separation is made between what a person actually perceives in his or her dreaming existence, and what is added to that experience through subsequent therapy, the analyst will be freed of an unnecessary task. For by dropping the notion that interpretation is possible "on the subjective level," he relinquishes all responsibility for deciding when to give preference to "interpretation on the objective level." In fact, both approaches to dreaming, subjective and objective, are equally groundless. "Interpretation on the objective level" would have made our present dream specimen out to be a transference dream. The patient would have been made to think that the murdered driver was a camouflaged version of the patient's father or analyst, something entirely different from what he was perceived as being. Of course, there is no concrete proof to support such speculation, just as there is no proof to back up the assumptions underlying a "reinterpretation on a subjective level."

At first, the dreamer was at a loss to explain what impelled him to murder someone else in his dreaming, and slowly destroy himself in his waking life. But appropriate therapeutic hints soon began to clear away his confusion. Once he had gotten a feel for the extent and nature of his present impairment, he was spontaneously flooded with memories of his mentors' misbehavior, and of his passive acceptance of it. He could now fully understand the contraction of his freedom, and the serious extent to which he had innocently fallen in arrears in realizing his full potential for living. This enlightenment granted him a much freer relationship to his own past, for reasons that were discussed in connection with our tenth dream specimen.[11] Of course, the dreamer was still far from utilizing all of the freedom that was his birthright. In order to inherit that birthright, he would need first to make thousands of attempts at practicing freer behavior toward those he encountered in his everyday life. Freud called this the "working through" of psychic contents brought to consciousness. Practicing and exercising freer behavior toward oneself and others describes the therapeutic phenomenon more aptly, however, than the Freudian formulation.

The patient pensively wondered why in his dream he had felt no guilt of his own about the murder. His attention had been concerned exclusively with the courts and the police. He was like a schoolboy after a nasty prank, fearing only the punishment that might come and anxious to destroy all traces of the act. The therapist's task here was to share the astonishment the patient felt upon discovering how childish and irresponsible he still was where existential culpability was concerned, referring to what he remained owing in regard to a full realization of his whole existence.

Example 12: Dreaming of a thirty-two-year-old male suffering from impotence.

Unable to stand up to the others in life, this patient has nevertheless advanced in his profession through hard work and conscientiousness.

Last night I dreamed I was walking across a field that was in front of my parents' house. I met a middle-aged man. He had a gun in his hand and threatened to shoot me. It was then that I noticed I too had a gun, not an ordinary one like his, but a machine gun. I shot the man who had threatened me, then mowed down a whole crowd that had suddenly appeared. While doing this, I experienced a tremendous sense of triumph, a kind of power surge.

On first glance this dream bears a striking resemblance to the one introduced in the previous example, but that appearance is thoroughly deceiving, since the only common feature is the fact that both dreamers kill others, rather than themselves. In the present example, however, the victim is not a philanthropist who stops to pick up hitchhikers; he is a villain with murderous intent. Still more significantly, the mood that follows the murders is fundamentally different for each dreamer. In Example 11, an initial indifference was succeeded by uncomfortable fear which prevented the dreamer from thinking of anything except the punishment that would come if his crime were discovered. Accordingly, that dreamer was intent on concealing all evidence of the crime. His guilty feelings sprang not from his own conscience, but from an external authority, the police. Still, in his case an extreme sense of guilt did exist. Dreamer Number 12, by contrast, did not experience the slightest remorse. The only anxiety he felt was at the very beginning, when he was being threatened and had not yet become aware of the means of defense he had on hand. No sooner had he discovered himself in possession of a weapon far more lethal than the one threatening him, than his mood—in sharp contrast to the course of events in Example 11—took a 180-degree turn, becoming one of a triumphant sense of power. He was elated to find that he had the power to cut down whole hosts of other people. Now, the only time an existence is attuned to triumphant joy is when it is able to burst through its everyday limitations to realize an unprecedented abundance of behavioral possibilities, an unbounded sense of freedom. For the duration of his dreaming at least, our gun-toting hero was capable of more action than had ever been granted him before, dreaming or waking. This man who had always run away from everyone and everything, who never dared to speak up, suddenly found himself in his dream the mightiest of men, with the power of life and death over everyone around him. His dreaming experience amounted to an immeasurable expansion of his existential capabilities. As might be expected, though, we shall have something to say about the precise character of that expansion.

The analyst might have done irreparable damage to the patient by taking the part of public opinion, representing its "moral reality," and chastizing the patient for his "destructive" dreaming behavior. That ill-advise action would have nipped in the bud a possibility of relating to others that had never before existed in the life of the patient. For even the ability to dominate others, even the triumph of ruthless aggression, even murder itself, constitutes a possibility inherent in every human existence. It is not surprising that our dreamer is destructive only of others, not of himself, since here for the first time he has a chance to give full rein to an expanded sense of his own power.

Freud has taught us that the moment at which a neurotically disturbed person is able to adopt an attitude of total honesty toward himself is also the moment at which recovery begins. Only after the patient has dared to face the myriad behavioral possibilities that comprise his particular *Dasein* and has acknowledged them as his own before himself and the witness analyst is he ready to set out toward a more healthy and mature, freer existence. It is an entirely different matter, of course, which of those constituent possibilities a person chooses to exercise in a particular context, and which he decides to leave unrealized. Consideration of that question does not belong in a treatise on the person's dreaming behavior; for it requires a thorough understanding of the human existence as a whole, the world it lives in, and the relationship between a human being and those around him, provided, of course, that such understanding includes an adequate ethical component.[12]

But there is another distinction which should be made in any theory of dreaming, namely, the crucial distinction between the mere *perception* of a personal existential possibility, and its *acceptance* as something demanding to be manifested concretely in one's behavior. People who dream of murdering others, for instance, often resume their daylight existence with extreme trepidation. They panic easily, in the false belief that the bearing they have exhibited while dreaming must inevitably and immediately be acted out in their waking lives. They do not realize that human existence implies the freedom to decide which behavioral possibility will be manifested at a given moment, and which left disengaged, remaining a mere possibility.

For all of the above reasons, then, it would have been disastrous for the therapist to have morally chastised the man who dreamed about the machine gun. It was the therapist's duty to say, no matter how horrified the patient was at his dreaming act of mass murder when he awoke, something along the lines of: "Thank God, at last you're breaking the pattern of your waking life by abandoning hypocrisy and permitting yourself to assert your independence triumphantly!"

That therapeutic measure contrasts sharply to the one taken with the dream murderer of Example 11. There the dreamer was asked whether, waking, he had a clearer insight into the meaning of his dreaming behavior than was given him during the dream. Did he realize that the dreamed murder of a masculine existence was analogous to something he had done to himself; since in the course of his life he had "burnt up, and scattered the ashes of," his own masculine behavioral possibilities?

In Example 12, however, the therapist strictly avoided directing the patient's attention to his dreaming destruction of life. He was careful not to ask whether, now that he was awake, the patient could more clearly perceive that he had killed off some of his own possibilities for living. Quite the contrary, here the patient's murderous dreaming behavior was praised as a first step on the road to freer self-assertion. Why this seemingly contradictory application of the phenomenological approach to dreams? Why, especially, when the twelfth example shows a destruction of human existence that is far more massive than that contained in the previous example? Why, also, when it is a fact that any annihilation of other life is tantamount to partial self-annihilation, whether it occurs in a person's dreaming or waking life, and regardless of whether the victims are human or not. For the world of human beings contains not only that which is ourselves, but equally that which is not ourselves but which speaks to us in the light of our existence and requires the perceptively open realm of our existence as a site for its shining forth and coming to its being. We are so dependent on all of the entities of our world that are not our own *Dasein*, that we simply cannot exist without them. For we only exist as human beings when we are able to reach out and take up residence (ex-ist) in our relationships to whatever impinges on us.

But if human existence is the sum total of the ways in which we can relate toward entities we encounter, then destroying such entities is equivalent to abbreviating our own existences (*Dasein*). The loss of an entity means the loss of possibilities for relating to that entity. And what is true of human nature as a whole naturally applies as well to dreaming human nature, as evidenced in Examples 11 and 12. Reasons of practical therapy cautioned against transmitting this insight to the patient in Example 12, however. It would have been very bad timing to alert him, in admonitory tone, to the devastation he had wreaked upon fellow humans in his dream world, and by extension upon himself. This would only have encouraged him to begin at the end of the process of self-discovery, instead of the beginning, causing him to totter and stumble. Before a person can practice altruism toward others, he must first find himself, that is, gather together all of his innate behavioral possibilities in order to render himself an independent selfhood. He must have himself at his free disposal before he is able to give of himself creatively. No matter how a person builds his concern for others into an attitude of self-sacrifice, without self-love it can never be more than vanity. A person who does not love himself will only use his concern to buy gratitude, because he cannot live without the assent of other people. Does not even the Bible command: "Love your neighbor as you love yourself," thus recognizing self-regard as a prerequisite for altruistic love?

That is why any therapist who does not allow a patient like the one in Example 12 to first triumph over others in his dreams will forever obstruct the patient's development toward existential independence. By dismissing the patient's dreaming murders as reprehensible, the therapist prevents him from experiencing an increased wealth of behavioral possibilities; and that experience is necessary if the patient is ever to act as a loving guardian toward the things and his fellow men that reveal themselves to him. The fact that dreamer Number 12 felt a triumphant sense of happiness the first time he dared to set himself up as lord over others indicates that he, in contrast to dreamer Number 11, has not yet taken the initial step on the way to finding himself. That sense of well-being is an unmistakable sign that what is occurring is a genuine broadening of the dreamer's existence, although as yet a first, provisional and insufficient step toward self-realization. Dreamer Number 11 experienced anything but a sense of triumphant well-being after murdering the man who was driving him; his was an act devoid of passion, one which gave him grim visions of standing before the bench, and so set his mind on concealing the crime.

The powerful difference between Dreams 11 and 12 should have been apparent to us from the first two sentences of each account. In the former, the possibility of standing hopefully at the side of the road, somewhere underway, far from the parental home, counting on the charity of another human being; while in Dream 12, we immediately hear about the dreamer's persistenc childish attachment to his parents. His whole dreaming life takes place right in front of his father's house. But what really gives away the impaired state of his perception is his statement, "I met a man [who] had a gun in his hand and threatened to shoot me." Here we see that the dreamer's vision is so restricted that it recognizes only the evil and threatening qualities of the only person he encounters—a killer—outside of his parents' home. This kind of limited vision corresponds to the prevailing state within the confines of a concentration camp.

Example 13: Dreaming of a thirty-one-year-old male, single, still chaste, with severely disturbed relationships with other people of both sexes.

I dreamed I had just gotten up after having a dream. I began to write down this dream—the dreams within a dream—for my next analytic session. What happened in the dream was that I was sharing a room with the Persian king Cyrus, who was about my age. He told me about his many victories and heroic deeds, and what an enormous empire he'd managed to put together. But then there were two other men in the room. They were wearing skirts made out of the gray material of Swiss field uniforms.

Here we have another example of the frequent dream types in which somebody dreams that he has awakened after having a dream. He then begins to do something with the "dream within the dream," in this case write it down for the next analytic session. This shows that this dreamer, even while dreaming, exists in outspoken relationship to the future as well as the present. At any rate, the patient here was able to link himself with an event that still lay ahead for him within the dreaming, allowing his future to determine his dreaming behavior at that present moment. Furthermore, the past of this dreamer is also seen influencing behavior within the dreaming. The next analytic session, in anticipation of which the dreamer writes down his account, is seen in the dreaming as a new link in a chain of past analytic sessions. That seemingly minor detail shows us how a person's dreaming world has, although rarely, the same property of openness as his waking one which we have shown to be an open realm both of space and time. So we see this dreaming world explicitly opening out into the three "ecstasies" of the past, the present, and the future.[13]

It is the Persian king Cyrus, one of the most powerful monarchs of the ancient world, who dominates dream Number 13. In his waking life, the patient had had only an extremely distant relationship to the exercise of power; in his dream, however, he came in close contact with that faculty in the person of Cyrus. Admittedly, the patient experiences that potential for power and rule only through someone else, not as one of his own existential possibilities. That someone else, moreover, appears to him only in the dreaming within his dreaming, indicating how doubly distant the acquisition of regal behavior seems to the patient at this moment. Still, the dreamer stood right next to Cyrus, that incarnation of masculinity, even staying in the same room with the king. Suddenly, though, the open realm of the patient's dreaming Being-in-the-world showed him a radically different sort of human nature. Two other men were present in the room, wearing skirts. Now a trace of femininity had entered the dream world, femininity that was still undifferentiated and vague, uniform. Also, the male gender of the skirt wearers, and the fact that the skirts were made from the material of military uniforms, combine to detract from the female element.

Based on what this highly timid patient witnesses while dreaming, the therapist should concentrate on bolstering his mood and strengthening his faulty self-respect by asking:

a. "Don't you find it very satisfying that in your dreaming you are now already able to stand very near to Cyrus-like strength and sovereignty?"

b. "Of course, in your dreaming that strength and sovereignty both exist only outside of yourself still. Are you more fortunate in your waking life, in that you perceive some of that masculine strength in yourself?"

The patient was not pressed to discuss the presence of the two other men, for good reasons. Their manifestation in the dream-world was so vague and distant that it could not be expected that the patient would have found much meaning in them.

Example 14: Dreaming of a twenty-six-year-old engineering student, with no specific symptoms of psychoneurosis, merely "full of" problems.

I dreamed I was far enough above the earth to see it as a globe. The conflict among the great powers on each had come to the point where an atomic war was imminent. The names of those powers were China, America, Russia, and England, but there were no living people representing them, no living politicians or generals, just inanimate blocks, stones, chess pawns. It never came to the worst. But one atom bomb fell into the ocean, and I knew that a big fish—or something—had the power to explode it there, more or less on purpose. I felt that was an added danger.

Following his account of the dream, the patient independently directed two questions to the *Daseins*-analyst:

a. "Does the earth in the dream signify my entire person?"

b. "Do the great powers in the dream refer to my own, embattled mental powers?"

From the *Daseins*-analytic point of view, both questions could be answered with a definite no. There is nothing in the dramatic experience of the dreaming itself to justify the assumption that the dreamed earth there was "actually" anything other than what it appeared to be. Equally unsupportable is the hypothesis that political powers of the dream carried any significance beyond the obvious one of political powers.

It is not only in a theoretical sense that the patient's attempt to "reinterpret" what he perceived while dreaming fails. Such a reinterpretation would have the effect of distorting the dream experience for therapeutic scrutiny. What the dreamer perceived was a set of events, taking place on earth, that did not affect him directly. For the duration of his dreaming, the patient has abandoned his planet for a stance somewhere far above it. The earth turns miles and miles beneath him. Of course, his "high" position allows him to see everything happening on earth. Yet in the end, he has a distant relationship to earth, not unlike that of an astronaut. His perception of earthly goings-on is correspondingly limited to what he can see at a great distance with his eyes. Even at such a distance, however, he becomes worried about the catastrophe brewing below. But he takes no further action. It does not enter his mind to participate personally in the battle beneath him; instead he remains merely a passive observer.

The earth is not just so many miles away from the dreamer, either. His relationship to it, and everything on it, is distant in a double, triple, and even quadruple sense. From all that he is able to record as a distant observer, humanity, animation, and warmth have completely disappeared on earth. What remains are merely stone blocks and wooden figures, with the exception of a single living creature: the fish. But the dreamer can detect even this creature only in the darkest depths, covered over by the tremendous water mass of ocean. Furthermore, the one remaining creature of the patient's dream world is just as threatening as the petrified, wooden inanimate powers. The only difference is that the fish's potential for destroying the world by detonating the atomic bomb has been displaced into the temporal distance of an indeterminate future, and into the spatial distance of the heavily obscured ocean floor.

Great care is necessary in applying phenomenological insights such as these in therapy. Naturally, the therapist is justified in asking a lot of questions. As we have said before, the patient could be asked, in his next analytic session, whether he could perceive more while awake than while dreaming. For instance, while dreaming, he had been concerned only with the destruction that might follow from an impending conflict among power blocs that were spatially and personally distant from him. However, it would be much too early to ask whether he began to sense that he, as a human existence, was threatened with the outbreak of a similar conflict among his own hostile life forces. Asking this might have dire consequences, causing the patient to retreat in fright to even more distant "heights," making him lose his footing on the earth even more than before. Worse still, asking this type of question might spark a devastating existential explosion that would send the patient's identity reeling off into the chaos of psychosis. For the fact that the atomic holocaust the patient sees in his dreaming can be postponed offers no assurance that mistakes in therapy may not damage his waking existence.

When a patient has lost his footing to the extent that this one has, the therapist is well advised to restrict himself to offering cautious suggestions for quite some time. At the start, the dreamer should only be helped to recognize his dreaming distance from everything earthly and alive, his "airy" stance high above the globe, and the conversion of human beings into things of stone and wood.

It might then be permissible to ask the patient whether, now that he was awake, he perceived not only as he did while dreaming his great distance from any entity that was not part of himself, but, above all, the existential and emotional distance which he kept toward everything and everybody he encountered. Only long after the patient had assimilated the fact that he compulsively kept himself at a great "social distance" would the time be ripe for inquiry into just what it was that motivated him to such self-isolation. If the therapist is able to time his question well, the patient will spontaneously get some idea of the extent to which his childish helplessness, in the face of those "great powers" that lay claim to every existence, motivated his existential ascent to distant heights—the ascent that he could perceive while dreaming only from his physical distance from the material earth. Precisely which "great powers" are responsible for frightening the patient is something that he can be made safely aware of only in the course of a prolonged *Daseins*-analysis.

Example 15: Dreaming of a young physician, suffering from chronic depression and an extreme lack of contact with his environment.

Shortly after his state medical examination, he dreamt as follows:

I am walking down the street with my old school friend N. We see little white packages placed along the sidewalk at regular intervals. They are disguised so that no one will know what they really are, but we know they contain explosives. I send N. off to the police, to report our discovery. Then I start to become afraid because the explosives are so near me; I want to go to the police myself and leave N. here. Suddenly, N. throws himself to the ground. I soon see why. The terrorist or freedom fighter who planted the explosives steps out of the woods nearby to check up on them. He aims his gun at us. I also throw myself to the ground and wake up terrified, knowing that my friend and I are finished.

In his dreaming state, the patient exists as an open realm of perceptivity and understanding which the following entities are able to come to light and *be*:

a. A country road
b. The dreamer himself
c. His former schoolmate N.
d. A terrorist, or a freedom fighter
e. Packets of explosives
f. The security police
g. The danger of being shot by the terrorist or freedom fighter

With regard to a: The fact that he is walking along a country road tells the dreamer that he is underway, moving forward as opposed to standing still.

With regard to b: Waking or dreaming, the patient knows himself as a stalwart, industrious, generally silent pillar of the middle-class bourgeoisie. Apparently he does not feel very comfortable with himself in either state.

With regard to c: The figure of his former schoolmate N. opens up to the patient a radically different kind of human nature. For, as the patient fully realizes in his dream, N. had developed into something of a "hippie" and drug freak, that is, a person who did not conform as he did to the societal rules followed by the "establishment."

With regard to d: The somewhat distant appearance of the terrorist or freedom fighter reveals to the dreamer a kind of human nature that is even more vehemently opposed to his own stalwartness than the passive bohemian existence of his schoolmate. With his explosives, the terrorist or freedom fighter presents a far more violent threat to the dreamer's own lifestyle. Yet what the dreamer perceives in both figures, the "hippie" and the terrorist, is more than just a threat to the existing order in which he has lived up to now. Both allow him to sense the possibility of greater freedom, which explains why the dreamer cannot decide whether the man emerging from the woods is a terrorist or a freedom fighter. Neither the "hippie" nor the other is repudiated totally: N. is envied for his unaffectedness, and the terrorist, as we have said, is not simply a destroyer; he is also fighting for liberation from inflexible norms.

With regard to e: On the other hand, in his dreaming state the patient has no intention of recognizing the behavior of the "hippie" and the terrorist as something possible in his own life, nor of adopting it for his own identity. To his dreaming eyes, the sorts of human nature exemplified by the "hippie" and the terrorist are entirely alien to himself, perceptible only from and through others. Of course, the mere presence in the dreaming of such "others" brings the dreamer into close proximity to those alien behavioral modes.

With regard to f: Quickly, however, his urge to keep himself just as he is and has always been wins out. He would rather expose the sort of behavior represented by the figure of his former schoolmate

N to the imminent explosion, electing to preserve for himself the behavior he has habitually practiced and to which he refers whenever he says "*I*" in the dreaming. Altering his original intent in the dream, he means to leave his bohemian friend behind with the explosives, while he places himself under the protection of the police, representatives of conventional, public opinion.

With regard to g: His instinct for self-preservation is activated too late. Both he and the passive, harmless "hippie" fall victims to the bomb. The terrorist, or freedom fighter, remains alive, as do the police, somewhere in the background.

In contrast to the therapeutic procedure used with dreamer Number 14, here the reawakened patient could be directly confronted with what he was known to have perceived while dreaming. This was because the patient here had remained firmly rooted to the ground in his dream, whereas dreamer Number 14 hovered high above it. In dream Number 15, the patient finds himself traveling along an ordinary, down to earth country lane. Only the danger of imminent explosion puts a halt to his travel. Yet in therapy, he should be strong enough to stand up to the danger, provided only that he is made aware, after he awakens, of the contrasting types of human nature that have defined his dreaming. There would be no risk in asking him straightforwardly whether he might not see now in his waking state much more and much more deeply than what he was able to experience while dreaming, although givens of essentially the same meaningfulness are present in both states. Dreaming, he had become aware of the physical walk along a country road, of the "hippie" friend, and of the terrorist freedom fighter. Thus the therapist would continue to ask the patient:

Can you now, awake, understand that you are on the way existentially, progressing as an entire human being? To what extent are you already able in your waking state to become aware of the fact that hippie-like and terrorist freedom fighter ways of relating to your fellow men also belong to your own existence? Or are you also waking still too much afraid of these existential possibilities as to dare acknowledge them as something of your own? May they actually, once you integrate them willingly into your own existence, explode the well-adjusted bourgeois structure of the acknowledged ways of conducting yourself that you have exclusively practiced up to now?

But it would have been totally irresponsible, from a therapeutic standpoint, had the analyst not begun, long before asking the above questions, by first of all stressing the patient's tendency to take flight. Actually, the patient became increasingly concerned in his dreaming state with self-preservation, that is, safeguarding the brand of human nature which up till then he had recognized as his own. To save this, he does not hesitate to sacrifice the amicable "hippie" figure, or flee from the terrorist—or freedom fighter—to the police. Since the police uphold the everyday public opinion he is accustomed to, they are the patient's asylum from all liberating change. It is a universally known fact that neurotically impaired people fear nothing more in analysis than entering into a broader, unpracticed freedom.

Example 16: Dreaming of a twenty-eight-year-old physician, depressive, with severely disturbed relationships.

In my capacity as a medical practitioner, I am called out on an emergency. Just as I start to leave the car with my medical bag, I see a young boy, maybe five years old, in front of the house. He is lying at the edge of a raised sidewalk. I think to myself, "That boy is very sick." His abdomen is swollen and hard as a rock. In my dream I remember that the only other time I'd encountered such a frighteningly hard abdomen was in a hopeless case of acute pancreatitis. After I have examined and partially undressed the boy, I take a transparent teflon tube, about the thickness of my thumb, from my medical bag. I push the tube down his esophagus slowly, but with considerable force. But no sooner have I begun to pour in a flushing solution, than the boy suddenly regurgitates a whitish mass filled with large lumps. He becomes cheerful immediately afterward, sits up and starts to talk. He thanks me for my help, then points to his stomach and says, "Look, it's soft and nice to feel again." And true enough, his stomach region feels like a soft indentation to me. Farther down along the abdomen, however, there is still an area of hard resistance. The boy tells me it will have to come out, but that it presents no immediate danger. Suddenly the sidewalk on which the boy has been lying is transformed into the stands of a circus or riding academy, and we, the boy and I, are watching a performance of trained white stallions."

The young physician dreamt this way just two days after he had first spoken with his future analyst, revealing a number of previously closely guarded secrets. Yet he waited several months to report the dream, telling the analyst after doing so:

> For some unknown reason I kept putting off the task of reporting the dreaming. I must confess that our first discussion forced me to say a lot of things that I had been carrying around inside like burning coals, experiences I had been unable to assimilate. When I left you and was driving home, I felt a strong, painful burning sensation not only in my chest, as I had before, but all the way from my neck to my abdomen. It was as if I had swallowed boiling water. After I awoke from my dreaming it immediately became crystal clear to me that I was just the kind of boy I had seen while dreaming and that, in a figurative sense of course, I was walking around with the same kind of stomachfull. But then I began to ask myself where I had gotten such ideas, since I never became the boy in the dream, always acting as the treating physician. Even in the subsequent circus scene, the boy was still the boy, and I was the doctor who had just finished treating him. For the whole duration of the dreaming, in fact, we remained two clearly distinct onlookers.

This man, a young physician finely trained in strict scientific thinking, utters a series of remarks that call into question once again the ordinary psychologistic "dream interpretation on the subjective level." He is on the right track, for the suffering boy of his dream world is at no time actually himself, the physician. Nor does the physician ever experience that boy as part of himself. Again, we could hypothesize an omnicient "superperson" "within" or "behind" the patient, capable of splitting the "ego-configuration," creating the image of a strange boy from one part, then projecting that image outward into the dream world, where it is held up as a mirror in front of the remaining part of the "ego." However, the facts argue a very different case. The dreaming patient is never allowed to see that he contains within himself behavioral possibilities quite different from those that are realized in the existence of a fairly successful physician, or someone watching a performance of trained circus horses. If he also exists as a five-year-old boy with a potentially lethal case of retention and restraint, he experiences it in his dreaming state only through another person, and even then only in the form of a decidedly physical intestinal blockage. Thus physical suffering calls out to him from within someone else. He responds to that call with the appropriate, somatic medical measures. He introduces a flushing solution into the boy's stomach, thereby causing a healthy physical release of the accumulated, stagnant matter.

He also realized, while dreaming, that his therapeutic efforts, though they saved the boy's life, still had to be completed. No wonder, then, that the dreamer and the boy were both perceived afterward as mere onlookers, incapable of facing horses in their natural state of freedom, seeing instead only trained stallions going through their paces within the narrow confines of a circus ring or riding hall. Also, the horses are as white as the wolves sitting in a tree in one of Freud's famous dream accounts.[14] Just as we must reject the arbitrariness of Freud's interpretation, which saw the white color of the wolves as a "symbol" for white linens of the parental bed, here we must permit the color white to be "merely" the color white. But in and of itself, white has many connotations. In contrast to the bolder colors, it connotes purity, innocence, and cool distance. While in the dreaming state the patient's perception was relatively limited, in the previous waking state, in his awareness of bodily discomfort, he could discern that he was emotionally suffering from much uncoped with and unfamiliar experience of his life history. Following the first conversation with the analyst, and before he dreamed of the physician-circus, the patient had felt an intense burning sensation, as if he were filled from top to bottom with hot water. His clear self-perception also returned to him immediately after he had awakened from the dream. If in the dreaming he saw himself as the healthy, active physician, upon awakening he quickly realized he was no less childless than the boy he had seen as existing outside of himself in the dreaming. He also sensed that he was suffering from a far more comprehensive blockage than the one afflicting the boy in the dreaming: namely, a widespread suppression affecting his entire existence.

One further detail of the dream is important. The sick boy "is lying at the edge of a raised sidewalk." Now, that isn't a very relaxingplace to lie, since at any moment the boy might fall off into the street. The patient was struck with this prospect even in the dream. When he first spotted the boy, he became afraid that the youngster might topple into the street and be run over by a car. The patient still remembered that fearful thought after he awoke from the dreaming, at which time the little boy's precarious physical posture spontaneously brought to mind his own persistent feeling that he himself had begun to slip as a human existence, with the possibility that he might end up run over by fellow humans.

If all of that had occurred independently to the reawakened patient, the therapist would have had to help him along by asking whether he now had at least a vague notion of a personal blockage, in the broadest, existential sense of the word. The only other task for the reawakened patient with his expanded self-awareness would be to confess his personal secrets in far greater detail than before. For only by expressing such things to another waking human being do we really face up to them, recognizing them as part of our own *Dasein*. Whatever we keep to ourselves, on the other hand, can always be passed off as something that never happened, or that does not exist. That is why silent "self-analysis" is hardly ever successful, whereas totally unrestrained verbal expression in the presence of the analyst has great therapeutic effect. It was one of Freud's most singular achievements to have discovered the therapeutic value of such communication on the part of the patient and to have coined out of it the one basic rule of analytic practice. It was the tragic genius of Freud, who felt it was his duty to back up his brilliant discoveries with natural scientific theorizing, which ultimately distorted the findings themselves.[15]

Example 17: Dreaming of a twenty-five-year-old female, single, suffering from frigidity and exaggerated shyness in her dealings with men.

Among others, she reported the following dream:

I am walking in the "Parc de la Solitude," looking for chestnuts that have fallen on the ground. I really like chestnuts, especially when they're still a shiny dark brown after popping out of their spiny, green shells. Suddenly, I remember I've been invited to a friend's wedding and still haven't bought her a wedding present. It's almost five o'clock, business closing time, so I go into the nearest department store. I buy my friend various household articles, a washcloth and so on, then ask for a vaginal mirror. But the salesgirl tells me they don't carry them.

The patient was exhorted to give a more precise account of what she had experienced while dreaming, but no more than that. Nowhere in the process of phenomenological analysis was there a need for any "free association" or "amplification," in the Jungian sense of introducing myths and legends with similar content. The patient was simply required to adhere strictly to those events and entities which she had visualized and immediately experienced during the dreaming period. She was told to describe them ever more precisely, and in so doing to report exclusively the significations and referential contexts given to her in the dream phenomena themselves.

According to the patient's own simple outline of the dreaming, as a dreamer she had felt as comfortable walking through the Parc de la Solitude as she did whenever she did the same thing in her waking life. For that park, she realized even in her dreaming, fully lived up to its name. You could walk there untroubled by other people, completely immersed in your own thoughts. In her dreaming state, the patient had been pleasantly engaged in gathering some of the chestnuts that lay along the paths of the park, exactly the same thing she did in her waking life on autumn walks through the park. She recalled vividly in the dream the many autumns she had enjoyed the shining, warm brown color of the chestnut fruit and remembered the marvelous necklaces she had made of them as a child. That is why she became so annoyed in the dream when her lonely play with the chestnuts was interrupted suddenly by the thought of her friend's approaching marriage. That reminder dispelled the peaceful contented mood of her solitary pleasure. It yielded to a state of distress and harassment attributable to her having to dutifully buy a gift at the last minute. The patient did not know why she particularly chose household articles, a washcloth and a vaginal mirror. It all seemed very natural in the dream. As a matter of fact, she really didn't know what a vaginal mirror looked like, waking or dreaming. All she knew was that it was an instrument that allowed gynecologists to see the uterus.

The above description of the dream experience reveals immediately the following peculiarities of the patient herself, her dream world, and her dreaming behavior:

a. Initially the patient feels comfortable on her solitary stroll through the park, whose very name is in fact "solitude." She is happy gathering, and playing with, the chestnuts, an activity that reminds the dreamer of her childhood. At first, then, her entire *Dasein* is attuned to peace and comfort. But no existence is comfortable unless it occupies a place in the world to which only those entities come that are familiar to the human being, and easy to deal with. In other words, a person can only feel comfortable in a world where things do not overtax him but, on the contrary, allow him to carry out freely the possibilities of behaving toward them that he has at his disposal, and so allow him a certain fulfillment of his existence. One of the existential possibilities capable of being realized by our dreaming patient was a walk through the Parc de la Solitude, the behavior of a solitary wanderer. She does not have to attend to any other human being there. She is exposed only to the harmless greens and warm browns of the plant kingdom, with which she learned how to play in her early childhood

b. Soon, however, another human being breaks into the playful, solitary world of her dreaming. It is her friend. Of course, the friend does not appear physically, she only "comes to mind." Yet even when someone only remembers another person, that other person is no less present. It is just that the presence is of another kind, corresponding to what we call "picturing," or "visualization." Here again, though, when we merely "picture" something "in" our minds, we still are completely in its presence out there where it has its place in the world, for our entire existence is engaged in a thinking relationship with that thing. The friend who enters the dreamer's world as a visualized presence unexpectedly speaks to her from somewhere beyond the narrow limits of the plant kingdom; it is the world in which two adults of opposite sex can be married.

But it is not the dreamer herself who is getting married, just a friend. The existential possibility of marriage is still so alien to the dreaming patient that she can perceive it only in someone else, though that someone else is a close friend of hers. Yet even the distant approach of that possibility is enough to transform the dream's predominant mood of happiness instantly into one of discomfort. That is the mood in which she sets out on her dutiful errand, finally buying the wedding gifts in an anonymous department store. When the subject of marriage comes up—even the marriage of another woman—then, the patient's dream world shrinks drastically. Only everyday household articles still have a place in it, in the foreground a miserable washcloth. Finally, whe decides to purchase a vaginal mirror. Now, the purpose of a washcloth is for cleaning up dirt. The fact that such a washcloth seems an appropriate wedding gift for a friend might lead the analyst to ask the patient what thoughts she had about this that had not occurred to her while dreaming. Was it possible that she considered marriage, involving the physical union of man and woman, as having to do with dirt that needed to be washed away?
      The dreamer's relationship to the vaginal mirror is at first only a remote need that cannot be fulfilled, for the mirror is nowhere to be found in the department store. But why should the dreamer want to give her friend a vaginal mirror in particular? Naturally, the impending marriage itself refers to the potential for complete love

between a man and a woman. But the dreamer's existence is too neurotically impaired for her to confront physical sex as a component of healthy, adult love. Instead, a vaginal mirror serves to point from a distance to a specific physical area of the adult female anatomy. By virtue of being a lifeless product of technology, the mirror puts the reality of the physical act of love at an extreme emotional distance. Out of the whole fullness of female love, the vaginal mirror is able to focus on only an isolated physical organ, the lower uterus. In addition, it belongs in the hands of a gynecologist and, by implication, in the realm of investigable diseases. The fact that the dreaming patient thought of buying the present at the very last minute, just as the stores were about to close, indicates her great temporal distance from marriage as well.

The full extent of the above phenomenological analysis could have been communicated safely to the reawakened dreamer. The therapeutic value of the analysis depends in fact, on how insights are communicated to the patient. As usual, of course, it would be better to propose each finding in the form of a question, beginning with something like, "Doesn't it surprise you that . . ." As already pointed out, this kind of intervention allows the patient much more freedom than she would have if presented with apodictic assertions. On the other hand, the references to her neurotic lack of freedom lose nothing of their clarity and impact.

Example 18: Dream of a thirty-five-year-old dentist, being treated for impotence.

This patient was very depressive, with acute feelings of inferiority.

Last night I dreamed I was way up north with my friend Erich, in a log cabin. Erich wanted to plant tomatoes around the house, and earn his living by selling them. I thought that was crazy, since the climate wasn't right for vegetables, but I didn't say anything. Then suddenly I had a peach pit in my hand. I started looking around for a place to plant it. First I looked around in a field beyond the garden, but the ground was too hard. Suddenly the garden was gone. It had turned into a tennis court, and I couldn't plant my peach pit there either.

When the patient is a very shy and depressive person, it is better to begin applying the phenomenological approach therapeutically by underscoring the positive traits of his dreaming behavior. The analyst therefore began by asking this patient,

Don't you find it refreshing that you were concerned with planting something new in your dream? Your friend wanted to grow tomatoes, you wanted to grow peaches, and both of you had in mind plants associated with southern warmth and sunshine.

The analyst then added:

Of course, the region your dream takes place in isn't exactly suited for growing such things. It is too cold and rainy. Also, the soil you mean to plant your peach pit in turns out to be the artificial surface of a tennis court, too hard to grow things in. Something else strikes me about your dream world, besides its coldness; namely, the loneliness. There is not a single female, and except for you and your friend, there isn't a single human being in that world.

The following questions were given to the patient during therapy:

a. Your dreaming existence has been able to perceive the coldness and hardness that are so detrimental to southern growth only from things outside of your being and responsibility: the raw climate of northern Norway, and the asphalt surface of a tennis court. Are you perhaps already more clear sighted in your waking state? Do you not become aware now, to some extent at least, of the same meaningfulness of coolness and imperviousness referring, however, to your own existential relationships to that which is encountered by you?

b. After that question had alerted the patient to the dryness and distance of his copersonal behavior, a second question could be ventured:

Are you also aware of some of the factors in your life that have caused your world to close up, to freeze it and make your "emotional" handicap seem second nature to you?

As usual, the second question called forth a whole slew of memories of situations when the patient had been warned by his mentors that the expression of warm emotion was unfitting. The same question also evoked situations in which the free expression of emotion seemed likely to dissolve the patient's self, allowing it to be abosrbed into someone, or something, else.

c. A third line of therapeutic questioning might run something like this:

It is very good that in the past few months you have learned, from numerous memories, just what behavior on the part of your mentors bound you, very long ago, at the start of your life, to the relationship of cool distance from the world, which you continue to maintain. After a time, however, it may become even more important to you to ask whether you want to live on in "captivity" for the rest of your days. Perhaps you could find the courage to use every future encounter, including those with me, your analyst, as a testing ground for freer, more open relationships.

In sum, then, the earlier questions pertaining to the motives leading to the neurotic impairment of the patient's existence are mere therapeutic forerunners. As such they have their own use, of course, and are indispensable. We said in relation to earlier dream examples that simply recognizing the biographical origins of disturbed behavior was enough to give the patient a freer relationship toward it. His behavior can be seen as something that has been grafted on to his life; that is not the result of innate, fated, immutable realtionship to the world. Yet if therapy is to be truly successful, the analyst cannot stop at questions of "Where from?" and "Why?" He must also ask "Why *not*?"—and this is an encouragement to experiment with yet unfamiliar, freer modes of behavior. "Why do you not try for once to laugh loud and heartily when hearing a good joke?" is an example of this kind of question. A human being is only healthy or healed when he has been able to make his own the possibility of freely disposing over all his inborn relational possibilities, and of choosing responsibly which he will carry to fulfillment so that he and all that he encounters out of his world develop their being to the full. A healthy human existence will have a range of behavior that encompasses every nuance, from selfless love of what is encountered to a merciless battle against what is experienced as evil, as well as against that which has outlived its time and has to give place to what is new.

Example 19: Dreaming of a thirty-three-year-old male, acutely depressive, in *Daseins*-analysis for two years.

> My dream last night was that I was an extremely worn-down carpet lying on the floor of a strange room. Many people, all of them strangers, were trampling around on me. I felt no pain at all. Then suddenly I was no longer two dimensional. I had three dimensions and was almost two inches thick. Now peoples' footsteps really hurt me.

The dreamer here perceives himself only as an object located somewhere. But even as a worn-out rug lying on the floor, he still exists in a human way and not at all in the way of an inanimate carpet lying in a room. In existential terms, he is still a creature that maintains an open realm of perception and receptivity for the multitude of significances revealed by the entities that come to light from their appropritate places of that openness. A simple carpet cannot do the same; it has no eyes or ears with which to perceive itself, or other things and there being in a world-openness.

Admittedly, our human carpet's perception is limited at first to a distant, numbed recognition of the fact that people are walking on him. He cannot yet see the possibility of establishing a close, "emotional" relationship to what is tramping across on top of him. Then suddenly in his dreaming he unexpectedly gains access to that possibility, as he physically expands to three dimensions. The formerly paper-thin carpet gains the novel spatial dimension of thickness. But the real proof that he has become existentially "thicker" and that he has appropriated also a new existential "dimension" shows up in his new sensitivity, for now he is able to suffer under the footsteps of those who walk over him, although his sensitivity still is restricted to the feeling of pain only. Feeling anything always means to have let it come close to oneself. It is significant that both the people above him, and the room he finds himself in, are unfamiliar to the dreamer. The scenario of the dream is alien to him in every respect, no bond of intimacy binding him to these people and things.

Never before in two full years of analysis had the patient been willing to face up to the fact that his Being-in-the-world was severely disturbed. This time a dreaming experience left his waking self defenseless, forcing him to open his eyes to the fact that, ever since childhood, he had allowed others to step on him, mistreat him, push him around, not only physically as in his dreaming, but in regard to his whole emotional life as well. It also dawned on him when he awoke that since his eighth year he had been trying, with increasing success, to block out all sensation, so that he would not have to suffer any more at the hands of others. His effort had prevented him, of course, from winning friends of either sex. In the loneliness he had known since puberty, he wrote poetry. His longest poem carried the title "The Alien from this World."

The analyst let the patient know that he fully understood how the brutality of a drunken father, and a powerful mother's failure to offer protection, had done him severe existential harm. At the same time, though, the analyst never tired of asking the patient whether such a background was reason enough to let others walk on him forever. Why didn't he himself ever attempt to step on others. When a person has been mistreated in such a crippling fashion that his identity appears in dreaming as a paper-thin nonentity, the mention of love could only have the very opposite of a liberating effect on the patient. Here it would be premature for the therapist to introduce the possibility of any loving relationship. It would be as brutally restricting as the exercrable behavior of the patient's father. Anyone who has been so thoroughly crushed must take the initiative by striking back on his own. Therefore, the same therapeutic procedure should apply here as was used in dream Example 12.[16] Only after the possibility of aggressive expansion has been allowed for a considerable length of time do genuine stirrings of afffection begin to venture forth.

Example 20: Dreaming of a twenty-four-year-old male who still behaves as if he were sixteen.

A philology student, he suffers from fear of exams and sexual impotence. After a year of intensive *Daseins*-analytic therapy, he dreamt as follows:

> The semester has ended, and I am returning home to the small town where my parents live. As I approach the house, I am horrified to see giant flames and clouds of smoke rising from it. The whole house is engulfed in flames, and my parents will surely die if I don't rush to their aid. Without thinking of myself, I storm into the burning house to search for my parents. I find them in the bedroom, but it's too late. The flaming walls collapse on us; there is no escape from fiery death for all of us! That's when I wake up screaming.

At his next session, the patient was very troubled. He asked the analyst whether his dream might have been prophetic, and as such, real reason to fear that his parents must die. If that should happen, he declared, there would be no point in going on, for they meant everything to him. It would be right that he should perish with them, as he had in his dream.

The analyst replied:

> Far be it from me to contest the possibility of prophetic dreaming. But dreaming of the kind you have just reported occurs very often in people who are engaged in a process of analytic growth, and whose parents are in the best of health. There is therefore no reason why you should feel uneasy. All that happened during this last dream state of your existence was that your perception was very clouded and constricted. This was the reason why only an external physical burning up of your parents' bodies and of your material parental house by a *devastating* physical fire could enter "the open field of vision" as which you existed while dreaming of all this. Now, waking, can you become aware that there might be another question of the

same meaningfulness as being "burnt up," but no such a burning up of physical bodies and material houses by a physical sensually perceptible fire, but rather the "burning up" of your parents *as* parents, i.e., as human beings existing as mothering or fathering relationships to you, and of you *as* a helpless small son; this "burning up" being the effect of the immaterial, unobjectifiable "fire of life?" If, waking, you could deepen your "field of vision" in such a way, you would no longer perceive this "fire of life" as a devastating one. You would experience the clearing away of the old order as making it possible for you to mature as an independent existence, to open up your own world and exchange your filial subservience for a relationship of adult equality with your parents. The clouded perceptibility as which you were existing as long as you dreamed did not allow you to know as yet that your parents can exist as more than mere parents and you can be more than just their little son. Dreaming, you also had to believe that your existence as their dependent small son is your entire existence, and therefore, you equated the dreamed death with the end of everything. You still were blind to all the hundreds and hundreds of more grown-up possibilities of reltionships which—as possibilities—also have been constituting your existence.

In this way there was at no time any need for the therapist to believe in the still common fiction that the holocaust in this dreaming was conjured up as a symbol of the patient's life processes in some mysterious fashion, by a wise all-seeing and all-powerful agent, housing somewhere behind the dreamer's own eyes.

Example 21: Dreaming of a very depressive thirty-one-year-old male, unmarried suffering from extreme feelings of inferiority

This patient was able to face others only with an attitude of distant indifference. He recognized, even before entering *Daseins*-analysis, that the people in his dreaming always stood around stiffly, as if they were figures in a dusty, old photograph. Soon after beginning analysis, he reported the following dreaming:

The other night I dreamed that a magnificently beautiful peacock suddenly flew toward me from the sky. It swept by me several times, as if it were trying to entice me to fly along with it. Then it rose back up into the sky. I was just an ugly, heavy bird who could flap his wings around but never get up off the ground. Saddened, I stopped trying.

What is most striking about this dreaming is how natural it seems to the dreamer that his body should be that of a bird. Of course, he is no more a mere bird than dreamer Number 19 was an inanimate carpet. For the duration of his dreaming, our patient was a bird with a human existence. Despite his outward form, the dreamer had something no "mere bird" possesses: the ability to perceive, and give verbal expression to, whatever significances impinged on the open realm that was his world. He was able to recognize, in every shade of meaning, that the peacock was a peacock, and that he himself was an ugly, heavy bird. Had he been merely a bird, the dreamer could not have desired something so explicit as flying up into the sky with the peacock; nor could he have realized, and been saddened by, his failure. At least most of us believe that animals are not gifted with the ability to think, for example, of the sky *as* sky, and so on.

The reason this dream is such an important addition to our series of neurotically disturbed dreaming experiences is that it hints at a better understanding of the puzzling problem of the human body. For the dream remains incomprehensible as long as the bodily sphere of human existence is treated as it has always been in the western world. Here in the West, and only here, the body is seen exclusively as a physical organism at hand at a definite point within some preconceived, hollow spatial realm and ending at its physical realm, and ending at its physical surface, its skin. That view leads inevitably to the insoluble riddle of how a "psyche" ever got put into such an isolated organism, and how the two things, "psyche" and physical organism, develop a reciprocal, symbiotic relationship.

If we agree to dispense with such ideas as those, however, and allow the dreaming experience to remain just as it revealed itself to be, it tells us of a human being fully engaged in an effort to mimic a peacock, by lifting himself up into the heavens. The dreamed peacock, unlike those we encounter in our waking life, was not only spectacularly colorful but had the flying ability of an eagle. In that from the very beginning, the dreamer was with his whole "body and soul" in his desire to follow the peacock, in that his whole existence, was also already in attunement with the striving toward flight in the heavens. It was so powerfully drawn into this desire and absorbed into it, that its form was that of a bird. This would presumably not have been possible, even dreaming, if the bodyliness of a man were not a fundamental existential trait of his existence. This seems to be so fundamentally true that the bodyliness of the human being cannot be understood other than as that realm of human existing that can, among other of its characteristics, be submitted to investigational methods allowing it to be measured, weighed, and computed. Exactly these methods, though, cannot comprehend anything specifically human.

True, people sometimes dream that they can fly even in their familiar human form using their own arms as wings. That the dreamer here was completely transformed into a bird may be seen as an indication of his radical obsession with flight, so that his whole existence was concentrated in that single behavioral possibility. And in fact, flight is the most striking characteristic of birds as birds. Often, it seems they can do little else.

When waking we think about dreaming in which our body and its movements participate totally in a willed mode of behavior, we are customarily left wondering, and puzzled. The fact that it could happen in dreaming leads us to suspect that perhaps in our waking lives, too, the nature of our so-called physical being belongs no less directly to our momentary relationship to the world around us than the existential realms of recognizing, thinking, and feeling. We may be less aware of this in our waking lives than while dreaming simply because, as far as the anatomical, measurable structural changes are concerned, our waking bodies are much slower to respond, and far clumsier, than the bodies of our dreaming.[17]

In treating this patient, a person permeated with feelings of inferiority, the analyst would be well advised not to comment about the ugliness and clumsiness of his bird-body in the dream, or about his failure to fly like a peacock—eagle. Emphasis should be placed instead on the fact that, at least for moments while he was dreaming, the patient was able to come very close to the meaningfulness of being beautiful and uplifting, although it only could be seen from and through an external materially sensually perceptible presence. In addition, while dreaming he experienced for the first time ever the desire to actively overcome total imprisonment in the earth's gravity. The patient might be asked whether his waking vision might not be more perceptive. Could he not see, instead of a mere high, high-flying concrete peacock, immaterial possibilities of his own for achieving great heights, perhaps, for instance, in the form of colorful creative fantasies, even of "castles in the air?"

Example 22: Dreaming of a forty-three-year-old female, married, no children, with many psychosomatic gastrointestinal complaints.

Last night I dreamed that my husband and I were visiting families dressed up as Santa Clauses. What I mean is that I was Santa Claus, and my husband was Santa's manservant, whom we Germans call "Schmutzli."I made a great effort to praise or scold children the way I was supposed to. It surprised me that another year had passed so soon. The previous winter had just ended, it seemed, and nothing had happened between last December 6th and the present one; there had been no spring, summer, or autumn in between. Yet here it was, December 6th again.

The most noticeable feature of this dreaming is the number of disguises the patient is aware of. She actually carries out a triple masquerade. First, she appears in the dreaming as a man, instead of what she is, a woman. Then again her relationship to her husband is that of a hard master to his unquestioningly obedient servant. Also, she does not appear as the mother who loves children unconditionally. She meets only strange children, and even then only as Santa Claus, a figure who judges the good and evil in children's behavior. Santa Claus is not even an ordinary, home-grown mortal, either; he is a man from the world of fairytales, who comes from afar to pay visits only once a year. In sum, the patient's dreaming relationship to the world is anything other than that of a mature sensuous woman, or loving mother. No figure who comes to visit only once a year can realize a woman's potential for motherhood. It is no wonder, then, that the dreamer stops at one place. She realizes in her dreaming that December 6th is repeating itself once more, and with it winter, when growth ceases and all nature is cold and frozen. The other, warmer seasons, the times of melting, blossoming, and ripening, are missing in the dreaming. The dreamer spends the lifetime given to her in the role of a legendary, male moralizer. Her "time," i.e., the unfolding of her own existence in its temporal dimensions, is at a standstill.

Dreamings of Brain-Damaged Individuals

Example 23: Dreaming reported by a twenty-six-year-old male immediately after he awoke from a month-long coma.

The coma was the result of a skull fracture suffered in an automobile accident.

I remember dreaming the following while I was unconscious: I am a plant rooted, like other plants, in a bed of soil. The gardener comes along. I watch her ripping out one plant after the other. She keeps getting closer to me, and I am deathly afraid when I see that she is going to tear me out, too.

Even at a time when this patient was incapable of waking up to experience the everyday human world, he experienced briefly a dreaming Being-in-the-world. He perceived himself as a plant, not just an "ordinary" one, but a plant that existed in the manner of a human being. For only such a plant has access to a world of perception in which it may recognize itself as a plant rooted in the soil and grasp the meaning inherent in the gardener's actions of tearing out plants. Possibily, something he perceived in the distorted and reduced vision of his comatose state brought on by the severe injury was made out mistakenly to be a gardener, one who destroys life rather than tending it. Perhaps that something would have been perceived by any healthy waking person as the nurse stepping into the patient's sickroom. Only after he had come out of his coma and had again opened up his existence to the perceptivity of a waking healthy person did the patient realize, from the memory of his dreaming existence as a plant and of the approaching killing gardener, how very near he had been to death, or to a permanent state of vegetation.

Example 24: Dreaming of a sixty-five-year-old male, suffering from organic, arteriosclerotic dementia.

One morning he gave his physician the following dream account:

Last night I dreamed some men had tied my feet together. They dragged me through the hospital ward by my bound feet, then threw me into the toilet.

The patient was in an anxious mood the whole day after he had dreamt in this way. As happens so often in the case of persons who become psychotic because of an insufficient flow of blood to the brain, the patient alternated between periods of confusion and some lucidity. In fact, at the time of his dreaming he was much more in touch with many of the repercussions of his fluctuating mental state than he usually was in his waking life. From his dreaming location inside the hospital ward, he recognizes his own suffering and need for treatment. Admittedly, even while dreaming he has no more than a fragmented view of the demise of his existence. What he experiences is merely a constriction of the physical realm of his existence, as seen in the binding of his feet. To his dreaming mind, it is other men who tie his feet together. Those men are intent on completely destroying his physical being, by immersing it in a toilet. The dreaming patient remains totally unaware that his existential freedom of movement has been severly impaired, and that death will soon follow. Nor does he realize, while dreaming, that the impairment originates in an overall existential decline, which his physicans have recorded from its physical expression as a decomposition of the brain tissue.

That partial blindness notwithstanding, this patient is an example of someone who is more clear sighted while dreaming than in the waking state, for then the patient knew of his general collapse only by his vague moods of anxiety; he did not even realize what was causing that anxiety. When asked after he awoke whether he felt hemmed in or bound up now, he answered no. He knew nothing while waking of his imminent death, which in his dreaming had been experienced clearly through the immersion of his body in the toilet.

In this case, the *Daseins*-analytic understanding of the dream phenomena could not be applied therapeutically. The nature of an arteriosclerotic dementia precludes any healing intervention through psychotherapy.

Dreamings of Psychotically Ill Patients (so-called endogenous psychoses)

Example 25: Dreaming of a thirty-eight-year-old manic-depressive male.

I am riding my bicycle through the little town of Berne, whose streets are as narrow and winding as they were when I lived there as a child. I come up to a big truck with a heavy trailer. Something tells me I am supposed to drive the truck somewhere, so I try to climb up into it. At first I don't have much luck, but then I find a kind of ladder that helps me get into the cab. I look around carefully to make sure everything is in order, clean the wind-shield and rearview mirror, and so on. Then I start moving, very slowly and cautiously at first. It's extremely hard to maneuver the big, heavy vehicle through the town's narrow winding streets. I feel pressured by the respon-sibility. But though it's very difficult, I manage all right. Finally I reach the expressway, where I really step on it. But instead of following the rule of keeping the truck to the right, I move over into the extreme left lane, the passing lane, then drive so fast that I pass all of the other passenger cars. While I'm passing these cars, I wake up.

That is the word-for-word account of a dream reported by some-one who was known to me only as a thirty-eight-year-old male. The account was handed to me by a colleague, who wanted to find out whether a *Daseins*-analyst could sometimes do anything with a dream even when he knew nothing about the life or habits of the dreamer.

In and of themselves, the experiences revealed in the dreaming, and the dreamer's behavior with respect to those experiences, tell us the following:

1. The dreamer finds himself in a small town, the site of his childhood. Nothing has changed there since that time: the random layout of the town has persisted through all the intervening years.
2. The most striking feature of the little town is its winding, narrow streets.
3. Initially, the dreamer is riding through the town on a bicycle. Now, a bicycle is a very modest means of transportation, deriving its motion from the physical power of its human rider.
4. The dreamer's self-propelled ride through the familiar world of his childhood is unexpectedly brought to a halt by a command. "Something tells me," the dreamer reports, "I am supposed to drive a truck which had suddenly appeared before me somewhere."
5. That command is obeyed by the dreamer without hesitation. He has a hard time, at first, getting to the steering wheel inside of the truck's cab.
6. With an almost pedantic meticulousness, he takes control of everything in the cab, clearing his vision forward and to the rear. Just as cautiously, pressured by the great responsibility placed upon him, he laboriously negotiates the narrow streets of his childhood domain.
7. Without injuring himself or anyone else, he reaches the open highway that carries traffic speedily out into the big, wide world.
8. At this point, his behavior changes drastically. What had been a very carefully, conscientiously executed procedure suddenly becomes a wild race. The dreamer no longer feels pressured; racing down the highway gives him pleasure. He nonchalantly breaks every traffic regulation in the book, shooting his massive truck past all other traffic at a mad, dangerous tempo. Even the fastest passenger cars are left far behind him.

Anyone will recognize how in this dream the patient's child-

hood, with all the existential narrowness of a small-town upbringing, is anything but dead for him. That living past retains such a
powerful influence on the patient, in fact, that it is able to absorb
him completely while he is in a dreaming state. All of the
relationships to the things that had made up his childhood existence
are very close to him again, close enough to see and feel as they hold
him captive within their little universe. At the start of the dreaming,
the dreamer moves through that universe under his own power and
volition, on a bicycle. But he soon exhanges that independence for
obedience to an anonymous, alien command. He performs the task
that has been assigned to him and, from the moment he begins, must
carry around with him a heavy burden, the tractor-trailer. About the
goal and purpose of the torturous journey through the narrow
streets of his native town, he knows nothing. Nor does he ask; instead, he conscientiously does what he has been told, anonymously,
to do.

To his great surprise, however, he finds his way out of the
narrowness of his childhood universe. No sooner has he reached the
wide expanse of the expressway than he abandons the caution that
others have taught him and begins to follow his own impulses, driving recklessly and having fun.

Only the transition from a depressive to a manic mood is
analogous to this patient's abrupt leap from the sort of obedient
self-control, learned in his small town, to mad recklessness. No
similar dreaming behavior has ever come to my attention, which did
not originate in someone who was manic-depressive in his waking
life. The therapist to whom I owed this dream report confirmed that
his patient did experience the extreme changes of mood characteristic of manic-depressive behavior. A few days following this dream,
in fact, he entered a new manic phase after a long depression.

Here, once again, the therapeutic value of the *Daseins*-analytic
aproach cannot be adequately measured. For once the manic phase
had begun, the patient never possessed sufficient awareness to learn,
from his dreaming behavior, to see new things about his own existential makeup. In his manic waking state, his entire being was

continuously thrown from one thing in his environment to another. There could be no hope of inducing the patient to reflect about himself until the manic phase of his psychoses had subsided.

Example 26: Dreaming of a thirty-five-year-old female manic-depressive, at the onset of a manic phase.

> I was walking along the street. Suddenly I started pouncing on other people's heads, using the heads as soccer and bowling balls. I kicked in their teeth with my shoes. In the dream I was a little surprised at my actions.

It might appear that this dreamer, more so even than the previous one, has been shown a highly "symbolic" version of the manic leap by which an entire human existence shifts into a violent, toying disregard for others. But that is not what has happened here. No "unconscious" portion of a dreaming "psyche" exists to note the severe existential disturbance, then mask it as a physical pouncing onto the heads of other people. Only an outside observer, say, a veteran psychiatrist, would be in a position to point out the existential import of the patient's dreaming behavior. In contrast to a healthy psychiatrist the dreamer herself is aware solely of an isolated sequence of rather absurd physical actions showing to her the meaningfulness of a jumping up above the other people, dancing on them from one to the other, recklessly damaging them. Dreaming, her perceptivity is not open enough to recognize that the basic meaningfulness masking up the essence not only of the physical but of the whole existential bearing of a manic psychotic. However, the reawakened dreamer herself, in this case a mentally disturbed patient, knows even less than she knew while dreaming. As a dreamer, she was at least moderately baffled by her behavior; the abnormal manic activity of her waking life does not strike the patient, while waking as in any way remarkable, much less psychotic. No, like most manically ill people, in her waking life she considers herself exceptionally healthy and normal. Therapy here would be esentially the same as that recommended for the previous patient.

Example 27: Dreaming of a schizophrenic patient.

Yesterday I dreamed I was totally alone somewhere on the Luneberg Heath. The sky became an evil, sulphurous yellow. I heard thunder, muted and subterranean. Then the earth began to shake, in preparation for a powerful earthquake. I was deathly afraid, thinking that this must be the end of the world. All of a sudden the ground fell from under me, and I was in the void of space, growing weaker by the moment. I dissolved into dust, disintegrating completely.

It is not uncommon, even in the dreaming state of only mildly psychoneurotically disturbed persons, for individual living things—animals, plants, other human beings, or the dreamer himself—to die. When, for instance, a dreamer is crushed and eaten by a giant snake, all that really perishes in this dream world can be recognized by a *Daseins*-analytic dream expert as referring only to the demise of that type of human structure—neurotic or not neurotic—which the dreamer presently knows as his Being-in-the-world. It is then only the reduced perceptivity of the dreaming state of an existence that keeps the patient from seeing more clearly. Actually, there is no point in his mourning that loss of his old existential configuration, for it had to make room for freer and larger existential structures. Here it has served to strengthen another living thing, the snake, for the snake not only survives in the dream world, it derives new energy and growth from its human meal. And the dreamed snake's meaningfulness can easily be recognized by the more clear-sighted perceptivity of an awakened existence as consisting essentially of vital, animal-like earthy possibilities of relating to what is encountered, and, as such, referring him to corresponding modes of relating that belong, at least, potentially, to his own existence.

In the dreaming at hand, however, a complete world- and self-dissolution both take place from the dreamer's solitary vantage point on the arid heath. The entire world collapses into an empty void. It is worth noting, once again, that the dreamer experiences all this destruction solely as the demise of the sensually perceptible, materially present earth, and the breakup of his own physicality. As a dreamer, the patient cannot immediately perceive what will become apparent after he has awakened: the existential extinction of his immaterial, not reifiable *Dasein* in a schizophrenic attack. Examination of over 100,000 dream accounts has convinced me that such dream experiences of a complete and malignant world- and self-dissolution occur only in schizophrenic patients. And in fact, the twenty-six-year-old lawyer who reported this dreaming was just beginning his fifth schizophrenic episode, following a two-year period of remission. However, the fact should never be lost from sight that the great majority of dreaming of schizophrenic patients cannot be distinguished from the dreaming of only psycho-neurotically ill patients.[18]

Example 28: Dreaming of a second schizophrenic.

A friend and I have enlisted in the war against Italy. We were very happy at first. We were told it wouldn't be a dangerous war. But as we pull into a station near the Italian border, I see a cripple with only one leg. All that's left of the other leg is a stump, tightly bound and bleeding profusely. A train leaves, and the cripple limps after it. He grins at first, then starts to grow thinner and thinner, as skinny as me, then even skinnier. Finally I myself am the cripple. I turn into a real skeleton, my head changing into a grinning skull. Terror grips me. Next the skull and the train station dissolve into blue mist. I panic and wake up bathed in sweat.

The above dreaming occured in a thirty-year-old schizophrenic who was in the middle of a very strong remission. He had been de-institutionalized for two years but, barely three months after so dreaming, had to be rehospitalized because of a new schizophrenic espisode.

The dreamer sees something that was never visible to him as a waking patient. He finds himself on the way to war. The enemy is Italy. Despite his initial assumption that the war will be a harmless outing, he comes upon misery even before crossing over the border. Initially, he perceives the possibility of crippling injury from the person of someone else who has lost a leg and may bleed to death. This is happening at a distance from himself but soon enough, he himself is caught up in the possibility of physical extinction. Not only does he become stranded by missing the train, he sees his own physical self turn into a skeleton topped off with a grinning skull. In the end, the dreamer is not even sure whether he still exists or not.

While dreaming, the patient witnesses merely the dissolution of his physical being. There is no mention, in his account of the dreaming, of any awareness of a schizophrenic loss of self and environment, not even an "unconscious awareness." The patient is even less cognizant of danger to his waking existence after awakening from the catastrophic dreaming. He feels very well and only the possibility of the psychotic annihilation of the patient's selfhood and its world. The physician alone recognizes the essence of the patient's existential state. He alone sees that the patient's dreaming behavior toward an external enemy beyond the Swiss border is no different in its essential meaningfulness from the one of his waking attitude toward the "Italian" possibilities of his existence. It is common knowledge that the Italian people relate to their fellow men in an emotionally much more open and warmer way than Swiss people are usually able to do in communicating with others. The patient can be said, therefore, to be at war with himself in his waking life, because he has been taught to regard any physical, sensuous relationship with others as something hostile and dangerous, even sinful.

The dreaming in question illustrates especially well the therapeutic application of the phenomenological approach. It makes transparent the radical differences in the *Daseins*-analytic treatment of neurotic persons, on the one hand, and psychotically disturbed persons, on the other. The first portion of the dream might just as easily have come from a "mere" neurotic, which such experiences as those contained in the latter portion occur exclusively in persons who suffer, in their waking lives, from schizophrenia. Accordingly, we will limit our discussion here to include only the first part of the dream. Had the patient been merely neurotic, he might have been asked the following question: "Now that you are awake, can you perhaps see more than you could while you were dreaming, such as, for instance . . . ?" Then the patient might immediately be given to understand the physician's insight into the patient's warring existential behavioral possibilities.

But since the patient was schizophrenic, it was necessary to use the dreaming as something that might help him avoid overly demanding interpersonal relationships. He had to be forcible dissuaded, for example, from becoming more deeply involved in a love relationship with a certain woman. He was exhorted to be satisfied with a male friendship of long standing. Only in those rare instances when the analyst is prepared to assume full medical responsibility for the psychotic patient over a period of many years, guiding him through all subsequent eruptions of psychoses, would it be permissible for him to apply the phenomenological approach exactly as he would in the case of a mere neurotic. Otherwise, the bolder approach might very easily worsen the psychotic's waking life, instead of making it better. Persistent *Daseins*-analytic therapy, meanwhile, would produce something more than simply a spontaneous remission, even in the case of a schizophrenic patient. For remissions are nothing more or less than successful attempts to put boundaries around existential problems. They do not lead to a freer use of inherent, but as yet unrealized, behavioral possibilities.

NOTES

1. M. Boss. *Der Traum und seine Auslegung.* (2nd ed.) (paperback). Kindler-Verlag, Munchen. 1974. P. 100.
2. S. Freud. *Gesammelte Werke.* Vol. II/III. London: Imago Publishing Co., 1942. P. 132. The italics are my own.
3. Cf. the discussion in Chapter V of the present volume and M. Boss. *Existential fundaments of medcine and psychology.* New York: Jason Aronson, Inc., 1977.
4. S. Freud. *Gesammelte Werke.* Vol. XI. London: Imago Publ. Co., 1940. P. 62.
5. M. Boss. *Grundriss der Medizin un der Psychologie.* Bern: 1975.
6. For the therapeutic exploitation of a similar dream, refer to the account of a severely disturbed neurotic in the present volume.

7. See Chapter 3 in this volume.
8. Cf. M. Boss. *Grundriss der Medizin un der Psychologie.* Op. cit., pp. 542ff.
9. See Chapter 1 of this volume.
10. See Chapter 1 of this volume.
11. See Chapter 2 of this volume.
12. M. Boss. Ibid. Ibid., p. 571.
13. M. Boss. Grundriss der Medizin un der Psychologie. Bern 1975, p. 253.
14. S. Freud. *Geasmmelte Werke.* Vol. XII. London: Imago Publ. Co., 1947. Pp. 54ff.
15. M. Boss. *Der Traum und seine Auslegung.* Op. cit., p. 35.
16. See Chapter 2 of this volume.
17. Cf. the chapter on "bodiness" in M. Boss, *Existential Fundaments of medicine and psychology. Op. cit.* New York: Jason Aronson, 1977.
18. M. Boss. *Op. cit.,* p. 163. The analysis of Dreams. Transl. by Pomerans Philosophical Library, New York. 1958. P. 163.

CHAPTER III

The Transformation of the Dreaming Being-in-the-World of Patients, in the Course of *Dasein*-analytic Therapy, in Its "Ontic" Concrete Fulfillment

Example 1: Series of dreaming sequences reported at the start of treatment by a twenty-six-year-old female, unmarried medical student.

a. Three months after the start of analysis:

Last night I had a strange "double-decker" dream. In the dream I woke up to feel a peculiar sensation, as if my mouth were full of pebbles. I spat out some of them, and was increasingly terrified to discover that they weren't pebbles, but that my own teeth had become rotten and broken off. That scare really did wake me up fully. I had to check to make sure what I dreamed wasn't really true. Luckily, it wasn't.

b. Eighteen months after the start of analysis:

We—my family, relatives and friends—are coming out of the church where my confirmation has just taken place. We enter the Hotel Swan nearby, and find the usual confirmation meal. Just as I'm about to bite into a slice of bread, I notice that all my cutting teeth are missing. All that's left of them are deep holes surrounded by black-and-blue swellings. only then do I remember that I've been going to the dentist. I am comforted by my dentist's promise that after he is through with me, everyone will think the new false teeth are real.

c. Twenty-seven months after the start of analysis, and four months after its successful conclusion:

I'm looking into the mirror to check over my teeth. In the dream I believe that I've been losing one baby tooth after the other during the past few months. I am delighted to see in the mirror that in many of the gaps, the tips of new, larger, and stronger teeth have already broken through. Still other gaps already contain powerful, well-developed teeth.

Freud was convinced that the loss of teeth in dreams should be "interpreted" as a "masturbatory symbol," simply because in the Viennese dialect of his patients, the phrase "rip one out" (*einen ausreissen*) was reserved to describe onanism. Yet people the whole world over whose languages make no such idiomatic play on onanism, and who above all at the time when they are just in the process of maturing through psychotherapy, continue to have dreams of losing teeth. On the basis of that evidence alone, the Freudian "symbolic interpretation" of such dreams should no longer be afforded serious consideration.

The phenomenological viewpoint prefers instead to seek out the essential quality of human teeth and of their potential loss. It means to discover the how and why of things, the inherent and prevasive meaningfulness that makes them what they are. The true nature of human physicality, of human bodyliness, can only be properly understood as an immediately belonging to human existence, as constituting a fundamental sphere of its Being-in-the-world, as we have intimated already, consists in nothing more or less than the sum total of a person's innate potential for perceiving and responding to the significances of entities that impinge on him from the open realm of his world. In its essence, physicality is that realm of human existence which is perceptible to the senses, submits partially to measurement, and is therefore often confused with *purely physical* objects or organisms that may be found at specific locations in space.

But human bodyhood is not merely another materially present object existing in the same way as other inanimate, material objects.

Rather, all the bodily or physical phenomena of the human being are nothing other than the bodily or physical sphere of the relationship to the world *as* which the human being at any given moment exists. Any attempt to grasp the nature of a human physical phenomenon should therefore begin with a search for the particular relationship in which the human existence in question is currently existing as Being-in-the-world. All physical phenomena would then be seen simply as realms of that relationship to the world. Teeth serve in a very specific realm of man's relation to his world, namely, the realm associated with seizing, gripping, capturing, assimilating, and gaining dominion over things. They are poorly understood, indeed, if they are seen simply as just another set of physical objects. In reality they are participating in the "bodying" of our capturing relationships to what we can eat in our human environment. They can also be said to constitute part of the bodily sphere of this possibility of capturing relationships.

With the proper insight into the nature of human physicality or "bodyhood," a therapist can attain a much deeper understanding of any "tooth dream." Naturally, this deeper insight affects therapy favorably.

In connection with the first dreaming of the woman in Example 1, the phenomenological approach warrants the following suggestions to the reawakened dreamer:

a. "Might it not be that you can see far more now, than when you were dreaming? Does it occur to you that you are a dreamer even in your waking life, exactly as in the dreaming? Do you still need to be properly awakened, as happened in your dreaming?"

b. "Might you perhaps recognize that it is not only your physical teeth that are being devastated, as in the dreaming, but that your entire existential relationship to the world to which teeth belong is in a state of upheaval? I am speaking of the potential for seizing something, for getting it into your power in order to assimilate it—and this does not apply only to material nourishment. There is another mode of grasping things apprehending them conceptually before "assimilating" them into one's understanding of the world. Have you perhaps begun to suspect, already, that in the course of your few months in analysis your previous manner of apprehension, the way in which you came to terms with your 'world,' isn't working? Is it possible that your old 'world-view' has fallen to pieces?"

c. "Now that you are awake, do you sense anything like the panic you felt over the loss of teeth in your dreaming? If so, can you realize now that you panic which you can experience now, in the brighter light of your waking state, results from the collapse of your previous relationship toward the world, along with the lack of any new way of getting hold of things?"

This approach to therapy avoids again the unfounded conclusions of other "dream interpretations" to date, in that it does not assume that the "dream image" had from the start already contained some "unconscious consciousness" about the mental comprehension, which a mysterious entity allegedly existing within the dreamer's mind has decided to disguise as the dreamed loss of teeth.

Once it is clear that the teeth are nothing less than the direct physical sphere of our grasping, apprehending relation to the world, it comes as no surprise that patients are regularly visited by dreamings of tooth loss whenever the therapeutic procedure has so challenged their neurotically impaired "world-view" that it is on the point of collapsing. During the dreaming, of course, the patients' "vision" is so limited, that of a collapse of the entire existential world relationship of grasping, seizing, and comprehending, he sees only a destruction of the material, sensually perceptible bodily sphere of that relationship.

The most important therapeutic insights deriving from the second dream might be formulated in the following questions:

a. "To what extent do you still think of yourself as a young girl on the point of confirmation, still under the protective wing of her family?"

b. "You still have a few teeth missing in this second dreaming, though far fewer than in the previous one. Yet the missing teeth are those most suited to grasping. Do you now suspect that, even waking, your ability to grasp and comprehend is defective, in a much broader, "metaphorical" sense? Just how deficient do you consider your behavioral potential for seizing, grasping, and comprehending the things of your world?"

  c. "Does it occur to you that in your dreaming you are unable to improve your ability to bite and chew on your own? Instead, you very matter of factly expect someone else, the dentist, to help you out. You are satisfied to receive a very realistic set of false teeth. Is there perhaps something in your waking life that is very similar to your dreaming expectations, only far more consequential? Might it be you realize, now waking, the extent to which you expect analysis to be a process whereby you simply sit there until your analyst implants a prosthesis in you, one that will allow you full use of your innate existential capacity for grasping?"

Such a question as the last one does not presuppose that the aptient has had a "transference" dream. There is nothing in the question to suggest that the dreamed dentist might actually refer to the ant. The only connection between the two, in fact, occurs because the patient's waking analysis has tuned her existence to the significance of medical treatment. That attunement has persisted in the dreaming existence; although it opened up this latter only in such a way that purely physical ministrations of a dentist could shine forth and appear. For as yet, the dreamer had no eyes to behold change on an "immaterial," existential level. Dreaming, she could not envision the correction of pathological impairment that could take place in her waking state in the course of her *Daseins*-analysis of her "immaterial," unobjectifiable, existential behavioral possibilities.

In the third dream of the medical student, occuring shortly before the successful conclusion of her *Daseins*-analysis, her initial panic has given way to its opposite. She is filled with joy at the growth of beautiful new teeth, stronger than her old ones. Admittedly, dreaming, she is still unable to perceive anything beyond a change in a material, sensually perceptible realm, her teeth. Yet the state of this realm in the dreaming is much improved over the teeth of her previous dreaming experiences. Only after awakening, was she in a position to realize that the altered character of her tooth dreams corresponded to a maturing of her immaterial existence, from the previous helplessness of a withdrawn compulsive neurotic to the independence and vivacity of an actively enterprising young woman. Thus relieved, she managed to relinquish also the analyst's help without suffering any withdrawal pains.

Just in passing, we might illustrate the dangers of blindly schematizing the dreaming experience with a dreaming of tooth loss occurring with a six-year-old boy. To his great delight, he dreamed that his two front baby teeth had finally fallen out. This was a boy who had watched with envy as both his brother, one year older, and his sister, a year younger than himself, had acquired permanent teeth. He had badgered his parents to tell him whether his own cutting teeth might not be loose enough to jiggle a bit. But even if that waking behavior were unknown, the dream account would in itself be sufficient evidence that the boy did not perceive tooth loss as an impairment of grasping ability, either waking or dreaming. Rather, the dreamed loss of his baby teeth held for him the unequivocal promise of getting bigger, of reaching his siblings' state of maturity. What he can only wish for in his waking life becomes accomplished fact in his dreaming. There is in the dreaming no hint of desire for something distant, only joy over present attainment. Therefore, while dreaming there is no wish-fulfillment occurring.

Example 2: Dreaming of a forty-one-year-old engineer, in a position of authority.

The patient's psychiatric diagnosis was acute narcissism, with a severe handicap in his ability to love, despite high intellectual development. He experiences life as meaningless and constantly feels as if he were existing in empty space.

First dreaming:

I am peacefully lying on a beach. At first, I am just *one* person, but suddenly another man is there, lying right next to me. I start to caress his back and arms. Then I notice, to my great amazement, that the person I'm caressing is me too. The thing is, I was really fond of that second man.

The intense self-infatuation experienced by this man in the dreaming state needs no further comment. Asked whether he had ever done anything similar while awake, he confessed that just before going to sleep he often derived great pleasure from stroking his own arms. It disgusted him, however, to touch the skin of a woman.

Second dreaming, two weeks later:

In the dream I notice I'm being robbed. While one man cleans out my house, another steals my wristwatch, and I can't do anything to stop them.

Dreams of being robbed, similar to this one, occur with this patient at least twice a week. He was asked in therapy: "Could it be that only those who are not prepared to give freely of themselves, feel that everyone they meet is robbing them?" The patient answers, "Yes, people are really a burden to me. I'm not interested in them, but they're always trying to get something out of me, they're oppressive to me."

Third dreaming, a year later:

I was in bed, just about to fall asleep, when I felt something moving on my back. I tried to shake it off, but the more I shook, the harder it held onto my back. Then I finally realized it was my mother clinging to me with a large pair of iron forceps. But because she was in back of me, I couldn't get at her to throw her off. I was panicked at not being able to get rid of this clinging mother.

When the patient was apprised of the powerful maternal bond evidenced in his dreaming, he said others had told him that as a boy, he had always been "tied to his mother's apron strings." He then poured out story after story to document his later relationship to her, which was miserable. True enough, when he was very young she had loved the smell of his hair, yet she had never been capable of showing him open affection. Nothing would give him greater pleasure than to strangle his mother with his own two hands. His father had always been warmer and more affectionate than his mother; but in contrast to her, his intellectual growth stopped at a relatively early age. If he was a good-natured idiot, still, that was not his fault. On the other hand, memories of cruelty and frequent beatings from his mother continued even now to bother the patient.

From a therapeutic standpoint, the patient should be advised to think over carefully the persistence of the maternal bond, as it had evidenced itself in his dreaming of the previous night. In his dreaming state, he could of course perceive that attachment only in the physical form of a forceps by means of which the mother held onto the back of his body. The therapist exhorted:

> But now that you are awake, try to enter fully into that feeling which binds you to your mother not simply in a crudely physical fashion, but in an overall, existential way. You are always complaining about her, it's true, and would like to kill her. But would there be any need for such a powerful defensive attitude if you did not have an "iron-clad" attachment to her, and if that attachment were not just with a physical iron forceps, as in the dreaming, but a "figurative" attachment of your whole nature?

Fourth dreaming, six weeks after the third dreaming:

> I am way up in the air over a football stadium, stationary as if in a helicopter. I'm watching two teams fight it out far below me. The players are so far away they seem like miniature figurines, as if I were seeing them through the wrong end of a pair of binoculars. I try to intervene in the contest by hurling apples down at them. I'm not sure whether I want to separate the fighting teams, or even whether I have a favorite side. Anyway, I miss my targets by a mile. My apples fly in every direction except the one where the people are.

The dream prompted the analyst to point out to the patient how high up in the air he had been, far above the bustle of human movement on the earth's surface. It was certainly worth noting, also, that the people he had perceived while dreaming were embroiled in a competitive battle, rather than an affectionate relationship. But the most important point was his mere observer's stance high above his fellow human beings. As time passed, he did experience a certain need to intervene in the human game below. The instruments he used were apples, living things, though inanimate fruits. But his attempts at intervention were uncoordinated and he missed his mark, failing to reach the other people. The first therpeutic question suggested by the *Daseins*-analytic approach would read something like, "If you really think about your waking behavior toward others, can you see yourself as the sort of mere observer you were while dreaming, not just one who perceives a football game with his five senses, but someone whose entire system of interpersonal relationships is subsumed in an attitude of distant observation?"

The second therapeutic question: "What you saw at a distance in your dreaming, optically, was an isolated football game. Are you now as an awakened individual in a position to 'see' more, namely, the fact that the only existential relationship conceivable to you is one of interpersonal competition?"

The third therapeutic question: "Do you sense, now that you are awake, that it is not only in your dreaming efforts to hurl apples that you fail to intervene in the distant activities of your fellow humans, but that all of your attempts to reach other people, emotional ones as well, are out of rhythm and unsuccessful?"

Fifth dreaming, a year after the fourth one:

I'm lying in bed in my parents' house, and I'm about eight years old. You, my analyst, come into my room, sit down on the edge of my bed, and put your arm affectionately around my shoulders. I tell you how nice this fatherly affection is. But you say, "It's motherly." As soon as I hear that word I spring up as if I've been bitten by a tarantula, and try with desperate strength to push you away. You remain, however, sitting on the edge of the bed, immovable as a granite block while the force of my endeavor sends me rebounding onto the hard floor of the bedroom. There I sit dejectedly, telling myself I'm apparently not as strong as I'd always thought I was.

Here the dreaming experience permits the patient his first interpersonal intimacy, in the form of a father—son relationship with his analyst. That shy bit of affection yields after only a few moments to a strong disinclination, brought on by the mention of maternal love. The dreamer does not even need to come face to face with a material mother, mere acoustic perception of the word "maternal" being enough to arouse his vehement resistance and throw the dreamer back into isolation on the cold, bare floor of the room. In addition, this dreaming casts initial doubt on the patient's narcissistic over-estimation of his own strength. The analyst proves far more stead-fast than he himself.

A therapeutic application of the above phenomenological insights into the patient's dreaming world and dreaming behavior would first of all require the analyst to tell the patient how pleased he was that as a dreamer, at least, the patient could countenance the fatherly affection of another man. Naturally, the analyst would also have to point out the patient's extreme defensiveness toward even a very distant maternal relationship.

Sixth dreaming, three months later:

I find myself in a room where a small wood fire is burning in the fire-place. It radiates a pleasant warmth. Before me stands a young woman, half undressed. But it isn't a real, live woman, more like a doll. Suddenly there is a whip in my hand. I use it to lash the doll-woman, the way children wind up tops. The woman gradually turns into a children's top, while I keep her spinning with the whip.

The patient's dreaming existence has broadened at least to the extent that it can find room for an attractive, young female, not just a hated mother. The fireplace also admits a bit of warmth into that world. Of course, the female quickly shrinks to the proportions of a mere doll, then is further reduced to become a top, an inanimate children's toy. The dreamer's relationship to that entity consists in whipping it harder and harder, to make it spin faster and faster. Here in his dreaming, as in his waking life, he is still miles away from a permanent love relationship toward a living adult of the opposite sex.

Seventh dreaming, four months later:

I'm at a village carnival, having the time of my life. But then I notice
there's a woman who keeps throwing knives, or axes, at me, and I'm in
danger of being badly hurt. I can still manage to dodge the weapons in
time, but it's getting on my nerves, so I go up to the woman, put her over
my knee, and give her a sound thrashing. As a final punishment, I rape her
brutally. I don't experience an orgasm myself.

For the first time here, the patient's somber mood, his sense of
meaningless boredom, give way to something akin to pleasant,
festive relaxation. This mood opens up the possibility of being happy with other people in the natural setting of a village carnival. Even
women don't immediately crumple up into lifeless objects. No
sooner does he allow himself a little enjoyment, however, than the
only female presence that stands out is perceived as a hostile enemy
who threatens his life with knives and axes. In sharp contrast to the
helplessness characteristic of his much earlier dreams, such as the
one in which his mother held onto his back with a forceps, here he
knows how to defend himself against the dangerous female. He ad-
ministers a punitive beating and finally rapes her as well,
demonstrating clearly that not every act of sexual intercourse constitutes surrender in a copersonal love relationship. Quite the
reverse, here coitus is to punish and humiliate another. No wonder,
then, that in such sexual intercourse lacking all traces of loving surrender to someone else, orgasm and ejaculation, the physical
manifestations of giving oneself up to the partner, are missing.

The analyst used the insights he had gained to best advantage by
sharing two reflections with the patient. First of all, he expressed his
pleasure over the fact that, at least for a brief time, the patient had
been able to exist together with others in a festive atmosphere. "It's
truly commendable," he remarked, "that in your dreaming at least,
you have come to experience human intimacy as something gratify-
ing and worthwhile." The analyst went on to say:

Of course, you still aren't able to maintain that mood for very long. It
immediately gives way to anger whenever a woman steps into the spotlight
of your attention. Any female capable of approaching you as an individual
in your dreams can only be interpreted as hostile and dangerous. Your

dreaming existence is still totally incapable of perceiving the enrichment that can come from a love relationship with a woman. On the other hand, it is no small matter that you have learned how to defend yourself. It is striking, though, that women are only permitted to appear as dangerous and hostile in your dreaming.

The therapist's third step was to direct the patient to look, more thoroughly than was possible in his dreaming, at the limitations under which his relationships with females had suffered since his early childhood.

Eighth dreaming, a few months later:

> In the heat of rage, I grab hold of a fat, bald, elderly man with a good-natured expression on his face, beat the living daylights out of him, twirl him around in the air, then tear out his windpipe, and all because I know that this man slept with my mother in the woods. That made me violently jealous.

Unlike the earlier dream experience, this one no longer shows the mother as someone clinging with iron forceps to the dreamer's back, or as something to be pushed away with every means at hand. Admittedly, the mother has not yet managed to emerge into the dreamer's immediate, and intimate, vicinity. But the extreme rage engendered against the mother's lover clearly points to the existence within the patient of an erotic desire toward his mother. Therapeutically, only the following hint might be ventured on the basis of the dream: "Is it possible for a person to break out in such a jealous fit against his mother's lover in a dream, if in his waking life that person has only hatred for the mother, as you keep saying you have?"

There would be no therapeutic sense, however, in speculating on whether the elderly gentleman appearing in the dream was "really" the patient's father, or his analyst. At least in the dreaming itself, neither of these was recognizable in the hated lover of the mother. Although his pleasant expression and portly stature were reminiscent of the patient's real father, the dream figure appeared as a total stranger. To declare that figure a "symbolization" of the father or the analyst, ignoring its patent differentness, means once again to accept as fact all of the ungrounded suppositions that have always been held out as the basis for symbolic representations. Not only would such reinterpretation of a dream entity lack all justification, it would severly detract from a proper understanding of the patient's existence itself. For it is in the unfamiliarity of the lover that we recognize the general deformity of the patient's "mental field of vision." That "oedipal" distortion may well have been stamped on him originally by the misguided behavior of his parents. But the original impetus is something very different from resultant perceptual limitations in the present, or reactive behavior toward what has been (mis)perceived. The anonymity of the patient's dreamed rival betrays the near-total distortion of his existence. For while dreaming, at least, the patient's existence is so restricted that it can perceive in whatever old man appears only behavior that is hostile and humiliating for him and disgracing for his mother.

Using insights gained directly from this dreaming, and not through the distortion of interpretive artifice, the analyst should stick to asking the reawakened patient whether in his waking life he could sense a basic attitude toward men analogous to the attitude evidenced in his dreaming world.

Ninth dreaming, a half year later:

I am traveling by airplane with a nice group of people. There is a kind of dining facility in the plane. We're all seated around a table, eating fondue. A charming young woman sits down next to me, and from the very first moment I am strongly attracted to her. But I don't dare let her know that. We begin to fly through a band of stormclouds. It becomes obvious that we've been hit by a bolt of lightning and are plunging toward earth. I am seized by a tremendous feeling of happiness, because under these circumstances I can tell the woman next to me how much I love her. At this point I wake up.

Here we have something that is wholly unprecedented, in either the patient's waking or his dreaming life. For the first time ever, he feels a direct, intense love for a female who does not belong to his immediate family. The new love is not just a derivative of the jealous desire for his mother, as seen in the previous dream. In fact, the only problem here is that he is so unaccustomed to interpersonal relationships of this sort that he cannot bring himself to show the woman his love openly. An extreme set of circumstances is required to pull him out of his shell. Only under the impress of approaching death does he find the courage to make a declaration of love, even in his dreaming.

A critic of this kind of approach to dreaming might object that in a neurotic such as our dreamer, a declaration of love is tantamount to a plunge to death, both entailing a dissolution of the accustomed neurotic existence. That, the critic may say, explains the connection between the threat of death and the declaration of love in the dreaming. But if we are faithful to the precepts of phenomenological observation, we can answer the critic: If we adhere strictly to the facts as they present themselves, considering only what they tell us on their own, it soon becomes patently clear that the plane did not fall *after*, much less as a result of, the declaration of love. The plane's sudden descent was known to the dreamer unequivocally *before* he declared his love; in fact, its imminence was the very thing that encouraged him to open up.

The patient might be given something else to consider, namely, his initial passivity toward the young woman in the dream. It is not he who sits down next to her, after all. He remains stationary while she comes up to him. Even a detail as minor as this is not significant. It might be used in therapy to discover whether the patient remembered any situations from his waking life in which he had displayed such passivity toward women.

Something else needs to be mentioned. The patient's unprecedented outpouring of love for a woman occurred in an airplane, high above the earth. That fact produces two important questions for the patient. First: "Does you latest dream flight correspond to your previous 'helicopter dream,' in which you watched a football game from on high? If so, does this mean that even in your dreaming, your capacity to love has not yet come down to earth, but is still hovering in the clouds? Or does the place where you dream— high in the heavens—result from the very 'elevated' sort of mood you are now able to experience, at least while dreaming? If so, again, does the 'elevated' mood originate in your newly acquired ability to enter into a love relationship, and shake off the weight of the earth's gravity?" The decision must be left entirely up to the patient. But the reawakened dreamer should not be permitted simply to reflect on his dreaming experience in a vacuum. Instead, he must be made to reexperience and reintuit it. When the present dreamer had completely reimmersed himself in the experience of his dreaming, his responses left no doubt that the second was the case, i.e. that he felt "elevated" while dreaming, because he was able to love a girl.

In the former of the two series of dreaming introduced above, we could clearly see the transformation of a single entity of the dreaming world—the dreamer's teeth—and an alteration of her attitude toward that entity. In the second dream series as well, it was not just the dreamer's attitude toward what he encountered that changed; the dreamed entities that could shine forth into and *be* in the perceiving openness of a dreamer's existence were caught up in a powerful process of mutation.

Because of that process of mutation, both dream series differ from all of our preceding dream specimens. They are useful not only as material for visual exercises in the area of dreaming experience, and as further proof for the therapeutic utility of a phenomenological, *Daseins*-analytic approach to dreaming; beyond that, they show that in concrete cases, the content of the dreaming experience is an excellent indicator of the effectiveness—or failure—of *Daseins*-analytic treatment. Whenever therapy is having little or no effect, the dream entities, and the dreamer's attitude toward them, usually undergo little or no alteration.

CHAPTER IV

Comparison of a Phenomenological Understanding of Dreaming with the "Dream Interpretation" of the "Depth-Psychologies"

INTRODUCTION

There are two main reasons I have chosen to make a clear distinction between the phenomenological approach to human dreaming and the interpretation based on the more traditional dream theories. First, such a separation will effectively highlight the true nature of the phenomenological approach, as it is applied in *Daseins*-analytic therapy. And second, a direct confrontation of phenomenological understanding of dreaming, on the one hand, and Freudian–Jungian "dream interpretations," on the other, will confirm that the latter do not actually interpret, i.e., make intelligible, the phenomena of the dreaming itself, consistently "reinterpret" without this "reinterpretation" having any basis in observable facts. Rarely if ever do Freud and Jung pursue the wealth of significance inherent in dream entities themselves, preferring instead to impose meaning on them from without to conform them with prescribed theory.

COMPARISON OF FREUDIAN REINTERPRETATION WITH THE PHENOMENOLOGICAL UNDERSTANDING OF THE SAME DREAM PHENOMENA

Comparison Dreaming A

In Freud's famous *Interpretation of Dreams*,[1] there is a particularly crass instance of how violence can be done to the dream phenomena by "interpreting" them. It was briefly mentioned in my first work on dreaming,[2] though without any *Daseins*-analytic emendation. I would like to make up for that now. Freud prefaced his account of the dreaming by identifying the dreamer as an agoraphobic female who in "real life" was the mother of a four-year-old daughter. She dreams, according to Freud, that:

Her mother (the child's grandmother) had forced her (the dreamer's) little daughter to travel alone by sending her away. She (the dreamer) is then traveling on a train with her mother, when she sees her daughter walking directly into the path of the train. She hears bones crunching (feels uneasy, but not really horrified), then looks out of the window of the train to see whether she can spot any of the parts (of her run-over daughter) to the rear. She then reproaches her mother for allowing the small child to go off by herself.

In order to come up with an infantile—her voyeuristic—instinct that will endorse his natural-scientific dream theory by serving as the dream's universal motor, Freud arbitrarily alters the text of the dreaming. The dreamer's statement that "she looks out of the window . . . to see whether she can spot any of the parts *"to the rear,"* is changed by Freud to read "whether she can spot any of the parts *from the rear.*" All that Freud is able to bring forward as a justification for this radical violation of a dreamed phenomenon is a so-called "free association" occurring to the patient during her next analytic hour when she was in a waking state again. Freud's argument however, is on its side based on merely another of Freud's arbitrary interventions. He thought it legitimate to change the mere temporal sequence of the so-called "free associations" into a chain of causes and effects. Where he finds the justification for this arbitrary change, Freud does not tell us at all. He simply believes in his right to change the words.

Once he has imposed the principle of causality on the temporal sequence of "free associations" it becomes self-evident for Freud that every later "free association" is the effect, and as such the basic meaning for each prior association. This logical manipulation enables Freud, indeed, to connect the dream component "to the rear," in its highly altered form "from the rear," with the dreamer's afterthought that she had once seen her father's sexual parts from the rear as he was standing in the bathroom; thus allegedly finding the infantile voyeuristic drive as his presupposed theory wanted it to have. Neither, however, the assumption that an infantile voyeuristic impulse has to be regarded as the basic motor producing the whole "manifest dream image," nor the violation of turning of the dream phenomenon "to the rear" into "from the rear" is made any less illegitimate a maneuver by these completely unwarranted mental constructions of Freud. They only keep him from seeing how casually and "unobjectively" he ignores the fact that looking to the rear at something does, from a phenomenological standpoint, mean exactly the opposite of looking at something from the rear. Isn't it at all possible that glancing backwards will produce a *frontal* view of an object? In reality, there is nothing about the dreamed entities to suggest genitalia viewed from behind, nor do those dreamed entities even remotely argue that the sending away of the little girl should be construed, after Freud's practice, as a "threat of castration." What is actually there in the open realm of the dreaming patient's perception, is something entirely different. For one thing, she finds herself in extreme physical proximity to her mother. She is chained to her mother in an emotional sense as well, so much so that the mother can command her to send her daughter off alone. At first the dreamer is unquestionably obedient, although that attitude places her daughter in great danger. The daughter is almost immediately killed, by the very car of the train in which the dreamer and her mother are sitting. Only after this does the dreamer venture to reproach her mother.

Rather than use so-called "free association technique" to pursue the patient's memory of seeing her father's genitalia from behind, the analyst should alert the patient to the supreme power her mother still holds over her in her dreaming. Hadn't her mother convinced her, in her dreaming of the previous night, to travel with her along the same track? Again, yielding pliantly to her mother's command, hadn't she then sent her one and only daughter away and, as it turned out, to her death? The appearance in dreaming of such a potent mother is in itself a sign that the dreamer continues to exist as a powerless child. The whole force of her infantile dependence on her mother is revealed in the dreaming, when the train in which she and her mother are sitting crushes her own little daughter. That dependence is so great that it buries the patient's potential for striking out on her own as an independent adult, a fullgrown woman and mother. For when her own child ceases to exist—and the child in the dream was her only child—she is no longer a mother.

The *Daseins*-analytic dream explication above neither distorts nor bypasses the facts of the dream experience and should be related in full to the reawakened patient. As a further therapeutic step, she should be asked to recall any waking situations, from her earliest childhood up to the present, in which she had shown a similarly infantile dependence on, and enslavement to, her mother. At every mention of such a situation, the analyst should express his surprise that the patient had actually endured, and continued to endure, tyranny like that from her mother. That would presumably help the patient to realize, for the first time ever, that it was possible to behave toward older women in ways radically different from the subjection she had always known, in both her waking and her dreaming lives.

Incidentally, insights about the dreamer gained from our *Daseins*-analytic investigation of her dream experience are confirmed by additional facts, which Freud, however, chooses to leave out of his "interpretation." He tells us that throughout the course of her waking life, even from the time when she was a small girl, the patient felt her mother's presence to be so detrimental to her own love relationships that she took on the behavior of a boy. Not surprisingly, she often heard herself accused of being a tomboy. A phenomenological approach would have exhorted the patient to become aware of her dependence on her mother, which in turn would have opened her eyes to her enslavement to such an extent that tendencies to break free of her fetters would soon have appeared in her waking life.

Comparison Dreaming B

A twenty-four-year-old psychology student had the following dream:

> I'm standing around with some friends and find out that the fiancee of another friend, who's been distant ever since he got engaged, had just died of cancer. Like everyone else present, I'm shocked at the news. I really feel sorry for my friend. After the burial, I find myself with mourners in a kind of self-service restaurant. Everyone's standing in a row in front of a buffet table, taking food. Before my turn comes, I look around for dessert, but there don't seem to be any sweets. I force my way through the crowd to see whether there might not be any dessert toward the front of the table. But there's nothing there. I return to my seat, still hoping to find something sweet to eat somewhere. But I don't find any and remain dissatisfied.

A therapist schooled in Freudian dream theory would begin by reinterpretating the dream as follows: "The fact that the dreamer's friend becomes distant after his engagement engenders, in the dreamer's unconscious, jealousy and a desire for vengeance against the bride who robbed him of his friend. The dreamer's anger at the woman spawns an unconscious death-wish, (which is) fulfilled by the fiancee's death in the dream."

A phenomenological approach to the same dream phenomena would counter the above reinterpretation by exposing fully the fiction of "unconscious desires." Only something already deemed worthy of desiring can be wished for. It is impossible to deem a thing desirable and, at the same time, not be aware of the thing's existence. Saying it is the dreamer's "unconscious" that possesses such awareness, rather than his own consciousness of his waking or sleeping state, adds nothing at all to an understanding of the given phenomena. Because the "unconscious" thus postulated is by definition unidentifiable, its introduction merely serves to explain a puzzling dream sequence on the basis of something still more puzzling, something whose very existence remains to be proved.

A particular phenomenological objection to the Freudian dream reinterpretation is that the dreaming itself does not contain the slightest evidence of any jealousy, or death wish, against the fiancee. The dreamer's genuine sorrow at her death would sooner point, in fact, to something opposite to a death wish, namely a wish that she might have stayed alive. Additionally, his friend's engagement confronted the patient, both in his waking and sleeping states, with the meaningfulness of a lasting love relationship between an adult male and female. Although the patient is not yet able to manage such intimacy with a woman on his own, his existence is now sufficiently open to recognize that intimacy as a behavioral possibility in a near acquaintance. Yet the potential for an adult love relationship cannot persist in his dream world even in that indirect fashion; where cancer claims the life of the fiancee, that relationship disappears as an immediately sensible presence, becoming instead merely something gone and to be mourned.

The second portion of the dreaming, containing the funeral meal with the missing dessert, would serve Freudian dream theory as proof of a libidinal regression to the oral stage. Here, once again, we must object that libido, as "psychic energy" cannot in any of its presumed stages manage independently to fabricate a human world. Nor can any unique mundane situation, such as a dessertless meal in a self-service restaurant, be fashioned from "libido." In order for a person to have access to such a situation, he must first be receptive to, in touch with the significance of whatever he encounters. The dreamer presently under discussion was aware from the beginning of the various meanings inherently associated with self-service restaurants, also meanings attached to desserts in general, even the absence of desserts. No manner of energy can fulfill these pre-requisites, which are prerequisites of human existence, in a world comprised of perceptible, significant frames of reference.

If we agree to put aside psychoanalytic speculation concerning hidden energies, reasoning that even if they existed, they could con-tribute little to an understanding of the phenemena in question, and stick instead to the given facts, the following can be said of the dreaming:

After briefly opening itself up to a love relationship between adult partners, the patient's existence quickly closes again, to such an extent that, of all conceivable possibilities for sensual enjoyment, it remains receptive only to that of eating almost alone in a restaurant where each person must serve himself. And even the op-portunity to eat is available to him only in truncated form: He can have the main course that is needed for physical subsistence, but not the dessert whose sweetness customarily completes the enjoyment of a meal. When even the sweetness of food remains confined to the level of desire, it is no wonder that, at the close of his dream, the patient cannot manage even a distant view of the far richer sweetness of love for a woman.

When the patient became acquainted with the Freudian reinter-pretation of his dream, the positive therapeutic effect was almost negligible. In fact, the Freudian scheme, which made the patient out to be a potential murderer, actually frightened him, sending him into a dangerous state of depression. He defended himself against insinuations of harboring unconscious death wishes, on the grounds that there was no factual evidence for such wishes in his waking or dreaming lives. His defense was interpretated as resistance to analysis. Yet the patient persisted in the belief that he was justified in defending himself against his analyst's unsupported reinter-pretation of his dreaming experience. Since patient and analyst could not come to an agreement, the course of treatment was soon ended, broken off by the patient.

The *Daseins*-analytic understanding of the same dream was

based solely on significances seen according to phenomenological criteria as being inherent in the dream entities themselves. This was immediately understood and accepted by the dreamer: To use the patient's own words, the new understanding merely articulated the perceptions he himself had vaguely had about the dream experience upon awakening. From that beginning, he gained a far greater awareness of his immaturity in love than had ever been available to him while dreaming. In the dreaming state, it was through two other human beings that he had perceived the possibility for forming a marital bond, as well as the impossibility of maintaining it. Now that he was awake—and only now—he realized that he himself had not yet acquired free use of his own potential for forming inter-personal bonds of affection.

Comparison Dreaming C

The following dream is taken from a previously cited work by von Uslar, although the appended "interpretation" might just as easily have come from a Freudian. Word-for-word, the dream reads:

> Once, when I had had a tooth pulled and my mouth was bleeding pain-fully, I dreamed a traveling companion of mine had been stabbed in the jaw (in the very spot where I was "actually" feeling pain.) The stabbing was some kind of shock therapy against schizophrenia. Now, my ego definitely wasn't split in the dream; my companion had the knife thrust into his jaw because *he* was schizophrenic, and above the door of the room where the shock therapy took place stood the words "Blood Room." I acted only as an observer and had nothing to do with it myself.

When the patient woke up, he felt a severe stabbing pain along his jaw, exactly where the knife had hit his companion in the dream-ing and, coincidentally, at the precise location of his own extraction. Because it was full of blood when he awoke, he easily identified his mouth as the "Blood Room." Here von Uslar's "depth-psycho-logical" interpretation takes over. He begins,

Looking at the dream as a dream, I can say it was not only the dreamer's ego that divided into an observer and an alter ego. That division was probably mirrored again in the form of "schizophrenia," or "divided consciousness." Not only that, the dreamer's own body was projected into space: his oral cavity became the "Blood Room," and the stabbing pain gave birth to a stabbing knife.

Von Uslar goes on to say:

A close examination of the dream reveals a clear, dramatically consistent sequence of events, in which nothing is split as long as we regard the dream as a dream, just as it was dreamed. On the other hand, there *is* a confusing splitting and inter-relationship of the split up components; there *is* an identity of "I" and "Thou," Body (oral cavity) and space ("blood room"), pain and instrument of pain. Simultaneously, the ego is split up into ego and alter ego, the body into body and space, thus making body and space, ego and other identical once again. What, then, is the reality of the dream: its simple dramatic development, or that great web of perplexity? . . . The answer, when we accept the dream on its own terms, is, both, for in its very essence a dream extends from matters of factual reality to the most subtle intricacies of ambiguity.[3]

The "dream reinterpretation" above is then described as having the advantage of almost entirely avoiding opinion and personal construction. While the writer admits that details might be subject to debate, he avers that no one would deny the connection between the patient's own pain and bleeding and the shock therapy his companion receives in the dream.

To my way of thinking, however, von Uslar's reinterpretation brings benefits diametrically opposed to the advantage he claims. It is exactly the plastic vividness of this reinterpretation that compels the phenomenologist to recognize that the alleged identity between the dreamed phenomena and wakingly perceived phenomena is but an unfounded assumption based on theoretical prejudgments. Further, it directs his vision to a relationship between the two of a quite different kind. For if the dream is taken precisely as it was perceived and recounted by the reawakened dreamer, it clearly shows a self-contained dramatic development. And it shows this not just within the dreaming, but on into the patient's waking life, long after the dreaming experience has become "merely" something that can be "retrieved from the past." At no time, however, do any ambiguities invade the past dreaming experience. So long as the patient's dreaming state persisted, all that he saw was a traveling companion who, for the sake of shock therapy, received a knife wound at a specific location along his jaw. Aside from that, there was a treatment room marked with the words "Blood Room," and finally the dreamer himself, though only in the role of an observer. A very special kind of observer, to be sure—for even as he dreamed, he was closely affected by the significances of both the schizophrenic illness, and a shockingly bloody treatment used against it. Any other entities which might have played a part in the patient's dreaming world never entered that dreaming world. There are no grounds, then, for supposing that some such entities may have been present unawares, as for instance in the dreamer's psychic "unconscious." The given phenomena do not offer a trace of evidence to support such claims.

If we remain faithful to the phenomenological research method, adhering strictly to the demonstrably present entities of the patient's dreaming world, we find it is no longer permissible even to say that the patient merely "misapprehended" certain perceptions that addressed him during his dream. Saying that would be judging the dreaming from the outside, from the standpoint of the subsequent waking state. It is entirely possible, of course, that while the patient slept his perception was somehow affected by that which he recognized, before falling asleep, as dental treatment, and which later on, after he awoke from dreaming, was felt as a stabbing pain along the lower jaw, accompanied by bleeding in the mouth. But we can never prove these things, since no one can place the reawakened patient back into the former dreaming state in order to elicit from him a detailed account of every background perception that visited him while he dreamed. We should also keep in mind that countless similar dreamings have occurred in people who did not have teeth pulled on the day before, and who did not wake up with bleeding mouths. Consequently, the appearance in dreams of such things as our patient's "Blood Room" or of his traveling companion who is treated for schizophrenia by having a knife stuck into his jaw, is in no way necessarily dependent on preceding events in the patient's waking life.

Yet when it comes to understanding the dreaming experience, it is not the etiology or motive behind a specific dream entity that is important, but grasping the nature of the phenomenon itself. What causes steam to rise from a kettle, for example, is the heat of the fire burning under it. But that fire is something very different, again, from the steam it engenders. Analogously, in the dream of von Uslar's patient it is not the original impetus attuning him to specific significances in the dream entities, that counts. From both the theoretical and the therapeutic standpoint, it is the entities themselves that are important, as they come to light in the open realm of the dreamer's world. For at the time of the dreaming experience, only those entities exist. Their existence is unequivocal. They also confirm the fundamental fact that every entity present in a human world corresponds to, indeed cannot exist without, the unique perceptive ability of the human being. For there is no shining forth and thus no becoming present, no being at all, where there is not primordially also a shining in the form of an open, lucid realm of perceptivity into which all shining forth beings can present themselves.

This is a fact that Freud himself recognized. Without its discovery, modern dream theories could never have grown beyond the simple stimulus-based explanations of the pre-Freudian era. We insert this little aside here because of its great relevance for therapy. Clearly in an attempt to resist therapy, many patients try to disown their dreaming behavior by foisting it off onto "external" events of the previous (waking) day. They do this as if there had never been a Freud to point out the "exaggerated importance, for dream-formation, attached to stimuli originating outside of the mind."[4]

Phenomenologically speaking, in any case, our "Blood Room" dreamer at no time perceives himself in that "other" person who has the knife in his jaw. Nor does he even begin to suspect, while dreaming, that a tooth has been extracted from his own jaw, or that there is blood in his oral cavity. It is only the speculation of the depth-psychological dream theories that assign ambiguity to dream entities and create the fiction of multiple meaningfulness, i.e., of a "manifest and a latent content," that allows them to be identified with wakingly perceived phenomena. For those later perceptions, the pain and associated bleeding, did not exist in the dreaming state. Again, the crucial question here is whether it is possible for something to exist independent of its perception by a human being. Isn't the manifestation and presence of things, instead, so inextricably tied up with their perception by existing human beings that, without that perception, nothing at all could be? The important little word "is," which comes to mind whenever we name a thing, would lose all meaning were it not for the open realm of human perceptive openness. And anything that simply *is* not in our dream, such as the presence of blood in the dreamer's mouth or pain from a tooth extraction, cannot be brought into a relationship of identity, or ambivalence, with something that does exist there. The facts of the matter will always be given a false context, therefore, if—by virtue of alleged "unconscious awareness," a contradiction in itself, on the part of the dreamer—the dreamed "Blood Room" were to take on the significance "blood in the dreamer's mouth"; the dreamed shock therapy by stabbing would be ascribed to a tooth extraction of the previous day; the dreamed traveling companion would also become the patient himself as a dental patient; and that companion's schizophrenic behavior would signify for the dreamer while dreaming nothing other than the fissioning of his dreaming ego. According to this approach, once the patient is awake again, that "unconscious awareness" need only be transformed into a conscious awareness of the multiple meaningfulness that always has been there, even if "latent."

The phenomenologist differs on yet another point about this dreaming: the dreaming experience shows no discernible motivation for the sort of concealment postulated by depth psychology. There is no evidence of any injured pride, or moral compunctions, that might have prevented the patient from openly displaying in his dream the blood and tooth extraction that existed in his waking life.

The dream reinterpretations posited by depth-psychological theories are not just theoretically untenable; they also prohibit the therapist from gaining the understanding of the dreaming he needs if he is to help the patient. A phenomenological-*Daseins*-analytical approach to the dreaming would have required, by contrast, that the reawakened patient be asked the leading question—whether he could not see more "deeply" than he could while dreaming. If the patient could not answer that question without further prodding, he might be asked whether the schizophrenia exhibited by his dreamed traveling compamion reminded him now, even vaguely, of any "mental," existential disturbance in himself, something that went deep down to his bones and therefore required therapy that penetrated, like a knife, "right to the bone."

Naturally, there is no rule that says the patient must be more clear sighted upon awakening than he was in the dreaming state. But the essential unity of both existential modes—dreaming and waking—within a single *Dasein*, and the distinctions between the two modes (as elaborated in the final chapter of this work) make such clear sightedness probable. Experience also shows that "deeper insights" occur far more commonly in the waking state. It is improper, on the other hand, to hold up a single dreaming as an exact diagnosis of schizophrenia in the patient. All that someone in my position can say is that, in over 100,000 dream reports, I have never seen one similar to this which has not come from a person with a severe existential impairment.

Comparison Dreaming D

Finally, we ought to give phenomenological consideration to the dreaming which, at the beginning of this work, helped us to see the discrepancies in "interpretations" proferred by a group of American Freudian analysts. The disagreement among them was so marked, we remember, that they were forced to conclude something must be fundamentally wrong with the art of Freudian dream interpretation. The dreaming in question is the one in which the dreamer, finding himself in a barbershop, discovered, to his great horror, that an area of baldness was rapidly expanding on the back of his head.

In order to make room for a phenomenological understanding of this dream experience, we must first recognize that the five psychoanalytic "reinterpretations" are entirely arbitrary and without any substantiation, especially when they designate the dream entities as symbols for anal, homosexual, and aggressive drives. What we are then left with is a situation that finds the dreamer in a barbershop. Now, the nature of a barbershop is in the nature of the service it provides. A person goes there to have his hair put in order by another person, namely, the hair dresser. In any case, a barbershop is that place where particular attention is paid to human hair. There, in comparison to the other beings of the human world, hair becomes unequivocally thematically dominant.

Hair is noticeable in the dreaming world of this patient in a very special way: it begins to fall out. The dreamer, surprisingly, sees the back of his own head, a region that is usually not visible to him without the aid of mirrors. This is possible because, in the dreaming state, he exists as visual perception that is unlocalized, able to fill the entire space of his dream. For as long as he continues to dream, that fact seems self-evident. Not until he awakens does it strike him as odd; not until he begins to visualize what he has dreamed does he discover that his vision did not depend on the location of his physical eyes, nor was it restricted to their optical field of vision.

Perhaps this feature of the dreaming state can tell us something about the fundamental nature of human existence. While dreaming, this person experienced himself mainly as immaterial vision, as something able to perceive the unique significances of things, something that cannot be located at a fixed point in space but that exists *as* perceptively spanning a realm of world-openness. That dreaming experience immediately points to a peculiarity shared also by waking human nature, one by which neurologists, ignoring the fundamental aspects of human existence, are still perplexed. Even in our waking lives, a soup bowl standing in front of us is always "seen" as a round, whole soup bowl. We never "see" it as just the flat, crescent-shaped facade that impinges on our eyes in a "purely optical" manner.

But back to our balding dreamer. He not only sees the back of his head directly in the dream, without the help of any mirror, but realizes that his hair, instead of vitally sprouting, is beginning to fall out. At first the bald spot is no larger than a saucer; however, it is expanding rapidly. Rampant hair loss sends the dreamer into panicked flight. His fear is so intense, so "real," that even after awakening he has to hold onto his bedsheet, to resist the impulse to jump headlong out of the bedroom window. Truly, what we have here is an apparently inexplicable, immoderate "emotional reaction" to the loss of a little hair! But that kind of characterization is totally alien to the phenomenological approach, for it refuses to take into account the abundance of meaning that human hair holds for the dreamer; instead, it assigns only "scientific factuality" to the hair. Hair becomes merely a collection of individual cuticular filaments, attached to the body at discrete locations, and having certain properties of weight, extension, color, and chemical composition. With that kind of tunnel perspective, it is impossible to bridge the gap between apparently purposeless physical appendages and the deadly fear engendered by their loss in the dreaming.

But in reality, there is no such thing as "empirical, pure factuality" except as abstraction, that which remains of things after they have been broken down by natural scientific analysis. Human hair is, by nature, far more than simply an assemblage of cuticular physical appendages. It is not for nothing that people speak about "sprouting." We give the same description to the growth of grasses and other members of tha plant kingdom. Human hair is an outgrowth of the human body. Being related to the fur of animals, it proclaims to man his relationship to animal being. In itself, animal being belongs to the fecundity and creativeness of the world of nature. The possibility of falling unfree under the spell of what is encountered belongs to this realm of nature, of animality, and hence is a constant possible mode of existence, not only for animals, but also for human beings. Furthermore, people are accustomed to speak of hair as a "crowning ornament." Advertising agencies constantly extoll the praises of ever more refined and exquisite hair styles and hair products. We like to imagine that a rich growth of hair goes along with vital masculinity or femininity, depending on where the hair grows on the body. It is no mere accident that the haircut Samson received from his beloved brought with it loss of his enormous physical prowess and sexual potency. As a physical adornment, hair is inherently connected with erotic attraction, and the intimacy of a physical love relationship. Such attraction may be exerted narcissistically on the person to whom the hair belongs, or on a partner of the opposite sex.

Seen from the phenomenological standpoint, the hair on a human head belongs very much to the body and, as such, belongs directly to that existential trait which is best described as the "bodyhood" or the "bodying" of human existence. And so, human hair cannot be considered just another physical object that may be isolated from the behavioral possibilities comprising the nature of human existence. Hair loss always brings with it, therefore, a certain *de facto* existential deterioration, which is often experienced as just that. It is not merely "symbolic" of that deterioration itself. Admittedly, only a peripheral region of human life is affected by deterioration associated with hair loss. Most men in good existential health are able to part with hair without suffering overly much. In women, hair loss is far more serious. Still, only people whose entire existence is already pervaded by an abysmal dread of existential collapse have such a deadly fear of hair loss as the patient presently under discussion. Such people cannot tolerate even the most veiled additional reference to their threatening existential deterioration without flying into panic. Then, they behave like any other panicked persons— what to an outside observer would seem mere trivial, totally unthreatening perceptions become for the panic-stricken harbingers of lethal danger to themselves. A state of panic obtains, meanwhile, only when a person sees himself, or simply suspects that he is, in grave danger, on the verge of having his entire Being-in-the-world annihilated. But in its very essence, extreme anxiety invariably indicates that the affected person has been thrown back on himself, having lost, or being in the process of losing, all contact with and all existential support from anything outside himself. It becomes impossible for him to give freely of himself to others. All that he "has" left, all that he now *is*, is his relationship to himself, and even that threatens to pass away. Of the little vitality remaining to a panic-stricken individual, a relatively large part resides in the hair on his head. That helps to explain why such a person, reduced to a narcissistic state, experiences hair loss as a catastrophe of the first order.

It is not only in dreaming people that seemingly harmless matters produce "immoderate emotional reactions." From time to time, we encounter instances of human beings who live in constant waking fear of hair loss. All of their energy is spent caring for each and every one of the hairs on their heads. Often enough, such people find their own behavior ridiculous. Yet both they and their therapists would do well to take their strong "feelings" seriously, and look into their meaning. Even in the waking state, a patient often continues to "dream;" his gaze fixed upon the surface of things. He is not sufficiently "awake" to pinpoint the actual source of the threat he feels, the origin of the panic that forces him to see everything, hair loss included, as catastrophic. Even people who are obsesses in their waking lives with fear of hair loss inevitably turn out to be people whose existence is threatened as a whole. They are so-called "borderline cases," for the most part. This means that they walk along the edge of schizophrenic dissolution, both of themselves and their world. Indeed, their lives *as* free and independent human beings are in grave danger.

As a naturally arising out of the phenomenological insights into the existential meaning of hair and hair loss, the following questions should be directed to the reawakened patient:

Question A: "Can you think of anything in your waking life that is like going to see a hairdresser?" The patient would not be hard put for an answer. "Well," he would say, "naturally coming to see you, my analyst, to have myself put into shape is like going to the hairdresser's. It's just that, with you, I don't just want my physical hair done, I want to acquire better possibilities of relating to the female sex, possibilities that as such are not visible to the eyes. Also, your treatment gives me better insights into personal defects that have so far remained hidden from my sight, and are the 'obverse' of my existence."

Question B: "Does the analytic relationship seem the same to you now, in your waking state, as a hairdresser's relationship to his customer? In the latter, after all, the customer doesn't have to do anything himself, just sit back and let the hairdresser take over." The patient was forced to admit that he tended toward a similar, passive stance in therapy, as also in every other interpersonal relationship.

Question C: "In the waking state that preceded your dream, you were aware, at most, of a vague discomfort and general lethargy in yourself. That discontent built, in your dreaming, to a horrible fear of losing more and more of your hair. But you never knew, while dreaming, just why that loss of hair seemed so unbearably frightening. It simply was. Has your perception cleared sufficiently, now that you are awake, to allow you the immediate insight into how the dreamed hair loss and some actual danger that threatens to cause rapid deterioration and dissolution of your existence as a whole belong together in the same meaningfulness of decay? Surely the formation of a bald spot in your dreaming is merely the visible tip of an iceberg. Although the hint is subtle, although the tip of the iceberg is all you can see in your dreaming state, still the tip, the hair loss, is a real threat. That being the case, your panic becomes understandable. Now does that material hair loss give you a clearer, fuller picture of what is really threatening you, something having to do with the loss, barrenness, or void in your own and entire immaterial existence?"

At first sight the first two of the above questions might give the impression that the phenomenological approach is equally guilty of reinterpretating dreams, for they do not seem to be satisfied with merely illuminating significances revealed by the dream entities themselves. In other words, it might at first appear as if even

Daseins-analysis took the dreaming to be a "transference dream," by assuming that already during the dreaming state the hairdresser was not really a hairdresser at all, but instead a "symbolic" disguise for the analyst himself. But phenomenology is far from committing that kind of interpretive error. It allows the hairdresser to remain simply a hairdresser throughout the dreaming period, since there is nothing at all to justify reinterpretating him as the analyst. In fact, the *Daseins*-analytic viewpoint assigns great importance to the fact that the dreaming patient *never did* catch sight of the analyst, the man who deals in immaterial behavioral modes, but saw only the hairdresser, the one whose concern is with the physical body and its periphery, at that, in the form of visible, material hair.

Yet even from the *Daseins*-analytic standpoint, the hairdresser's appearing in the dream, and the patient's going to see him, are not wholly unrelated to the course of therapy in which the patient was then engaged in his waking life. We find the same circumstance mirrored in two previously discussed dreams, Number 5 of the second chapter and Number 2 of the third.[5]

It is highly unlikely that the patient would have dreamed about the hairdresser and the bald spot, had he not been in analysis. The only question, once again, concerns the nature of the connection between the dreamed hairdresser and the analyst from the waking life. There is nothing that would point to a relationship of concealed or open identity between the two. The sole connection between the events dreamed by the patient and the content of his waking world results from the fact that his analysis directed his entire existence, and indeed thematically, to the significance of being treated. The immersion of his waking existence in that significance of being treated persisted into the dreaming state. While the patient was in the dreaming state, however, it was not his analyst nor an analytical treatment that originated from that existential common denominator, but instead a hairdresser and an expanding bald spot. We are not yet ready to discuss precisely why the patient's existence was claimed by a physical defect and a barber shop in his dreaming, rather than directly by the analyst in the *Daseins*-analytic setting.

The final chapter of this work will be devoted to that question. Only then will we begin to discuss the fundamental distinction between the waking existential mode and the mode we call "dreaming." There we will also explore why the dreaming patient sees himself threatened by loss of physical hair, instead of by deterioration of his immaterial existence.

COMPARISON OF THE JUNGIAN REINTERPRETATION OF A GIVEN DREAMING WITH PHENOMENOLOGICAL UNDERSTANDING OF THE SAME DREAM PHENOMENA

An article Carl Jung wrote in 1936 carries the title, *The Nature of Dreams.*[6] Here Jung formulated his dream theory in a few, pregnant precepts. As if in anticipation of our practical needs, he inserted a concrete dream specimen at the start of his work. It reads:

A young man dreams of a great serpent who is guarding a golden chalice in a subterranean vault.

Before reinterpreting the dream in light of his own theoretical assumptions, Jung cites Freud's contention that no adequate understanding of a dream can be gotten without the cooperation of the dreamer; he then applies that procedure, which he himself claimed to have developed, of "gathering of context" (*Aufnahme des Kontextes.*) It consists in employing the dreamer's associations in order to "establish the nuances of meaningfulness in which the most striking dream phenomena appear to the dreamer."

Jung then tries to show that this typically phenomenological method alone is inadequate on the basis of the same concrete specimen. The only thing that the patient could think of in connection with his dreaming was the time he had seen a giant snake in a zoo. Jung tells us:

Besides this, he could supply no possible motivation for the dream, except for the memory of fairy tales. Such a disappointing context would lead us to believe that the dream, though filled with powerful emotions, has only negligible significance. But that would leave its explicitly passionate nature unexplained. In such a case we *must* defer to mythology, where serpents and dragons, caves and treasures represent a rite of initiation for the hero. It then becomes clear that we are dealing with a collective emotion, that is to say, a typical emotional situation that is not primarily, but only secondarily, personal in nature. It is a universal human dilemma that is overlooked subjectively, and therefore penetrates human consciousness objectively. . . . In such a case, the patient-dreamer will labor in vain to understand the dream with the aid of a *carefully* gathered context; for that context is expressed in mythological forms that are alien, and unfamiliar, to him.[7]

If we examine Jung's statements about dreaming more closely, we find that they are filled with surprises for the contemplative. They are replete with erratic conclusions that can hardly be followed. Moreover, in many instances, they advance unverifiable supposition as proved fact.

Condrau pointed to these shortcomings as early as 1967.[8] He also countered Jung's arbitrary interpretation of the dreaming with one based on the *Daseins*-analytic method. What follows here is based on Condrau's work, but takes that work farther by illuminating innate therapeutic possibilities unearthed by *Daseins*-analytic understanding.

The first thing worth mentioning is that, from a *Daseins*-analytic standpoint, Jung's interpretation of the dream fails in its stated purpose of "carefully gathering" the pertinent context. This is especially so if the word "context" is used in its original Latin sense, to indicate everything that "speaks with" the matter at hand. In order to perceive such a "context," it is necessary to listen attentively and with great respect to all of the meanings and frames of reference making up the essence of a dream entity. To achieve the proper state of attentiveness, the analyst must repeatedly encourage the reawakened dreamer to visualize the entities that have appeared in the light of his dreaming existence, then describe what he has visualized in the most minute detail. He should be asked to portray with equal refinement the behavior with which he responded to the call of entities in his dream. This procedure neither projects meaning onto the dream phenomena nor reinterprets them in any way; it is, pure and simple, a way of apprehending more and more succinctly what someone has actually dreamed and then succeeded in visualizing once again after waking from the dreaming. This method is no different from the one we normally use to recall any past events in our waking lives.

For this "gathering of context," however, Jung was satisfied with the patient's two memories of a visit to the zoo, and of past hearings of fairy tales. Presumedly, those memories do not even belong to the "context" of the dream, in the strictest sense of the word. It could hardly have been the dreaming encounter with the dreamingly concretely, materially present snake; that alone and of itself, referred the reawakened dreamer to the zoo snake and the serpents of fairy tales heard as a child. Such associations more likely belong to the reawakened patient's general appreciation of the concept "snake."

A genuinely careful fathering of the context perceived by the dreamer would have to focus exclusively on the particular snake he encountered, along with what he realized about that snake while dreaming. Merely stating the first thing that came to mind, that it was a "great serpent," does not nearly exhaust the matter. In a *Daseins*-analytic procedure, the patient would be expected to give a verbal account of everything else that the dreamed snake communicated to him. A phenomenologically oriented therapist, in other words, would not begin as Jung did by directing the patient away from the concrete snake of the dreaming and toward other more abstract and distant mythological notions of snakes. Instead, he would insist on a simple, yet strictly detailed, description of directly perceived characteristics of the giant serpent and its environment. Presumably the patient would then portray a "context" very similar to those reported by scores of other patients who have dreamed about serpents guarding the subterranean path to golden chalices. I will try to summarize their descriptions as well as the meaningfulness and referential contexts which the dream phenomena disclosed to my vision:

The patients' worldly dwelling place in such dreaming is a dark, narrow underground cavern, entirely enclosed by earth, and cut off from the bright and spacious world of daylight above. Here the dreamers meet up with a giant snake. We have asserted before that the mere frequency of dream phenomena such as this does not justify the invention of a collective mental archetype.[9] It is more important to simply see that snakes are animals of a specific kind. Whether we encounter them in our waking or in our dreaming lives, we are addressed from them by their characteristic ways of living. They can then remind us that potentials for similar manner of existing always belong to the human existence, too. We share these potentials with all animals, even a dreamed giant serpent.

We have already said that animal life is distinguished from human existence in that the former is firmly bound by instinct in its relationship to its environment. Animals are compelled to react to what they encounter in more rigidly determined ways than is man. Even though their lack of speech prevents us from appreciating the precise quality of their relatedness to the "world around them," we can state that it stands in sharp contrast to man's open relationship to what he meets, where there is a free choice among numerous behavioral responses.[10]

A particular feature of the snake, as opposed to, say, a dog, is that it is bound even more markedly to the earth. The snake has no legs or warmth of its own to separate it from the soil it lives in. Moreover, between the snake and mankind there exists a special relationship of abhorrence and mistrust. With a few exceptions, snakes frighten people far more than warm-blooded, domesticated dogs do; not to mention the fact that snakes can actually endanger human life with their potential for poisoning and strangling. Because those are essential traits of snakes in general, they inevitably disclose themselves to us whenever we encounter any single snake. The same meanings apply as well to giant serpents encountered in the world of dreaming.

Frequently enough, snakes like the one in Jung's dream specimen are somehow more imposing than the snakes we adults might encounter in the course of our waking lives. Dreamed snakes are often at the same time snakes with human existences, insofar as they possess a humanlike ability to perceive the significance of things and, like people, to exercise freedom of will in performing certain actions. Otherwise a dreamed snake could never recognize that something is a golden chalice needing to be guarded. (Needless to say, snakes have never been trained as watchdogs by man!) Still, the presence in the human dreaming world of such snakes does not necessitate an assumption of mythological knowledge. How often do children, in their waking playing, experience animals, and even things that adults see as inamimate objects, as being endowed with specifically human abilities of perceiving and speaking! Furthermore, in the dreaming state, even adults often encounter insignificant things, which waking appear to them only as lifeless material and which appear nowhere in mythology as existing in human manner. I know of a case where an adult dreamed that a dust bunny crawled under his door in an attempt to pull him down and and envelop him. Based on all of this, it would seem that mythological figures and images are derivatives of the concrete experiencing of individual human beings, rather than that myths are the common ground from which the animals and things of human dreaming spring.

The patients we have been discussing saw snakes in the caves they dreamed of, and something else: golden chalices. Now, no matter whether we are awake or dreaming, a golden chalice is always golden and cup shaped: those traits constitute its very nature. No object can be a golden chalice unless it possesses those traits and addresses them to human perception. A human being cannot truthfully report seeing a golden chalice while dreaming, unless the meanings of both "goldenness" and "cupness" are known to him. For instance, "goldenness" is normally "brilliant," "genuine," and "indestructible," while the essence of a cup centers around the concavity which allows it to accommodate something within itself, but also to pour it out again. That something may simply be water from a mountain stream, a reveler's wine, or it may be holy water in a sacred chalice.

To a mind reduced to the viewpoint of modern technology, the properties of a chalice enumerated above will likely seem "subjective, poetic construction." "Pure," or "empirical" reality, in the technological view, consists solely in data obtainable from a chemophysical analysis of the isolated chalice. But where does the technological approach find its justification for independently defining where "objectivity" and "reality" end, and "subjectivity" and "fantasy" begin? Is there anything more "subjective" than the data of technological measurement? At any event they exist *as* data only when there is a human perception to receive them as such. Are technical data then not for this very reason even more "subjective" than the emptiness of a chalice's concavity and its immediate reference to fullness and pouring. The chalice at least reveals its meaning directly from itself *as* a chalice, whereas measurement and the data derived from measurement do not belong primordially to the chalice itself but are derivatives of that human way of encountering worldly beings, of technically measuring and analyzing, in accord with the principles of natural science.

Last, but not least, the dreaming Jung recounts exposes the dreamer's relationship to the two things that define his dreaming world, the chalice and the snake. The chalice is seen as a guarded object, which indicates that the dreamer is enticed into the vicinity of the chalice but is denied free access to it. His way is obstructed by a dangerous, hostile serpent that guards the chalice. All of these qualities helped make up the concrete details revealed to Jung's dreaming patient. The entities of the dreamer's world addressed him with those qualities, which explains why he was able to picture them again after awakening. It is hint enough that the serpent and golden chalice did not have an indifferent effect on the dreamer but, understandably, put him in a "highly emotional" state and left him in no way indifferent. None of the significances inhering in the dream entities needed a "dream interpreter" to classify them as "unconscious," "symbolic" productions of a separate component of the human "psyche." There was no need, either, to transform the entities into what they "really" meant; nor was it ever necessary to defer to mythology. When Jung says we "must" do so, his use of the verb "must" feeds on two sources, both of them foreign to the spirit of the dreaming. First of all, Jung was almost totally blind to the wealth of meaning inherent in the concrete phenomena of his patients' dreaming. Second, he approached dream analysis with a preconceived theory based on the assumption that dream phenomena were elaborations of archetypal forces and structures acting out of a psychological collective unconscious. Jung's "must" is therefore highly reminiscent of the "must" used by Freud, the one which impelled him to value presumed tendencies above directly perceptible phenomena, all for the sake of a prescribed theory.

We have pointed out that Jung's exemplary dream phenomena do not of themselves demand a reversion to mythological matter. Quite the opposite, their concrete meanings and therapeutic potential do not become clear unless the analyst has resisted Jung's imperative. Once there is no longer any "objectivity" need for soliciting mythological matter, then, in contrast with Jung's opinion, it is no longer apparent why the dreamer's excited state would have had to originate in a "collective emotion"—whatever such a "collective emotion" might be.

The dreamer himself experienced his "emotional situation" as highly personal in nature, not at all, as Jung put it, "a universal human dilemma that is overlooked subjectively, and therefore penetrates human consciousness objectively." We might also mention that the meaning given in this context to the terms "subjective" and "objective" remains obscure.

Both the nature of the dream and its therapeutic message will emerge, contrary to the Jungian viewpoint, without any support from mythology or folklore, without any knowledge of primitive psychology or comparative religion, without any aid at all from psychology. In fact, no doctrine of "psyche" is required. The therapist might instead share the following perceptions with the reawakened patient:

a. While dreaming, the patient became aware of being in a concrete, sensual, perceptible underground cavern. Might he be able to realize, upon awakening, that his dreaming location in a material hollow cavern was not just an accident, not just a one-time affair, but that in an existential sense he himself remains encapsulated, as yet incapable of reaching and enjoying daylight, and opening voluntarily toward the wide world?

b. From the temporally present, sensually perceptible giant snake, the dreaming analysand perceived that impressive, compelling, and for him dangerous proximity of that mode of living as an animal, earthbound and rigidly unfree in its relations to what it encounters. Dreaming, he experienced all of this as belonging exclusively to an unfamiliar and alien snake outside and separate from his own selfhood. Might not the patient see more while waking than he could while dreaming?

c. The giant serpent disclosed itself in the dream as being a hostile, frightening creature that obstructed the dreamer's way. Can the waking patient see something more here as well, namely, that his own possibilities for animalistic behavior are threatening that structure of his existence as which he had up to now known himself to be, i.e., as an impeded, conformistic wayfarer? Might it not be that if he should recognize and accept the full vitality and strength of his own such possibilities, that his present constricted, conforming existential structure would be doomed to make place for something new and previously unknown?

d. While dreaming, the patient knew the quality of "cupness" only from the sensuous, material form of a concrete chalice. Now that he is awake, can he see a deeper connection to his own nature, in that human nature is also chalicelike in its very essence *as* an open, perceptively receptive realm into which the phenomena of world shine forth, and only so come to their being? Is there not something chalicelike about the human being when, in response to his existential tasks, he pours himself out in his answering response to the address of the beings of his world?

For reasons previously stated, the dreamed chalice is obviously something other than human nature itself, or a symbolic version of human nature. Any comparison between a physical object and human existence is bound to be clumsy. That applies equally to the analogy we have been using between the brilliance of physical light and the bright, clear realm of openness that is spanned as indwelling by the human being as an illuminating realm of perception, and that constitutes that necessary immaterial, unreifiable realm into which beings appear and so be.

e. Finally, might there not be still another way in which the patient is more clear sighted awake than while dreaming? In the dreaming state, his way to a highly enticing golden chalice was blocked by the frightening physical presence of a serpent. Might he begin to recognize, now that he is awake, that the fear he felt was a fear of himself, which made him build up the limitations of his immaterial existence? It would be an abiding fear of his own existential potential for becoming enslaved, in the manner of animals, in an "earthy," erotic relationship to the things he encounters. Yet as long as the patient fails to realize those possibilities for living, keeping them so distant that they appear hostile, like the dreamed snake, he is merely existing halfway. For not only can he not bring the force of those existential possibilities to bear in his waking activity, he must expend enormous energy to hold them at arm's length.

Another noteworthy fact is that, of all the creatures on earth, the one usually considered "lowest," "most primitive," "most earthly"—the snake—is charged with guarding the golden chalice, the most valuable and important entity in the world of the dreaming. Isn't that circumstance powerfully reminiscent of Nietzsche's admonition that anything bent on reaching the sky must have deep roots?

The questions the *Daseins*-analytic therapist decides to direct to the reawakened patient, and their precise formulation, depend on that therapist's assessment of the patient's strength at the time. It is always better for the analyst to begin by adjusting his questions to the reigning conceptions of the person seeking his aid; otherwise the questions will not be understood. My first two decades of analytic practice were under the strict aegis of Freudian metapsychology. It came as a pleasant surprise, after I had exchanged the Freudian vision for the *Daseins*-analytic one some thirty years ago, how much more directly my therapeutic questions were received and understood by my patients and how more efficient they proved to be.

Another dream about a snake, this one by a thirty-two-year-old neurotic, serves to show that Jungian adherence to mythology is not merely therapeutically useless ballast but often enough seduces the patient to take refuge, from the personal and concrete, in something distant and alien which does not oblige the patient in any way to become more responsible for the concrete ways of living his day-to-day life.

> A big snake is coiled up in an armchair. It seems creepy to me. At first it's just lounging around, but then it drops to the floor and starts coming toward me slowly. I stare hard at it, more frightened with each moment. Then it occurs to me that it is the snake of the Jungian unconscious, the archetype *ouroboros* who holds the world together. From that point on, the snake doesn't make me uneasy anymore.

The patient might be asked in therapy whether he had ever caught himself, in his waking life, trying to charm away his inherent, but unfamiliar possibilities for animal behavior with the power of intellectual speculation.

One of Jung's leading pupils, H.K. Fierz, applied Jungian dream theory to a dreaming that came at the close of a patient's three-year program of analysis.[11] Fierz labeled it an explicit "transference dream." The dream was reported as follows:

> Dr. Fierz was operating to save my (the dreamer's) life by making two abdominal incisions. Suddenly, a large, powerful, white-haired man came along, offering to cut out two pieces of his own flesh to fit into my incisions and save my life. The man made his offer out of pure, unsentimental love.

"This dream shows," Fierz tells us, "that I was just a vehicle, while the real life-saving operation was dependent on a powerful old wise man, a higher figure of mythological nature."

But if the dreaming is not subjected to reinterpretation based on a preconceived, inappropriate theory, if, in other words, the analyst does not put on the spectacles of mythology and archetypes, then there is nothing "higher" or mystical in the phenomenon of the white-haired man, not even to the wildest imagination. What happens in the dreaming is that Dr. Fierz appears along with a powerful white-haired man who, despite his uncommonly mature sense of selfless love for the threatened dreamer, is a flesh-and-blood human being. All that may be said from a phenomenological standpoint is, therefore, that the waking patient had witnessed Dr. Fierz practicing psychotherapy with patient and personal sacrifice. The patient's attunement to the theme of medical treatment persisted in the dreaming state, admitting the presence of Dr. Fierz in the form of a physical surgeon. Above and beyond that, while dreaming the patient sees the possibility for an interpersonal relationship that is masculine, mature, philanthropically selfless. He perceives that possibility in the figure of the powerful, white-haired stranger.

The fact that the dreamer does not know who the kind, selflessly loving stranger is tells us by itself that the human nature in this most mature state of altruism is very unfamiliar to the dreamer as yet, really unknown still to him, far stranger to him than what he could see in Dr. Fierz's behavior.

It is most common that certain patterns of human behavior address themselves to people for the first time in their lives in dreaming states, and these states from existentially far away, unfamiliar strangers. Their existence is not yet open enough, neither dreaming nor waking, to enable them to perceive that the same possibilities of copersonal relationships are part of their close friends' lives or of their own existence. The above-mentioned dream events of Dr. Fierz's patient are just one more example of this state of affairs.

For practical therapeutic purposes, the radically *Daseins*-analytic approach to dreaming is important in two respects. First, it should bother us a bit that the dreamer submits to a *surgical* procedure. Surgery is very much the opposite of analytical treatment, in the sense that in surgery the patient is entirely passive. Rendered totally unconscious by an anesthetic, he usually leaves 100% of the therapeutic effort to his physician. In analysis, by contrast, the patient has most of the work to do. But we should be even more suspicious about the fact that the life-saving operation in the dreaming was predicated on the transplantation of foreign tissue;

"recovery" did not come about as a result of independent tissue regeneration. It can only be hoped that the patient in question contributed more to the banishment of his ailment while waking than he did in the dreaming state. For only then can we be certain that he will not in his waking life reject foreign matter that has been transplanted into him, especially when that matter is existentially behavioral, rather than physical, in nature.

Daseins-analytically speaking, any patient who dreams like the one under discussion is not ready to be released from therapy. Much time would have to be spent discussing whether he felt better simply because he had borrowed certain possibilities for living from his analyst which, not originating from his own being, might soon be abandoned after he and the analyst parted company, much in the way that behavioral features imposed upon a patient by hypnosis rapidly disappear.

Summing up, then, the *Daseins*-analytic questions we have recommended for the three patients who had undergone Jungian analysis have as little to do with dream interpretation at the "subjective" or "objective" level—in the depth-psychological sense of those words—as the questions we formulated earlier in this chapter when several Freudian interpretations were discussed. In contrast with depth-psychological notions, our *Daseins*-analytic questions do not presuppose that during the dreaming state some "unconscious knowledge" existed somewhere in the "psyche," through which the snake, the chalice, the cavern, the pieces of flesh were able to disclose to the dreamer other significances over and above those that are inherent in these things *as* these things. Consequently, the *Daseins*-analytic approach can dispense with Jung's speculation that each dreamer has a hidden double who knows more than he and who hides that extra knowledge from the dreamer behind "symbolic dream images." *Daseins*-analytic questioning appeals to the patient's greater awareness and perceptivity in the waking than the dreaming state. For then the possibility exists that the analysand can perceive meaningfulness which in his dreaming he could only perceive from the sensually perceptible presence of concrete events and beings, as being analogous to the essential meaningfulness of behavioral possibilities belonging to his immaterial and nonreifiable existence.

During dreaming there were exclusively snakes, vessels, and pieces of flesh present as concrete beings. Presumably, the dreamer cited by Dr. Fierz would have to awake before he could perceive his own inherent existential "fleshy" modes of behavior having to do with "belly," as being of essentially analogous character. At this point, it should be stressed once again that nothing can be there, i.e., nothing can be at all, unless there is an available realm of perceptive openness where it may appear. One could, however, to a limited degree, compare this indivisible unity of being and perception to the way in which light, physically conceived, and entities of the physical world require each other to manifest themselves.

NOTES

1. S. Freud. *Gesammelte Werke.* Vol. II/III. London: Imago Publishing Co., 1942. P. 366.

2. M. Boss. The Analysis of Dreams. Transl. by Pomerans. Philosophical Press, New York. 1958. P. 33. Critique of the Foundations of Freud's Dream Theory. *Op Cit.*

3. Detlev von Uslar. *Der Traum als Walt: Untersuchungen zur Ontologie und Phenomenologie des Traums.* Pfullingen: Gunther Neske Verlag, 1964. Pp. 17−18.

4. S. Freud. *The Interpretation of dreams* (*Die Traumdeutung*). *Gesammelte Werke.* Vol. II/III. London, Imago Publ. Co., 1942. P. 44.

5. See Chapters 1 and 3 of this volume.

6. C.G. Jung. Vom Weses der Traume. *CIBA-Zeitschrtft*, 1936, *3*(36), 101.

7. The italics are mine.

8. G. Condrau. *Einfuhrung in die Psychotherapie.* Olten and Freiburg: Walter-Verlag, 1970. Pp. 230−231.

9. M. Boss. *Der Traum und selne Auslegung.* (2nd ed.) Munchen. (paperback). Kindler-Verlag, 1974. Pp. 129ff.

10. Cf. the remarks on animal nature in the introduction to Chapter 2 in the volume.

11. H.K. Fierz. *Methodik, Theorie und Ethnik in der analytischen Psychotherapie.* Ed. by the Klinik und Forschungsstatte fur Jungsche Psychologie. Zurich: 1972. P. 8.

CHAPTER V

The Nature of Dreaming and Waking

HISTORICAL NOTIONS OF THE DIFFERENCE BETWEEN WAKING AND DREAMING

Not until we have succeeded in making a fundamental distinction between the waking and dreaming states of human existence, can we claim to have contributed anything or worth to the understanding of dreaming in itself.

We all recognize that dreaming is somehow different from waking. As soon as we begin to define that difference, we find ourselves groping in the dark. Throughout the ages, the greatest human minds have labored to formulate a set of characteristics on which the distinction between waking and dreaming might be based. Nearly twenty-five hundred years ago the Chinese sage Chuang-Tse used his own experience to illustrate the philosopher's dilemma. He wrote,

I, Chuange-Tse, once dreamed that I was a butterfly, flitting to and fro with a butterfly's goals and motivations. I knew only that, like a butterfly, I was following my butterfly whims; there was no awareness of my human nature. Suddenly I awoke, and there I was, "myself" again. Now I am left wondering: was I then a man who dreamed of being a butterfly, or am I now a butterfly dreaming that he is a man?"

Little has changed in the intervening years. Even what Pascal, a modern thinker, has to say about dreaming does not sound very original. If events followed one another sequentially in dreams as they do in waking reality, he was forced to confess, there would be absolutely no way of distinguishing the two states. Schopenhauer admitted, with equal resignation, that the only sure criterion for separating waking from dreaming is the absolutely "empirical" experience of awakening. But because awakening is not part of dreaming itself, Schopenhauer was forced to conclude: "If one assumes a position of judgment outside of both states, no specific difference can be found in their natures, and one is compelled to agree with the poets that life is one long dream."

Perhaps we could make considerable gains by beginning to discuss dreaming with greater phenomenological precision than we have used till now. For we drag into both our colloquial and scientific speech a bundle of unexamined presumptions, piling these up against the actual phenomenon of dreaming and thus making a new viewpoint impossible. The fatal consequences of that practice have been evident enough in our previous discussions of concrete dream specimens. We have tried to dismantle our prejudices, piece by piece, to clear the way for a phenomenological attitude adhering strictly to what has been seen and experienced in the dream phenomena themselves. Now comes the time to gather together all of those popular and scientific prejudices and subject them to careful scrutiny.

First of all, there is the myth that we "have" dreams. We talk about "having" dreams in almost the same way we do about "having" a pair of shoes, or a car. The French, it seems, can even "make" their dreams: *"J'avais fait une reve cette nuit."* But since dreaming does not exist as a physical object, we cannot have, possess, or make it. We should, therefore, never speak about "having" dreams, in that very possessive sense. At most we might say we "have" them in somewhat the same way we "have" fears. For this latter "have" no longer implies possession, but rather a state of being—I *am* frightened. Analogously, I only "have" dreams because I *am* dreaming, because I *am* existing as a dreamer. To "have dreams" is thus to be or to exist in a specific way which is a mode of existing other than that of waking. If, on the other hand, we talk about "having" or "making" our dreams, with implied possession, we have already objectified that specific existential mode, our dreaming Being-in-the-world, into some matter at hand located at a given spot in space. The next step usually consists in comparing that object "dream" with an equally possessible objectification of the waking state of our nonreifiable existence. Yet, because neither waking nor dreaming exists as an independent object in physical space all comparisons on the basis of such conceptions are doomed from the start to failure.

We do a severe injustice to that which we dream, moreover, should we simply regard it as hallucination, as was historically once the case. That is a judgment from the viewpoint of the waking state, and as such is alien to the nature of dreaming. By calling dreaming "hallucination," we are thus merely making a negative pronouncement, merely saying that dream events and beings, like any hallucination, can be perceived by no healthy, awake person as something being sensually perceptibly present other than the "hallucinator" himself. We still do not have a positive definition of dreaming. Furthermore, "hallucination" is a false label at best; for in its meaning of "sensory illusion" hallucination is, strictly speaking, impossible, owing to the fact that the organs of sensation cannot independently misconstrue—only the whole human being can misunderstand something, not his organs in isolations.

If the dreaming experience and its contents are called "hallucination," they are equated with nonreality. But that makes even less sense unless we have first defined what "reality" actually is. Denying dreaming its own specific reality most likely follows from the idea that "dream-objects" are engendered by the dreamer's "subjectivity," created within his psychic "unconscious," and then projected outward into the world.[1] In the phenomenon of dreaming itself, however, there is nothing to substantiate the definition of dream contents as independent creations of the dreamer's mind.

Admittedly, in recent times dream contents have been given more stature than that of unreal hallucinations. It is conceded that so long as we continue dreaming, dream contents are experienced as thoroughly real, but that no sooner do we awaken than those dream contents are accessible only as things of the past, and not even a real past, at that. The fact of awakening nullifies the reality of dream contents, so that we say, "It didn't really happen."[2] And so, while waking up does not erase memory of the dream, it does extinguish its being—what it actually was and is—its "living reality" as it happened. So, in this view, the dream is said to retain its reality as a dream from the viewpoint of the waking state, but it is a *representation* of reality, not itself reality. Such a representation, however, is not of the same reality which the dream objects had for us while we were still dreaming.[3]

The opinions outlined in the preceding paragraph, though they do not dismiss dream contents as unreal hallucinations, cannot stand close scrutiny. For one thing, there are instances in which dreaming is immediately and directly accessible to our perception during dreaming *as* dreaming, and not merely as something having been dreamed in the past. People occasionally enter a state of mind while still dreaming that permits them to recognize that what they are currently experiencing is "only a dream," although the perceived dream entities continue to be sensually present. "Thank God! It is only a dream!" they usually say to themselves within the dreaming. The dreaming condition may then persist and be recognized as such by the dreamer for quite some time before he finally reawakens again to "everyday reality." For another thing, there are people who dream the same sequence of events over and over again, each time telling themselves while dreaming at the start, "Oh, no, here comes that horrible dream again," then consciously experiencing the old sequence of events as dreamed, i.e., as consisting of the same sensually perceptible present entities. Finally, it is even possible at times that dreaming persons question themselves, while still dreaming, about the nature and meaning of what is being revealed to them at the time. Such "dreamed dream inquiries" are admittedly rare: I have heard of only nine, three each from philosophers and psychologists, one from a farmer, one from a merchant, and the last from a housewife. Yet if in even a single instance it has been possible to question whether what is being experienced in the dreaming state is being dreamed or not, we can say that dream contents are by nature accessible in other ways than as merely having been dreamed in the past. However, generally speaking, it is true that dreamed experiences are perceived from the standpoint of the subsequent more waking state as something belonging to the past.

Here the comparative "more waking" is adequate, because it is possible to dream that one is falling asleep and to dream this or that during this dreamt dreaming state, only to—still going on dreaming—"wake up," thereby being aware of the dreamed dream entities as having become mere dream entities. Only in a further step after a more or less prolonged dreaming state the dreamer may then wake up fully into the waking state of his ordinary everyday life.

Then again, the being of dream contents is by no means "nullified" or "extinguished" through our visualization in the subsequent waking state. For could we begin to visualize anything that no longer existed for us, whose existence we had done away with? True enough, in the waking state a person is hardly ever able to bring a dream to mind other than as something that happened in the past. But even past being persists in the present. Insofar as we are able to visualize them while waking, then, dream contents retain their being, though their presence may now be solely in the mode of a dreamed past having been present during now-past dreaming. And finally, the assertion that what we have dreamed is available to us afterward only in the form of "representations of reality" raises two difficulties. First, it contradicts experience when we consider how vividly the entities from our dreaming sometimes persist in the consciousness of our waking lives. Second, we must wonder what is meant by the term "representation" in the first place. But nowhere do we find any satisfactory definition of this notion.

The boldest, and at the same time most widely held, definition of dreaming centers around Freud's claim that the "manifest dream" is a product of self-deception whereby the dreamer is very purposely fooled by his own "unconscious." This view is axiomatic to all depth-psychological dream theories. It holds that dreaming is never "in reality" what it appears to be; and dream phenomena are by their very nature nearly always "symbolic" facades; "in reality," dreamed entities usually represent, or embody, or signify something very different from their appearances, at times even the very opposite. For instance, the reality hiding behind a dreamed banana is the significance "male member." In the Jungian view, analogously, a slice of mortadella might conceal, say, the "archetype pharmakon." That would be seen as the fundamental reality of the dreamed salami.[4]

Based on such assumptions, "depth-psychological" dream theories could hardly avoid reinterpreting dreams, and in a manner—as we have seen—that does not shrink from the wildest distortions. Not only that: both Freud's original "depth-psychological" dream theory and all others that have imitated it in defining dreams as attempts at self-deception inevitably end up in a series of logical impasses, the same sort of paradoxes that lurk behind Freud's metapsychological explications of slips of the tongue and hysterical symptoms, as Kohli-Kunz pointed out forcefully not long ago.[5] Making self-deception characteristic of all those human existential phenomena, she wrote, is saying not merely that the hysteric, or the dreamer, errs *in relation to himself.* Instead, the view of the "depth-psychologists" implies that those persons are deceived of and *by* themselves. In the self-deception of the dreamer, that is, deceiver and deceived are one and the same. Neither Freud nor any subsequent depth psychologist has been able to throw any positive light on how such a state of affairs may have come about. Quite the reverse, Freud had to content himself with hearing Sartre reason:

When I lie, I recognize the truth that I am distorting—the same truth that I do not recognize as the deceived person I also am. As deceiver I am aware of my intent to deceive. But if I know that I intend to deceive myself, I am no longer able to be deceived; for I can only be deceived if I desire to know the truth.[6]

Freud himself recognized this logical difficulty, acknowledging that the phrase "unconscious awareness" was a "contradiction in terms."[7] Kohli-Kunz adds that "The problem with explaining away dream distortion as self-deception is in the implied paradox that I must first be aware of something in order to keep myself ignorant about that something." Kohli-Kunz then goes on to demonstrate how Freud tried to escape this impasse by developing the self-relationship in question by analogy with the interpersonal relationship of deceit. The latter, she writes, "concerns a relationship to someone else: I, recognizing the true facts, deceive someone else; that someone takes my deception to be the truth. Where deceiver and deceived are two separate persons, there is no problem."

In order to create the duality needed in a self-deceiving dreamer, Kohli-Kunz explains, Freud inserted a second personality into the individual human being, calling it "the unconscious." That insertion ignored the fact that we experience ourselves as integral personalities. The wholeness of human existence was split by Freud into two parts, the "conscious" and the "unconscious." These two can then exist in the same relation to each other as two distinct human minds, as for instance in the matter of deception. In dreaming persons particularly, we might add, the Freudian "unconscious" employs the method of "dream-work" to deceive the dreaming consciousness, by transforming "latent dream thought" and "infantile desires" into "manifest dream images."

Such a theory—if we may repeat this point of paramount importance once more—demands a personal agent with the dreamer's own personality who recognizes, first of all, what is unconsciously present in the dreamer, and who decides, second, what to provide to or withhold from the "dreaming consciousness" and then is able to subject the releasable material to more or less intensive camouflaging. Freud actually invented such an agent, naming it the "unconscious dream censor." Of course, if we were to ask what traits enable the censor "to exercise those functions"—here Kohli-Kunz is speaking again—"the theoretical solution of the depth psychologists runs aground. Once again, the censor can only be an unconscious consciousness. Thus the dilemma to be solved for the terms psychic and reality remain obscure. Indeed it is exactly the prevailing obscurity of the meaning of reality and being that underlies the confusion in the traditional theories of dreaming. Although a thorough analysis of the question of reality and being is of fundamental significance for any attempt to clarigy the nature of dreaming, it lies beyond the scope of this work. That belongs in the realm of philosophy. We draw, however, on the insights offered by Martin Heidegger's life-long concern with these problems. A particularly penetrating philosophical analysis of what is meant by "reality" is to be found in his essay *Wissenschaft und Besinnung* in the volumes *Vortrage und Aufsatze* (Neske-Verlag: Pfullingen, 1954.)

Here, it must suffice to point out that such a penetration philosophical analysis of the meaning of "reality" leads inevitably to the conclusion that the beings and events of our dreaming have the specific character of reality. That which we humans encounter in dreaming—just as in waking—is such that it appears into the openness of human perception and is so brought to its presence, to its being. We never experience that an "unconscious system" fabricates of itself the "stuff of dreams," this system being postulated as the deepest component of an allegedly existent psyche. And how such subjectively produced dream images can then be projected outside the psyche is a mystery. In any event, no evidence for such processes has as yet been adduced.

Certainly, in that the realities of the dreaming existence, as well as of the waking existence, are brought into an openness (*Unverborgenheit*), they refer out of themselves to an origin in a hiddenness (*Verborgenheit*.) Openness and hiddenness are then mutual determinants of each other. However, this origin of the "real" in a "hiddenness" has only so much to do with the "unconscious" of the depth-psychologies, in that this latter is a very abstract, distant, anthromorphic, and reified derivative of that primordial hiddenness from with the human existence has to win a clear realm of world-openness.

Any fundamental consideration of "reality" such as that above will end in assigning a reality to what we dream that is autonomous yet equal in importance to waking reality. For what impinges on us as dreamers is no different from what we see while waking, in that it too comes to being in the light of human perception and persists "there." Nowhere does our experience alert us, however, to an "independent creation of dream images" by a human subject, or by his "unconscious." And, of course, no one can say how such a subjective creative process operates in the dreamer to produce images, then project them outward.

Both dreaming and waking reality, comprising what has been disclosed, naturally point to their origins in concealmant, for disclosure and concealment are mutually dependent concepts. We could say the "unconscious" of depth-psychological theories is not entirely unrelated to the aforementioned concealment. For the "unconscious" is a subjective descendant—distant, abstract, anthropomorphized, objectified—of that prehuman, in fact, preontological concealment from which every human existence must wrest a region of illumination of the world.

WHAT WAKING AND DREAMING HAVE IN COMMON

At first sight, it would seem that the *Daseins*-analyst comes to the same conclusion as the aforementioned prephenomenological philosophers. At first, all we will see are things that waking and dreaming have in common. The possibility of making a clear distinction between those two states of human existence will seem to retreat more and more into the distance. As early as twenty years ago, I was able to dismiss one of the most widely held distinctions on the basis of over 50,000 dream accounts that I had listened to.[8] I referred then to one of Ludwig Binswanger's early articles, which stated that dreaming meant submitting passively to a stream of images, being a plaything of life, now knowing what was happening to oneself, simply living on without intellect or mental history.[9] Erich Fromm later supported Bergson's claim that dreaming was the state into which people fell when they ceased to exercise volition, and that, conversely, waking and willing were one and the same.[10] Even colloquial speech describes the dreamer as one who allows life to pass by him in fleeting images.

But observation will show that such statements describe only one among many of the behavioral possibilities open to the dreamer. Again and again it happens that a dreamer purposefully decides to intervene int he dream events, then carries out his decision to the letter. Even people who don't quite know what is happening to them in their waking lives, allowing themselves to be driven by their momentary moods, often show an astounding strength of will while dreaming.[11]

Just as voluntary decision making concerning entities characterizes both waking and dreaming existence, so every other mode of behavior open to waking human beings may occur also during dreaming. In the course of my own research, I was able to identify and demonstrate the existence of the following behavioral modes in dreaming persons:

1. Being frightened or appalled
2. Resolute, willed behavior
3. Brooding, pondering behavior
4. The relation to visionary beings of the dream world
5. Scientific reflection over a problem
6. Lying
7. "Unconscious slips of the tongue" and other analogous behavior

8. Ability to "interpret dreams" in the course of dreaming
9. Ability to awaken while dreaming
10. Artistic, creative relationship to the dream world
11. Moralistic judgment
12. Relationship to divinity
13. Telepathic and "prophetic" perception during dreaming
14. The relationship to one's own personal mortality[12]

But waking and dreaming share something even more profound than common possibilities of relating to encountered entities, for both states are modes of existing of one and the same individual human being. One's waking and dreaming belong always and exclusively to one as an individual human existence. And although waking and dreaming are different, they are equally autochthonous conditions or states of one and the same human existence. The waking and dreaming existence of a given human being belong fundamentally together in a unique, human *Da-sein* and selfhood that endures uninterruptedly lifelong and is strictly and ever mine, i.e., strictly personal (*je-meinigen*). Consequently, proper insight into the nature of human *Da-sein* and selfhood, which at one time carries out its Being-in-the-world waking and at another time dreaming, is the immaterial, unreifiable prerequisite not only for an adequate understanding of individual human existential phenomena, but also for a clear distinction between the dreaming and waking states.

The existence, or *Da-sein*, which is the common matrix of both waking and dreaming reveals itself to an unbiased observer as an "ecstatic" opening up of that clearance which we call "world." It is the eruption of a worldwide realm of sensitivity, of meaning—understanding openness.

This world-openness, *as* which each human being fundamentally exists, is very different from the emptiness of a physical container into which at times things can simply fall and then "be there." Instead, when we think fundamentally, we see ourselves existing as nothing other than a unique illuminating realm of understanding openness spanning an entire world. Thus our being "open" never exists as something in itself and as itself. Our existence is openness "only" insofar as it is claimed by that which is encountered. It is exclusively an openness *for* something, i.e., for the perception and the responsive handling of the givens of our world. In contrast to nonhuman beings, we cannot be characterized by the description of objective physical qualities. Instead, as a realm of understanding openness, the basic feature of human existence is of an absolutely immaterial, unobjectifiable, unreifiable character. It consists of a perceptive openness *for*, and a responsivity *to*, whatever presences come to appear, and so be, in that worldly realm of openness, *as* which the human being exists. It consists of the ability to comprehend understandingly the totality of significances and referential context, which make each single presence to that which it *is*. Thereby, our basic nature as such perceptive, responsive openness and ability to comprehend understandingly is always and enduringly spanning the time–space field of the whole world. It extends or "exists" as far as the temporally and spatially most distant beings and events that address us with meaning. As such a realm or world-openness, our being reveals itself to us as that place which serves all that is *as* the place where it may appear out of "hiddenness"; i.e., where it may come to be and unfold its being to the full. Human existence is then existentially claimed by all that has to be.

Humans do not perceive themselves primarily as unspecified "subjects," "egos," or "encapsulated consciousnesses." We do not see ourselves as machinery of alien construction. Were we by nature simply "things" occupying space, mere vague immanences or spirits inhabiting physical forms, we would at some time have had to fabricate a blueprint of the world without any benefit of external evidence. It would then have been necessary for us to impose our blueprint, with all of its subjective meaning, onto some initially insignificant *factum brutum* present in the world beyond our encapsulated psyche. That, in fact, is precisely the description given to fundamental human nature by both Sartre and Binswanger, showing that both men pay lip service to the Heideggerian term "Being-in-the-world," while actually abiding by the older Cartesian subjectivism. In the writings of both men, it remains a mystery how subjectivity, taken to mean primary immanence, ever "transcends" itself to apprehend objects of the external world. How might such subjectivity ever come to intuit that anything like an "external world" even exists? But no one experiences himself in that way. In German the "subjective projection of meaning into brute matter is commonly designated as *"Welt-ent-wurf"*, i.e., as it is subjectively understood, "the throwing out of world" (out of a capsule subject onto previously meaningless matter.) However, the original meaning and derivation of the German word provides an insight into the essential nature of the phenomena meant by this term. The *"ent"* means rather *"weg"*—"way," or *"auf"*—"up to." *"Welt-ent-wurf"* means in respect to its origin "the opening up of the world." Likewise, Martin Heidegger's term of *"Entschlossenheit"* is frequently mistaken to mean "resolution" in the sense of a subjectively willed relation to beings and world. He uses the term, though, in its original sense of *"Er-schlossenheit,"* i.e., the "opening up of a realm of openness and freedom." A person can see for himself, as I have said before, that he exists fundamentally as an open realm of receptive perceptivity for the presences of beings. At once, the significations and referential contexts that constitute the essential nature of whatever is encountered are immediately illuminated for him; that is to say, the nature of whatever he meets is accessible to his perception. This applies equally to all encountered entities, whether they are themselves human or not human. Yet, even though it exists in a nonphysical manner like this, human *Dasein* is from the very start "out there" alongside the entities of the world—to such an extent, in fact, that no "subjective, inner world" can be demonstrated. For even when we are supposedly just picturing something "inside," "internally," "in our mind's eye," we do not limit ourselves to viewing some mere imaginary intrapsychis representation of the thing. Instead our perception, i.e., we ourselves *as* existing human beings, is from the beginning by the visualized entity, there, whence it addresses us in the mode of visualized presence, from its location in the time–space field of world. For waking or dreaming, how could we ever perceive or comprehend anything in its true significance, i.e., *as* that which it is, or respond knowingly and understandingly to it, if we were not already *by* it *as* fundamentally perceptively open beings. If, for instance, I had to catch a train at the station in half an hour, I would never be able to find my way there physically if I, though still bodily present in my apartment, were not already *as* an ability to perceive something *as* that which it is, there by the visualized station and train in the center of the city, where they are to be physically found.

There is a further point: in order for the train station, or any other entity, to come into being in a way that may be experienced by humans, there must first exist a corresponding human ability to perceive. Without the openness, the range of that perception, there would be no "there" in general, and no specific locations in which things might manifest themselves. Even the tiny, yet portentous words "is" and "being" would surrender all meaning in the absence of the openness of human existence.

For the sake of analogy, human existence may be compared to physicalistic light which illuminates a specific area. The latter is likewise "with" things from the very start, in the sense that, without light, nothing is visible, nothing "comes to light." And just as all the individual rays of any physical light source contribute to the brightness of the illuminated area, so too every human being helps to make up the illumination characterizing the species' perceptual openness to the significances of entities encountered in the world. Inherently and at every moment, we exist alongside the same objects of our shared world. Never do we experience ourselves primarily as isolated, subjective capsules which, if they are to feel and apprehend other entities and humans, must in some inexplicable manner first step outside of themselves. On the contrary, whenever we think of ourselves, we automatically think of other human beings as well. For how could one person learn where to direct the "empathy" required to know another were that other human existence not already known to him?

To be sure, the analogy between the human being as a perceptive world openness and physical light is inadequate because light can of itself never perceive something *as* something, *as* that which it is. It cannot see. Further, that realm of worldly openness (*Lichtung*) which is maintained communally by all human beings cannot be better understood through an analogy with the concept of physical brightness. The openness (*Lichtung*) of that worldopenness (*Weltlichtung*) is rather to be compared to the clearing in a forest (*Waldlichtung*), a free and open area that has been wrested from, and must constantly be defended against, darkness and concealment. Without that primary openness the spatial component of the human world, with all its locations, could never be, nor would there by any place into which physical light could shine, nor would there be "mental vision" in the sense of insight, nor any kind of perception. It would not even be possible to hear, touch, taste, or smell things with discrimination.

But just as little as physical light may be regarded as "making" the beings that come to light in its brightness, so too our characterization of human nature may not be misunderstood in the sense of a definite philosophical idealism. For human beings, though they are engaged as that open realm in which all that is has to appear to be at all, do not themselves "make" things from nothingness.

We have said that human nature inherently dwells by whatever entities it encounters, and exists in relationships defined by the perceived significances of those entities. So each individual human existence consists in the sum of innate possibilities for behaving toward what is perceived. Human existence existence also possesses an innate attunement, to sadness, happiness, boredom, or any other mood. And each and every attunement shapes, in turn, the momentary character of an individual's perceptive openness. An existence attuned to panic, for instance, only has eyes for that which is threatening.

Human nature also finds itself situated at varying distances from the entities it resides with, depending on whether they affect the human perceiver closely, only marginally, or leave him altogether cold. Here lies the true basis of human spatiality, not in the secondary, measurable distances of geometric space.[13]

There is another way in which the innate spatial nature of man's waking and dreaming existence expands beyong the geometric: Part of his placement with respect to the entities he encounters consists in a retention of things that once have been perceived in the past, thus multiplying the locations in which he dwells. Things of the past do not leave human beings; they remain as codeterminants of their present behavior. This fact makes man essentially historical, and man's inherent historicity underlies every phenomenon of memory, whether it belongs to waking or dreaming existence.

At the same time, however, human existence is historically determined by what is approaching it from the future. Much of our present behavior is, for example, directed to the possibility of a nuclear explosion. So human existence extends over the three dimensions of time as well as space. It is opened out temporally to the three "ex-stasies" of the past, the present, and the future. To sum up, human existence is therefore essentially an illuminated realm of time and space. Basically, it is a nonphysical, insubstantial capacity for apprehending the presences, and significances, of things that impinge on its open realm of perception. It manifests itself, as the being that is, for its potential for acting toward retaining and envisioning presences that have spoken to its open realm of perception from near or far in space or time; with great or little effect.

Waking and dreaming, as but two different modes of carrying to fulfillment the one and same historical human existence, belong fundamentally together in that one existence. That explains why the continuity of historic self is uninterrupted, even in dreams. While we dream, our historical continuity is preserved to the extent, at least, that we recognize ourselves as the same persons we were when we were awake. Of course, it happens quite often that when we fall asleep and start to dream, entities that had been physically present to our senses are no longer so. Instead we meet entirely different objects and people in our dreams. Yet we never confuse our essential selves with the existence of other human beings. True, occasionally in dreams I may find myself transformed into some person or animal that I see walking alongside me. Through all such transformation, however, I remain myself, the same "me" I always was. I am the "me" that existed in my previous waking state, notwithstanding the fact that I may suddenly have become the Emperor of China, or a rag moving across the floor, or a lad of twelve instead of my waking fifty years, or—although this is rarer—an octogenarian, complete with wrinkles.

To that rule, I know of only a single exception, where the dreamer loses all sense of personal continuity. He does not know who he is during the dreaming, nor who he has been, nor even whether he still exists at all. The mood of such dreams is normally one of considerable anxiety, sometimes actual naked horror. Dreaming experiences of such extensive self loss occur, so far as I have seen, only in persons who have also felt loss of self and world in their waking lives. Without exception they are people whose waking existential manifestation is deficient in a manner that psychiatry would describe as schizophrenic.[14] Yet even waking schizophrenics retain some rudimentary sense of self, and of their dwelling in the world, for otherwise they could never experience a loss of those things, waking or dreaming. And if the loss of those essential human traits were in fact total, such persons would no longer be human beings.

Consequently, the schizophrenic experience argues for, rather than again, the historical continuity of our personal existences, through both our dreaming and waking lives. This is corroborated further by the frequency with which some dreamed occurrence strongly affects subsequent waking behavior. Occasionally, for instance, the mood of a dream will continue to hold the dreamer captive for some time after he has reawakened. A simple instance of this is given in the experience of a patient with arteriosclerosis. In point of fact, though—and this was stressed in relation to von Uslar—everything about our dreaming, including ourselves as "former dreamers," persists as genuine being in our subsequent, waking Being-in-the-world.[15] The only change is that which occurs at the moment of awakening, when the contents of the dream assume a new mode of presence. What had been immediately, sensually present to our dreaming Being-in-the-world addresses us, when we have awoken, as the "merely" visualizable being and events of a former dreaming state of ours. But the new mode of presence of dream beings and events to the human being does not annul what happened in the dreaming. Even in their altered mode of presence, dreamed experiences influence a person's waking behavior. Additionally, whether we are aware of it or not, they help to determine our waking plans for the future. In earlier times the dream contents of kings and military commanders sometimes persisted so powerfully in their waking life that they determined the fate of entire nations.[16] Contents of past dreaming have the same historical character, for the most part, as contents of the past waking life: Both can later be recalled to mind. The past tense in the title of this book is, therefore, technically incorrect, for the nights we spend dreaming never disappear and are gone. They remain as vital a part of our present and future lives as any past event of waking life.

Wherever we turn our gaze, then, we find that both existential modes, dreaming and waking, share the same basic characteristics. The most important of these are primordial spatiality, temporality, attunement or mood, historicity, mortality, and bodyhood.[17] Were that not so, we would of necessity experience ourselves while dreaming as "mere dreamers," not fully alert human beings. Some exceptional occurrences we have mentioned—moments of transition from dreaming to waking existence, when we declare with relief, "Thank God, it was just a dream"—only prove the rule.

Pascal averred that the only peculiarity of the dreaming state, the only thing distinguishing it from its waking counterpart, was a nonsequential ordering of events. But even this does not always hold true. For there are recorded cases in which a single individual experiences up to six distinct dream states in the course of one night, each of them separated from the others by a brief awakening into an entirely different second world (within the larger dream.) Each of the successive dream states in these cases picks up where the previous one ended, carrying the night's dreaming a step further in a continuity that ends only with dreamer's final awakening in the morning. Admittedly, such continuity of the dreaming world is uncommon, whereas our final, morning awakening is regularly accompained by a return to the familiar objects of our physical environment (unless a noctural apoplexy strikes our existence so that we wake only to a state of confusion.) It is entirely possible, of course, to move a sleeping person into a bed in a new location. He will nevertheless awaken with an expectation of seeing the objects he saw while falling asleep in the first bed. The very foreignness of the things he physically perceives in his new location confirms that the old ones have remained with him somehow. It is just that the old objects must be visualized, no longer having an immediate, physical presence. Yet even in this visualization, those objects stand exactly where they stood when he was carried away from them while sleeping. Now, the same sequence of events can occur while dreaming, such that the dreamer finds himself falling asleep in a certain bed, in a certain room, only to wake up—still within the dreaming—somewhere else. But such dreaming is almost unique; dreamers rarely find themselves in the same surroundings two nights in a row. In the second night's dreaming, the dreamer is likely to be in an entirely different situation, as for instance, sitting for his matriculation examination under the watchful eye of a former teacher. The new dreaming world of the examination room no longer accommodates the thematic presence of either of the beds of the previous night's dreaming, neither the bed sensually perceived in the dreaming, nor the one visualized during the dreaming as having been dreamed.

As has already been mentioned, however, even as dreamers we have sufficient access to the past to experience a persistence of that perception of self we refer to when we use the pronoun "I " Yet whatever entities are not part of ourselves, as well as our behavioral modes with respect to those entities—all, in other words, that determines our Being-in-the-world directly before we fall asleep—retreat from our field of perception in our subsequent waking state. For the most part, they are absent, also, from the world of the next night's dreams. Thus the isolated periods of our dreaming do not, as a rule, vouch for the continuity of our existence to the same extent as its waking phases. This is so, in spite of the fact that something like one-third of what we see while dreaming is retained in our waking memory to exert an influence upon our subsequent life history.

Only two types of dreaming seem to follow waking life in maintaining historical continuity of existence. One sort is the stereotypical dream that places the dreamer, night after night, in the same relationship to an identically endowed dreaming world. Yet it is just such dreaming that shows a singular lack of history, in the sense that it is mere repetition of a fixed sequence of events (whether or not the dreamer recognizes this.) In waking existence, by contrast, the same things cannot possibly occur twice in the same way, for each event influences, and thereby irrevocably alters, the future. Stereotypical dreaming, which results from a halt in the development of free access to existential behavioral possibilities, ceases once the individual becomes sufficiently aware of this fact in his waking life. They stop recurring as soon as he seriously sets to work overcoming his arrested maturity.

There is another kind of dreaming that supports the notion of historical continuity carrying on into the dreaming state. I refer here to dreams in which we simply continue what we were doing just before falling asleep. Actually, the dreamer himself is unaware that such dreaming is a continuation of the activity of the preceding waking states. It no longer occurs to the dreamer that shortly before, he was awake and exhibiting precisely the same behavior as now. He will not realize this until after awakening from such a "continuation dream."

On the other hand, there are certain states—perhaps not exactly dreaming states but deep dreamless sleep—that seem to belie my contention that, come what may, nothing ever entirely interrupts or nullifies the historical continuity of personal identity. Or does it happen that each time we fall into sleep so deep that dream activity fails to register even on an electroencephalograph, our exsitences, as open realms wherein entities and their significances are perceived, break down completely? Certainly not! For if the state of deep sleep, or other "unconsciousness," renders us nothing more than biophysical mechanisms, how is it that we immediately realize, upon awakening, that we are the same people we were when we dozed off, and how do we recognize the objects around us then as familiar fixtures of our everyday environments? What we experience each morning, a renewed knowledge of all things that comprise the human world prior to dreamless sleep, as well as their interrelationships, can never have been manufactured from mere molecular "engrams" existing within a purely physical brain. Biophysical matter can produce only other biophysical matter, not anything as "intellectual" as the ability to perceive specific significances in things. Even in dreamless sleep, therefore, we continue—in a way that is alien to our waking lives—to recognize that we are unique individuals, and that certain things in our worlds carry particular meanings. Were that not so, none of us could ever become reoriented after awakening. Of course, the western mind has never devoted much thought to the way we exist in deep, dreamless sleep. In fact, many an eastern thinker has pointed to this as the reason why so little is known in the Occident concerning the true nature of waking human life.

But our present concern is with the third mode of human existence: dreaming. As yet no trait has come to light that would serve as a clear basis upon which to distinguish dreaming from waking existence, and thus enable us to define the former in its own right. Not even the experience of awakening is limited to waking existence, for it sometimes happens—as several examples have already shown—that, after sinking into sleep we dream that we have woken up to remember what we have just "dreamed." Very occasionally, someone who wakes up "in a dream" will even begin to subject the beings and events of his previous dreaming to psychological analysis before awakening eventually to the "true waking state."

What is that ultimate process of awakening which renders the immediately preceding experience "just a dream?" For the time being, no more can be said than that it is a transition to a state of alertness which adjudges itself "more awake" than any waking state in dreaming. Since with the exception of a very few borderline situations it always seems to us in dreams that we are fully awake, we must begin to speak of such a "waking state in dreaming." For while we are still dreaming, we usually do not begin to suspect that a more alert state is available to us, namely the one that follows that final, "true" awakening. As "truly awake" people, therefore, we are acquainted with one state of existential alertness more than is known to us as dreamers.

The existence of more than one "awake" state may lead us to wonder whether that ultimate waking state is really the most genuine, that is to say, the most alert possible. It may be that the ordinary mortal simply cannot imagine a state of greater alertness than the one he is currently experiencing, whether the latter is a waking or a dreaming state. Yet the continuity of our waking knowledge, through dreaming and dreamless sleep alike, should caution us against categorically denying the possibility of states more alert than that of everyday reality.

The dreamer's complete ignorance of his own sleeping body has often been cited as an important difference between the waking and dreaming states. In particular, it is claimed that the neural synapses connecting the brain to the motor system are interrupted in dreaming. Dreamers have frequently been described, in fact, as bodiless. Yet such is obviously not the case. We can say the trait of bodyhood belongs just as much to dreaming existence as to its waking counterpart. No dreaming behavior lacks a corresponding bodyliness, just all phenomena of waking human existence are also bodily. Even the vision of encroaching baldness constituted sensual, optical perception, though it occurred beyond the scope of the subject's physical eyes.

It is true that the bodyliness a dreamer experiences usually bears no relation to what a waking observer would recognize as the dreamer's attention completely. This is not to say that the sleeping body no longer exists; the results of contemporary EEG-experimentation affirm that, though the dreamer is usually unaware of it, the sleeping body continues to belong fundamentally to his existence. Such findings indicate that alterations occur in the body in conjunction with dreaming behavior, exactly as they do in conjunction with similar waking behavior. If, for instance, a person dreams of performing strenuous physical labor, his sleeping body will register rapid eye movements, as well as increased blood pressure and pulse rate, etc. The dreamer's physical activity is very different- ly manifested, however. While waking observers see him fast asleep in bed in Zurich, the dreamer may feel that he is skiing, with con- summate physical grace and pleasure, down an Alpine slope. The questions now is, which body is the "real" one, the body that others see lying in bed, though the dreamer is unaware of it, or the body that the dreamer himself feels so intensely but that no waking observer can perceive? We are at a loss for an answer, probably because the question is inadequately formulated. We may discover that both bodies, the recumbent and the active one, belong equally to the bodyhood of the sleeper's existence. In any case, however, physicality has shown itself to be no criterion for distinguishing between the human waking and dreaming states.[18]

THE ESSENTIAL PHENOMENOLOGICAL DISTINCTION BETWEEN WAKING AND DREAMING

A crucial and, in my opinion, very real distinction between the waking and the dreaming existential modes seems to inhere in the markedly different character of that realm of perceptive openness and freedom opened up and maintained by the dreamer's existence in the two states. In the preceding chapters we noticed this essential distinction at every turn, whenever dream specimens were in- troduced as exercised in the phenomenological, *Daseins*-analytic viewpoint. It is astounding that philosophers and psychologists have not, to my knowledge, focused on this as *the* fundamental variance between the waking and dreaming modes of existence.

If we attempt to examine phenomenologically the basic character of the human dreaming state, it would first seem that when we dream, we dwell in a more open, broader, more free, less constricted world than when we are waking. When compared with the beings of our dream world, are not those beings by which we dwell in our waking state mostly rigidly fixed objects made up of ponderous inert masses, which can only be changed or mutated with the greatest difficulty? By contrast, the beings we encounter dreaming are often of a fleeting and mutable character, like mere cloud masses blowing in the wind. Cannot a dream mouse suddenly become a lion, a bare railway waiting room an imperial palace, the black and white projection of a battle of a screen a colorful battle between men of flesh and blood?

In fact though, the reverse is true, when we direct our attention to the breadth, the freedom, and the openness of our Being-in-the-world. Provided we do not suffer from a neurotic or psychotic disorder, we are waking able to choose the existential relationships in which we dwell, exist. We may dwell in far or close relation to sensually perceptible presences of the present, to things of the present or past that we are merely visualizing "in our thought," and to what still has to come to be present from the future. Waking we are able to dwell from moment to moment, relatively free in the totality of the time—space field of the understanding openness of that worldly realm as which we "ek-sist," that we hold or bear open and free. On the other hand, what appears to us out of the openness of our dream world appears predominantly—though not exclusively, but to an imcomparable greater degree than in waking—in that mode of being present of an immediately sensually optically, auditively perceptible, temporally present presence—as distinct from visualized presences, remembered presences, or expected presences. This is so, even when those presences of our dream world are of a more mutable character than those of our waking world.

The much extolled occasional hypermnesia of the dream state does not negate but confirms that the openness of the dreaming existence is largely limited to admitting only to the sensually perceptible presence of what is encountered as being temporally present. *Freud* saw correctly in this hypermnesia a further argument against the degradation of dreaming to a disturbed state of mental existence. It actually happens that we repeatedly dream of people and things of whom we no longer know anything when waking. However, do we really remember them? This would be the case when what we dreamed of was present as something that once, at some given time, had been. In truth though, that which has long disappeared from our waking world confronts us in our dreaming world as an immediately sensually perceptible, temporally present presence.

There is a second and equally fundamental distinction between the worldly realm open to understanding the significances of the encountered as existed by the waking human being and that by the dreaming one. What appears to us dreaming is not exclusively, but incomparably more frequently than in waking, revealed in the mode of sensually perceptible, temporally present presence—materially visible things, or the equally sensually visible bodies of human beings, animals, and plants. As such, the beings of our dream world, in their immediate sensual visibility, come impressively, and at times uncomfortably, close to us. Waking, we are "seeing" being also in a second sense, that of "insight." This has only peripherally to do with the "seeing" of the sensually, perceptible "external" characteristics of materially present objects. It refers rather to the thematic perception and recognition of the immaterial basic character of things, namely their significances and referential context, and the equally immaterial inobjectifiable existential behavioral possibilities of human beings in their encounter with world. This distinction between waking and dreaming necessarily gives rise to a third. The significances and referential context (the totality of interconnecting significations) that constitutes our dream world address us predominantly from "external" beings, which we ourselves are not. Dreaming, we rarely reflect on ourselves in the attempt to gain insight into our existential state. It scarcely happens that we perceive from ourselves our own existential condition, that we perceive of what inobjectifiable, "immaterial" behavioral possibilities we are constituted.

Freud, and before him Scherner, got close to the matter, without actually putting his finger on it. In 1900 Freud claimed that the camouflaging techniques of "unconscious dream-work" tended to "transform thoughts into images," while Scherner, as far back as 1861, described a "lack of conceptual language in the dreaming imagination," as well as the dream's conversion of innter life into external, "plastic vividness."[19]

Actually, of course, dreams do not begin with endopsychic thoughts—whatever is meant by the word—or desires that must then be transformed. From the very start, we are in relationship with whatever presences may address us from "out there," from their unique locations within our open world of perception.

The woman whose jungle dream was given earlier,[20] for example, existed in her preceding waking state—though she was not specifically conscious of it—amidst the furniture of her living room. Chatting with her friend ther, she was at the same time consciously attuned to the omnipotence of living nature, and to the claims it made on her, in the form of pregnancy. She was also pondering over the future birth of the child she carried. But once she began to dream, this same woman found herself in the immediate, sensory environment of a luxuriant primitive jungle, where she perceived that she was a mother elephant concerned for the welfare of her newly born twins. Her dreaming existence was therefore bound up exclusively in relationships toward sensually present entities.

Another woman, who hasn't been mentioned as yet, dreamed that she was together with her best woman friend and this friend was suffering from a serious heart disease (which is not at all the case in her waking world). The friend had an advanced stenosis of her heart valves. Waking, this young dreamer was already—though to a very limited degree as yet—aware of "heart trouble" in a metaphorical sense. In her waking state she had fallen in love with her analyst. She herself suffered in waking some emotional pain as a result of the inevitable frustration of this love, but she did not want to admit it. Dreaming, her existence was still much less perceptive than in her preceding waking. Dreaming, she perceived none of her own suffering in her "lovesickness." The meaningfulness of ailment and pain addressed her, in her dreaming state, solely from a disturbance of the material, bodily heart of another woman.

At this point the dreamer gradually woke up. In the course of the unusually slow process of her awakening, the dreamer herself became aware of an amazing kind of opening up of her existence. She noticed a sharpening and farther reaching out of the perceptiveness and responsiveness of which she consists. Within the more clear-sighted and farther reaching realm of her awakening existence she came to realize ever more succinctly that she herself and not her friend was suffering terribly from a "heartsickness." But as her friend's bodily heart disease, which had disclosed itself to her so distinctly within her dream world, transformed itself by and by into an ailment of herself, it also changed its form completely. The basic meaningfulness of trouble, the meaningfulness of ailment remained nevertheless the same. But the more she awoke, the more completely this meaningfulness of pain addressed her in the form of an emotionally painful affection, arising out of her frustrated love for her analyst and no longer from a material bodily organ.

This self-observation of a slowly awakening dreamer gives particularly convincing evidence of the way in which a dreamer's existence as perceiving and responsive world-openness had been dimmed and restricted in comparison with the realm of understanding which then constituted her following waking state. In her dreaming state the meaning "heart trouble" had disclosed itself to her existence's understanding only from a bodily sphere, from a diseased heart organ. This certainly is a more peripheral and distant region than is the "heart" in the sense of the core and center of one's feelings. In addition, it had not even been her own heart organ which had been sick while she was dreaming, but the still much more remote one of another woman, although this woman was her closest friend. Her dreaming existence had become completely blind to her emotional suffering from her frustrated love, although it had already been present to a certain degree in her previous waking state. More than only this: her hurt feelings simply did not exist at all within her dream world. They had totally fallen out of it. Nothing whatsoever justifies the assumption that her emotional "heartsickness" nevertheless did continue to be there in her dreaming state as a "psychic being" but was only temporarily "symbolically" hidden behind the "dream image" of a diseased bodily heart organ. Any dream theory that pretends to know of those kinds of psychic mechanisms is committing the inadmissible logical mistake, long since called a _"petitio principii"_ by the classical philosophers, i.e., already putting into the presuppositions what would have to be deduced, demonstrated, and proved as a result of logical thinking.

Still another female patient had concealed all of her feelings about her sexuality, and about her analyst, during the actual therapeutic session. The next night she dreamed: "I'm not coming here for the session; I'm staying at home because I just don't feel like coming." both in her dreaming and waking existence, she finds herself addressed by the same significance. She is attuned to withholding herself as someone who is in love, as someone who is erotically drawn to her analyst. In her waking life, that attitude is realized simply through the nonverbalization of her desire to engage the analyst in love play. The same interdiction, "Away from the analyst!" appears in her dream as a refusal to attend therapy.

The fourth dreamer saw himself standing on a rubbish heap near his church. The rubbish came from the ongoing total renovation and expansion of the church. In waking state of the previous day, the subject had realized the large extent to which the religious commands imposed on him by a bigoted mother, and an even more bigoted pastor, had given way during the maturing process of analysis to a far freer, and more loving, relationship to the Divine. While awake, then, he could recognize the crumbling of a narrow "intellectual" relationship toward God, and its replacement by a novel relationship of freedom, whereas his dreaming perception responded only to the sensory presence of a material building. Not just any old building, of course, but a church, an edifice inherently associated with things religious. Still, the fact remains that in the dreaming state he perceived nothing except the material, sensory presences of the church and rubbish heap. The alteration of his "intellectual" relationship toward God, so clear to him during his preceding waking state, was totally inaccessible to his dreaming perception.

To give yet another example, a forty-year-old woman sees her three-year-old daughter plummet downward from a mountaintop. The woman reported,

> At first, the child's fall is broken when she becomes caught on a projecting ledge. But soon she falls off onto another ledge, where she also remains hanging for a while. If I don't come to her aid, she won't be able to hold on much longer and will finally plunge to her death. But I can't figure out how I can get to her.

The above dreaming occurred following an analytic session in which the patient finally realized that her powerful, adolescence-tinged desire for her analyst would never be fulfilled. That realization had sent her into a deep depression in her waking state. At that time, whe was aware of falling in the immaterial sense from the heights of infatuation into the equally immaterial existential mode of depression. But in her dreaming she perceived only the physical fall of another person, from a high mountaintop to a series of ledges below. The fact that it was her child who fell, rather than the dreamer herself, naturally has a certain import, but it is secondary in the present context. For even had she seen herself fall, while dreaming, from a physical mountain into a physical abyss, the relationship of her dreaming to her waking perception would not have changed.

The distinction between the two modes of perception appears in yet another way in this dreaming. The patient's existential plunge from infatuation to depression came about as a result of the analyst's intervention. He said things to her that dealt a death blow to her immaterial, existential love relationship. In the dream sequence, the unstoppable crushing of the child's body likewise threatens a love relationship. But in the dreaming, the death of her daughter merely precludes a physically intimate manifestation of love. Under certain circumstances, mourning and reminiscence are particularly intimate expressions of immaterial love. The dreamer here does not recognize that existential possibility, however, in her relationship toward her analyst.

A sixth patient told of her dreaming at the age of six, and of how she has remembered the dream beings and events ever since. She said:

> I am standing alone in the middle of a big courtyard. There are high walls on all four sides. From out of all the apartment doors, lions are coming to pounce on me. In the midst of this emergency I notice that the courtyard has a roof, and a lamp is hanging down from it. I manage to jump high enough to get hold of the rope holding the lamp. There I am, swaying high above the lions, when I see, to my horror, that the rope is about to give way. I wake up terrified just before it gives away completely.

That was the dreaming of a seven-year-old girl born into the most miserable of social conditions. Her parents fought constantly and were divorced when the child was six months old. Afterward the mother had little time for her daughter. When the daughter was six, the mother died. The daughter was placed in an orphanage, where she was once again left entirely to herself. She had never been able to rely on another human being. Her brother, an acute schizophrenic, was committed for an indefinite period to a psychiatric clinic. All that would lead us to suppose that the patient herself had little to help her overcome her disadvantages and attain to independent selfhood. Though she never experienced the same sort of severe schizophrenic disruption as her brother, she remembers vividly how, on the day preceding her childhood dreaming, she felt totally isolated from others and in gravest danger. And so, as the now mature woman remembers, it was "a matter of pure survival" for the six-year-old girl to apply all of her powers to the task of getting a grasp on things. She did this by burying herself in her schoolwork. Owing to her native intelligence, she was able to assert herself among her fellow humans, at least in the realm of pure intellect. During the period when the dreaming occurred, the patient purposefully "leaped" out of an existential isolation brought on by parental fighting, rising to the "heights" of academic achievement. That waking leap took her abruptly from one possibility in her immaterial existence to another. In the dreaming state, however, her loneliness was expressed in physical isolation within a large courtyard. Here, too, she leaped high in the air, but in an entirely different manner. This time she leaped physically away from the earth's surface, seizing hold of a physical rope that kept her suspended at a measurable distance, of, say, ten feet above the courtyard pavement. Her dreaming leap had been motivated by the charging, physical bodies of lions that were intent on tearing her physically to pieces. In her waking life, by contrast, it was her immaterial existence that was threatened with dismemberment. She could not overcome that kind of threat, as she could in her dreaming, with a simple physical leap. Instead, she had to elevate her existential relationship to the world, until it consisted in a purely intellectual consideration of things. In a child of her age, an "intellectual" leap of that kind may be somewhat overambitious, bringing with it the danger of an existential tumble. The girl in question might easily have sunk into deep depression. No wonder her dreaming was filled with the danger of falling! Here again, though, it was not that the danger threatened her immaterial existence; as a dreamer, the patient could perceive only the danger connected with the breaking of the rope that held her body physically suspended, and the possibility of dropping into the decidedly physical jaws of the lions who were waiting below.

The patient's dreaming points once more to the differences between the things that define her waking existence and the determinants of her dreaming world. In the former, there is nothing but immaterial, intellectual, existential behavioral possibilities, things accessible only to experience and insight; in the latter are the massive physical presence of the earth, of heavy stone walls, the lion's bodies, the thick lamp rope, the dreamer's own body, her physical leap upward into the air, the fraying of the rope, and the danger of a physical fall to the level of the courtyard pavement.

Even a nun who, in her waking life, was accustomed to living within herself, giving highly intellectual consideration to abstract problems, always met up with the physical presences of other people in dreams. Before going to bed one evening, she had been reflecting on the value of celibacy and what it meant to be married, all this in abstract theological fashion, with no relation to herself or other actual persons. Next morning she reported the following dream:

> I am walking down the stairs with Sister K., telling her that Father S. has just finished reading a lovely prayer for the newlyweds at a ceremony in the church. I go on to say that I had never realized two people could pray together as well as that young couple did. I could marry a man who prayed with me as well as that. Sister K. thought that celibacy was nevertheless a higher value.

The nun's dreaming life differed from her waking existence in that it was not spent wholly in lonely reflections of an abstract nature. While dreaming, she no longer lived "in her thought." Marriage was no longer merely a concept to her, it now addressed her as an act performed by a flesh and blood priest, Father S., on behalf of a flesh and blood couple who stood inside a tangible, massive, stone church. In fact, the possibility of marriage to a flesh and blood male even confronted the dreamer herself. She heard an opinion about the alternative, celibacy, from the lips of her physicall present colleague, Sister K. As she dreamed, she was also aware that both she and the other sister were "living, breathing" celibates. Admittedly, the dreamer continued to exist "in her thought" to some degree, as evidenced in the discussion of the concept of celibacy. Yet her participation in abstract relationships was minimal in comparison with that of her waking life.

It may be beneficial, in this context, to recall the young physician's dream of being called out on an emergency. He had to pump out the stomach of a young boy whose abdomen had become clogged and rock hard. A whitish mass filled with large lumps was regurgitated in the process.[21] Immediately after waking up, but only then, the patient was cued by the physical regurgitation of the dream to recognize a relaxation of his own, existential restraint. This was communicated to the analyst in a verbal "throwing up" of thoughts that had been held back. Just as spontaneously, the sick boy's precarious perch on the edge of the sidewalk led the reawakened patient to discover the danger to himself of a nonphysical, "figurative" fall: namely, the decline of his integral human existence. For quite some time he had been feeling, in some hard to define way, that he was gradually deteriorating.

We began by saying that this patient, while dreaming, perceived all the significances that were given him solely from sensually perceptible, material beings and events. In the more clear-sighted, more perceptively open waking state, he could comprehend these significances in another, in an existential sense, namely, as significations *also* characterizing his relationships to his "world." Now that the fundamental difference between waking and dreaming has been examined more deeply, the usual distinction between sensually perceptible, temporally present presences, which dominate the dreaming state, and the immaterial, unobjectifiable, existential significations that can be comprehended waking becomes questionable. This latter perception of the analog character of one's own existential possibilities of relating to the perceptible characteristics of the sensually perceived dream entities is often termed figurative or metaphorical. Closer examination, however, reveals that this latter perception is "more true," or better, more fundamental than the perception of the sensually perceptible, temporally present, objectifiable entities of dreaming.

Even a very minimal evidence of concepts, such as the nun experienced, is rare in dreams. The great disparity that most often separates the nature of what we see in dreams from things in waking life is clearly visible in the following dream of a forty-year-old, single male. Before falling asleep, he begins to grapple with the problem of human freedom. He sketched out for himself a contrast between the freedom characteristic of life in the people's republics of eastern Europe. Before he has fully fallen asleep, his world has already shrunk to such an extent that he finds himself penned up within a pigsty. His "prison" is located near Checkpoint Charley, just east of the Berlin Wall. He considers escape. Through a little opening in the Wall, he can see a broad, sunny meadow in the west. He gazes upon that open land with longing.

In his dreaming existence he can no longer do what he had done while awake: reflect on the freedom of entire nations. Now he finds himself in the sort of "concrete" situation that gives rise, in waking life, to such abstract concepts as freedom and compulsion. Freedom and its deprivation exist concretely only in the form of an individual's behavior toward the entities of his world. The concrete elements of his dream alone revealed to this dreamer the fact of his imprisonment, as well as his hope for physical release from confinement. Both things, in other words, were perceived solely through visible, material objects that the dreamer encountered in his dreaming world. Those objects were the narrow pigsty, the Berlin Wall, the weapons and uniforms of the East Berlin border guards, and the wide open strip of land in the west.

But the realm of perception maintained by this person while he dreamed was less open than its waking counterpart not only to mental abstraction, it was explicitly more restricted in yet another way. In the dreaming state, the patient's ability to "see," the very opposite of conceptual abstraction, was far more limited than in his waking life. I am referring here to "vision" in the second of its two senses, meaning "insight," a mental rather than merely optical apprehension. What I mean by the "opposite of conceptual abstraction" is that which is even more basic than the single visible objects and specific modes of personal behavior revealed to the dreamer. The most basic of all things, what remains hidden from the dreamer's mental focus, is that without which it would be impossible for any object, or person, or human behavior to exist. That predicate of all being is *the penetrability of the essences of things*. We could never perceive a tree as being a tree, for instance, if some tree essence were not already known to us, at least intuitively. And without first recognizing, no matter how vaguely, the nature of freedom and human beings, we could know nothing at all about freedom, or the lack of it, in human behavior.

Generally, of course, just the reverse is held to be true. When someone pronounces the word "tree," it is assumed he has called forth an abstract concept, one that has come about through dropping the peculiarities of individual trees to reveal what is common to them all. But it is impossible to take away—abstract—something from nothing. The formation of the abstract concept "tree" is therefore feasible only after some concrete tree has addressed us with its individual essence, its uniqueness, that which pervades it most thoroughly and which henceforth becomes apparent in every pine tree, apple tree, birch tree, etc.

The human freedom mentioned above not only gives rise to every human attitude of freedom or compulsion, but, so long as it exists, persists as the common essence of those attitudes. Thus all human attitudes, all relations to the world, are "grown together" in one fundamental essence. Now, the Latin word meaning "grown together" is *concretus*. It seems proper, then, to say that the essence of a certain thing, immediately visible to the "mind's eye," is the most concrete thing of all. In any event, it is anything but a metaphorical abstraction.

Yet are we really fully aware, while waking, of the nature of everything that presents itself to our senses, as well as past and future things that may be visualized? Certainly more aware than when we dream. But considering the extent to which that essence escapes even our waking gaze, it might justly be claimed that we go right on sleeping and dreaming in our waking lives.

Finally, there is another way in which a person's dreaming existence is usually less open then the waking states that precede or follow it, as illustrated by the following case. A middle-aged man had just returned from a Greek island, where he spent two weeks vacationing with his lover. He had thoroughly enjoyed the vacation, remembering it as one of the nicest, most fulfilling times of his life. During the first nights after his return, he regularly found himself situated once again on the Greek island, reliving in vivid detail all that he had experienced there on his vacation: beautiful sunsets, the shadow of the ship's bridge upon the golden sea, even the cozy hotel room shared by him and his lover. Each time he awoke from such a dream, he had difficulty—less with the passing of time—convincing himself that what he had just experienced with such sensory immediacy actually belonged to his past, that for days now he had been back at his job in his town in Switzerland.

This man's dreaming existence is not only restricted to entities perceived through the senses, but it lags several days behind its waking counterpart. His *Dasein* does not extend *temporally* as far as the waking present.

In a great many neurotically ill persons, such temporal foreshortening of the dreaming existence is even more marked. It is quite common for fully grown adults to see themselves in dreams as high school students taking difficult examinations. The temporal extent of their manifest *Daseins*, the bodily component included, is thus cut in half at least. Under the direction of a knowledgeable therapist, such people are usually led to realize, upon awakening, that they are not nearly as mature as they believe themselves to be, at least not where emotions are concerned.

Even with respect to the examples I have introduced to illustrate the distinction between our waking and dreaming states, the long-established precepts of traditional dream theories are as seductively dangerous as they have proved to be in our earlier discussions of dream reports. Such theoretical speculations can deceive us into believing that an awareness of insubstantial, existential attitudes, of the kind that puzzled our pigsty dreamer in his waking state, is already present in dreams. Of course, that awareness is transformed in the dream into the concrete "image" of physical confinement within a pigsty, along with the sensory perception of an open landscape. Yet there is no evidence in the dream to show that this man's existence, after shifting from the waking into the dreaming mode, retained an awareness of the relative freedom enjoyed by nations located behind, and outside of, the Iron Curtain. Rather, from the moment the dreaming began, the dreamer perceived only his own physical confinement within an enclosure of a specific nature. There was nothing else for him. And if there was nothing else in the dreamer's world, there was nothing capable of being transformed. Once the patient woke up, of course, he not only perceived more than he had while dreaming, but more than he had in the waking state that preceded his dreaming. Now he could not only reflect on the problem of national freedom but also—based on his own dreaming imprisonment within a physical pigsty—give thought to the lack of freedom in his own existence.

The very same traditional speculations might imply that the man who dreamed of the church renovation, or at least "something in him," recognized, even as he slept, the renewal of his "intellectual" relation to God.[22] All of the physical objects, the church, the rubbish heap, the process of renovation, would be seen as "actually referring to," or "actually signifying," the dreamer's insubstantial existence. The "dream," or the "unconscious," had employed those physical objects in order to "symbolize," or "camouflage," the underlying existence. Thus the need for "dream interpretation," the uncovering of what is actually meant by the entities in a dream.

But if the dreamer cannot perceive his own existential renewal while he dreams, it is senseless to claim later that the renewal has been there, concealed in the dream entities. For in order for anything to "be," or have meaning, in the world of a human being, there must be an adequate awareness of that thing, an ability to perceive its significance. Just as nothing can be seen in the absense of light, so nothing can "be" outside of the indissoluble union between the entity's presence and the open realm of human perception. Outside of that union, the words "is" and "being," "mean" and "signify," would make no sense whatsoever.

The many other illogical creations of depth-psychological dream theories have already been discussed. Among them, "dream," as a noun, and the concept of "the unconscious" were especially stressed, both of them abstractions without any demonstrable psychic counterparts. Since they do not exist, they can hardly be at work in the wings of dreaming existence, as superdemons who symbolize and project their superior awareness.

If we avoid speculation that is by nature unprovable, we find that the following facts remain:

1. The realm of perception opened up and "occupied" by the dreaming existence of a human being permits the manifestations only of such sensory presences, and personal behavior, as he himself can perceive. Dream entities neither "mean" nor are anything other than what they reveal themselves to be to the dreamer.

2. After waking up from dreaming, a person may become clear sighted enough to recognize the sensory presences of the dreaming, though in the dreaming they had nothing to do with his behavior, as being pointers to personal existential traits, whose significances are analogous to the perceived significances the dreamed entities.

The qualitative differences elaborated so far between waking and dreaming perception may help us to understand the sharper discontinuity which divides the world of a dreaming state from that of the succeeding waking state—or even the next dreaming state. The fact that in its dreaming state human existence responds, far more than is the case with waking life, solely to the sensory presences of objects means in turn that the dreaming world has no place for all of the other things that go to making up the world of waking existence. All of the things that exist in waking existence alongside of sensory presences—visualizable past, present, and future—are not permitted to come into the foreground of the dreaming world. Whenever some significance addresses a dreamer, it does so as the sensory presence of an entity; and as such, it drives off whatever sensory presence previously held center stage. For no two entities can occupy the same space at the same time. If a table comes into view, it is impossible for a piano to assume an equally vivid sensory presence. Each time a dreamer is addressed by a new significance, a radical change of scenery must take place among the entities of the dreaming world. Only the dreamer's sense of self pervades his awareness continuously.

Our waking world is not populated, by contrast, with just a handful of predominant sensory presences of entities. Instead, it has a place for all of the things that formerly came to light in the open world of our perception, as well as those that have yet to do so—for the whole of the visualizable past and future. That is not to say that each of those things is equally in the foreground of our waking awareness. Yet even when merely an unthematic presence, it nevertheless remains "there," in its specific location within the open realm of our waking world. Were that not so, it would not be possible for us to turn our attention to it thematically whenever we desired. In dreams, on the other hand, much of that which is not immediately evident as a sensory presence seems to have retreated, for the duration of the dreaming state, to an extreme distance in the background.

The incomparably richer collection of entities that gathers from diverse temporal modes to comprise our waking world manifests itself in the same, familiar way after each daily awakening, endures throughout the entire waking period, and thus vouches for the broader historical continuity of the waking state. It also speaks for the waking state's greater openness and freedom. So the waking state provides us with realms of meaning not available in the dreaming condition. Furthermore, the nuances of awakening, of the transition from sleep into dreaming, of dreaming within dreaming, lead us to the general conclusion that every state of greater alertness is distinguished from a prior, or subsequent, state of lesser alertness. This seems reason enough to assign the highest rank to the most alert existential state, for the greater the alertness, the more it is possible for *Dasein* to develop and attain freedom.

The process generally recognized as "awakening" therefore leads toward the full unfolding of our being, out of the confinement of dreaming Being-in-the-world, on up to the maximal existential freedom of the waking state, which is to say, the attainment of the true purpose of our existence or out Being-there (*Da-sein*.) It should not be lost from sight that in any state of our existence we generally believe, and are convinced—as long as we are existing in this state—that we are fully awake. We are, therefore, in no position to deny the possibility that there may be an even more awake state of human existing than that in which we dwell at this very moment when we are reading these lines in a state of so-called everyday waking.

I might mention, finally, that the above discussion of the differences between the waking and dreaming states of a healthy
human being may contain the basis for a better understanding of the
sort of pathological waking phenomena which have until now been
clothed in the polite phrases "hallucinations" and "delusions."[23]

Conclusion

The very peculiarity of the dreaming state highlighted in the
preceding chapter, that is, its limited existential range relative to the
waking state, lends dreaming its great importance for therapy.
While it may be said that dreaming existence is less open than its
waking counterpart, often enough a person is exposed to unfamiliar
significances *for the first time ever* while dreaming. Of course,
significances that have never yet been countenanced in waking life
tend to appear in dreaming, as every meaning does, only from alien
sensory presences of entities. Yet there is some advantage in the fact
that in those massive, materially visible forms, significances do not
merely suggest themselves but strike the dreamer forcibly. Owing to
this special circumstance, the dreaming mode of existence proves to
be of decisive therapeutic value. In the hands of a practiced
therapist, dream contents are often consummately suited to alerting
the patient, in his more clear-sighted waking state, to identical
meaning of as yet unrealized, behavioral possibilities within his own
existence. This helps the patient to clarify his relation to his waking
behavior and, consequently, also to himself and the world around
him.

It is easy to see, then, why even interpretations based on depth-
psychological dream theories often meet with some success; this
despite the fact that their assumptions are purely speculative, while
conclusions drawn from those assumptions, such as the posited

relationship between "latent" and "manifest" dream contents, have no basis in fact. Entities that the patient has previously fended off and unrealized behavioral possibilities are capable of addressing the waking patient through layers of misleading interpretation, compelling him—though now in a brusque, harmful way—to come to terms with them. But because the natural scientific approach from which all depth-psychological dream theories spring is gradually relinquishing its absolute hold on the human imagination, in the future more and more patients will refuse to pass blindly over the inconsistencies hidden in traditional dream theories. Increasingly, they will defend themselves against depth-psychological dream interpretation, many of them finally offering such "resistance" that analysis will be terminated—thereby throwing out the baby with the bath water. The readiness and ability of patients to complete a course of *Daseins*-analysis will, on the other hand, probably grow by leaps and bounds. That will in turn decisively increase its therapeutic value. I feel capable of judging these events, having myself trafficked for ten years exclusively in Freudian and Jungian dream theory, and having applied that theory in therapy, before opening my eyes to the far more appropriate, and in a certain sense more "objective," phenomenological approach to human dreaming.

The sole intent of the present work is to instruct others in the art of helping neurotically ill human beings. Whatever measure of success this enterprise reaps will finally depend on therapists and patients taking the dreaming world seriously, as one of the most integral facets of human "reality."

NOTES

1. S. Freud. *Die Traumdeutung. Gesammelte Werke*, Vol. II/III London: Imago Publ. Co., 1942. P. 538ff.

2. Detlev von Uslar. *Der Traum als Welt. Untersuchungen zur Ontologie und Phanomenologie des Traums.* Pfullinger: Gunther Neske Verlag, 1964. P. 310.

3. Ibid., p. 14; and Rollo May. *Op. cit.*, pp. 19 and 27.

4. Cf. for instance, C.A. Meier. *Zeitgemasse Probleme der Traumforschung. Kultur- und staatswissenschaftliche Schriften der ETH* (Zurich), 1950, No. 75, 19-20.

5. A Kohli-Kunz. Das sogenannte Unbewusste. *Psychosomatische Medizin und Psychoanalyse.* Goettingen and Zurich: Verlag Vandenhoek & Ruprecht. 1975. Vol. 21. P. 284-298.

6. Jean-Paul Sartre. *L'etre et le Neant.* Paris: Gallimard, 1943. Pp. 94ff.

7. S. Freud. *Gesammelte Werke.* Vol. XI. London: Imago Publ. Co., 19. P. 100.

8. M. Boss. *The Analysis of dreams.* (transl. by J. Pomerans). New York: Philosophical Library, 1975. P. 129.

9. Binswanger. Traum und Existenz. In Ausgewahlte Vortrage und Aufsatz. Vol. I. Bern: A. Francke Verlag, 1947. Pp. 96ff.

10. E. Fromm. *The forgotten language.* P. 146.

11. See the concrete evidence of this in Boss, *The Analysis of Dreams.* Transl. by Pomerans. New York. Philosophical Library. 1975. P. 129.

12. M. Boss. Ibid, *The Analysis of Dreams.* Transl. by Pomerans, New York. Philosophical Library. 1975.

13. Cf. M. Heidegger. Bauen Wohen Denken. In *Vortrage und Aufsatz.* Pfullingen: Gunther Neske-Verlag, 1954. Pp. 156ff.

14. See the chapter in the present work devoted to the dreams of psychotic patients.

15. See p.

16. Cf. Boss, *The Analysis of Dreams.* New York. 1975 Philosophical Library. P. 13.

17. Cf. M. Boss. *Existential fundamentals of medicine and psychology.* New York: Jason Aronson, 1977.

18. Refer also to p. 000 for a discussion of the physical component of human existence.

19. (a) S. Freud. *Die Traumdeutung.* In *Gesammelte Werke*, Vol. II/III. London: Imago Publ. Co., 1942. P. 660. (b) A.A. Scherner. *Das Lebem des Traumes.* Berlin: 1961. (Quoted in Freud, ibid., p. 88.)

20. See p.

21. See dream specimen 16, p.

22. See p.

23. Cf. M. Boss. *Grundriss der Meditin un der Psychologie.* Bern: Hans Huber, Inc. 1975. Pp. 503ff.

Index